LUNDY
ISLAND

Bris...

Bideford Bay

...LE

HARTLAND
POINT

BIDEFORD

River Torridge

Morwenstow

Stratton

BUDE

Bridgerule

Millook

Area of inset at left

St. Gennys
Crackington Haven

River Tamar

BOSCASTLE

Tintagel

PENTIRE POINT

Port Isaac

TREVOSE HEAD

PADSTOW

PLYMOUTH

NEWQUAY

Bristol Channel

N
W E
S

TRURO

Mylor

St. Just

FALMOUTH

St. Anthony's Light

0   10 Miles

0   10 Kilometers

Lizard

Cornwall and North Devon

D0671879

Treachery at
Sharpnose Point

Also by Jeremy Seal

The Snakebite Survivors' Club

A Fez of the Heart

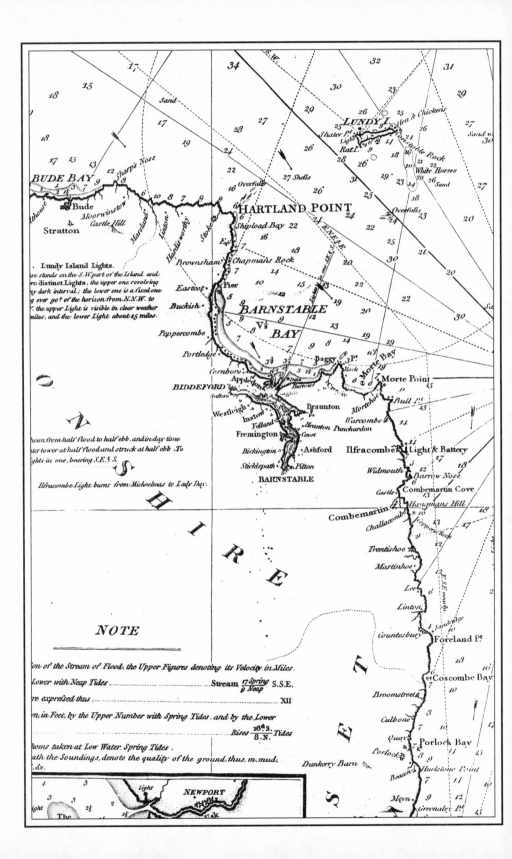

JEREMY SEAL

Treachery at Sharpnose Point

Unraveling the Mystery of the
Caledonia's Final Voyage

HARCOURT, INC.
New York   San Diego   London

Copyright © 2001 by Jeremy Seal

All rights reserved. No part of this publication may be reproduced or transmitted in any form or by any means, electronic or mechanical, including photocopy, recording, or any information storage and retrieval system, without permission in writing from the publisher.

Requests for permission to make copies of any part of the work should be mailed to the following address: Permissions Department, Harcourt, Inc., 6277 Sea Harbor Drive, Orlando, Florida 32887-6777.

www.HarcourtBooks.com

Library of Congress Cataloging-in-Publication Data
Seal, Jeremy.
Treachery at Sharpnose Point: unraveling the mystery of the Caledonia's final voyage/Jeremy Seal.—1st ed.
p.   cm.
Includes bibliographical references.
ISBN 0-15-100524-9
1. Caledonia (Ship) 2. Shipwrecks—England—Sharpnose Point.   I. Title.
G530.C235 S42 2001
914.28'7—dc21   2001024980

Designed by Linda Lockowitz
Text set in Fournier TC

First edition
K J I H G F E D C B A

Printed in the United States of America

To precious A and A,
with my love as always

Every cove, almost, has its bit of wreckage; every churchyard its memorials of the drowned; the very fences are made or mended with spars and planks.

—J. L. W. PAGE: *The North Coast of Cornwall* (1934)

Significant, how an agricultural people is generally as cruel to wrecked seamen as a fishing one is merciful.

—CHARLES KINGSLEY (1849)

Treachery at
Sharpnose Point

Chapter ∞ *1*

She stood in the graveyard and stared at the sea, as if to understand the hurt it had once done her.

The first I knew of her was when my dog began to bark. The din ejected the crows from their roosts in the sycamores and drove a black cloud of them among the four tall chimneys of the vicarage. As the footpath emerged from that building's lee, scraps of sea spume streamed inland on the afternoon wind. They collided against old stone walls and slate headstones patterned with lichen, or planted salty drying kisses on my seaward ear.

She stood beneath oaks and sycamores on high ground, close to the lych-gate and the stone outhouse that formed the graveyard's southeast corner. A train of celandines lay about her feet. She was dressed in a tam-o'-shanter and a sporran, and held a cutlass and a round shield on which a flowering thistle was carved. A sash hung from her left shoulder, and beneath it was a glimpse of chain mail like mermaid scales. Painted white, she was almost life-size.

At my approach, the incensed dog backed into a whimper. And as he slunk away to ponder that woman's mysterious motionlessness, I marveled at her effect upon the somber surroundings. She conjured a more beguiling atmosphere than that of the average graveyard, where the standard expressions of regret are whispered and mortality is conceded with a shrug. She defied the quiescent epitaphs on the headstones—*Thy Will Be Done, Rest in Peace, Watch for ye know not when your Lord doth come*—striving for life in a place that would not have it. She brandished her cutlass undaunted and advanced, it seemed, with a goose step or the high kick of a reeler on the nearby church and the sea cliffs three fields to the west.

The figure, then, of a martial Scottish maid from another time had ended up in a remote Cornish graveyard. But that hardly explained her. I laid an exploratory hand upon her shoulder. I'd expected dense statue metal and was surprised by the wood grain there, a faint responsiveness pulsing beneath the paint under my fingers. Then, behind her, I noticed the stone Celtic cross that stood close to the lych-gate. Beneath a peeling crust of lichen an inscription read: *To the glory of God, and in memory of shipwrecked sailors buried in this graveyard unknown and yet well known. He sent from on high, He took me, He drew me out of great waters.* All at once a crowd of images stumbled over each other in an eagerness to present themselves: the white maid high on a prow, steep seas breaking over her and flinging themselves among flailing shreds of canvas. She was a ship's figurehead.

By the nineteenth century, heyday of the figurehead tradition, ship decoration in general had long since retreated from the excesses of the Elizabethans. Like superstition, which had largely inspired it, the tradition fell back before the advance of the machine age. But while the elaborately carved, painted, and gilded sterns, cannon ports, rudder posts and masts, galleries bearing coats of arms, and Gothic pillars had long since gone, the tenacious figurehead flourished, as if the old impulse of embellishment had not been abandoned but merely concentrated at the bows in a single adornment.

The figureheads of nineteenth-century merchant ships were by all accounts a colorful cast. Included among them were rajahs and American Indian chiefs, Arthurian knights, sprites and fairies, characters from Scott and Shakespeare, Gypsy brides and sea creatures, revered admirals and statesmen, and even favorite daughters; they all spoke of their shipowners' origins and enthusiasms.

That it was a Scottish ship that had come to grief here went without

saying. The figurehead maid was no less than Scotia, the spirited national embodiment of the eras of Burns and Scott. Though the Scots, currently reclaiming their sense of nationhood, had good reason to invoke her, their fiery lass had long since fallen out of use. What had endured, ironically enough, was her British rival (if only upon the change in my pocket where stately Britannia appeared seated on the fifty-pence coin, with a compliant lion alongside her and an olive branch in her outstretched hand). It was easy to see why the two had not got on.

The figurehead tradition had graver origins, however, in ancient rites performed to placate the gods of the sea. Even in Victorian times, as mechanization loomed large, the figurehead served as a heartfelt appeal for divine protection, shielding sailors from the misfortunes of their hazardous lives. Dark irony, then, to find this white maid resurrected in the alien element of a graveyard's soil, for which one explanation alone could account. Ripped from her deck fixings in an unknown upheaval, she had failed her ship and the crew she now stood over, their talisman to fortune recast as a memorial to disaster.

௧௭

I had seen the early photographs. I had seen the rended planking that remained when ships ran ashore among these vicious jags of sandstone, slate, and shale. Time and again, the shore from Bude to Hartland Point lay awash with snapped masts and yards, broken staves and strakes, gunwales, hold beams, cleated deck timbers and varnished cabin paneling, staved barrels and chart tables, buckled packing cases, oars, and tinderized longboats.

The wreckage did not lie there long. Trees were scarce on the windswept cliffs, and the landowners proved zealous protectors of their thickly wooded hollows. The local people lost no time in gathering what timber washed up on their shores. They built barns or homes with it, or burned it on their hearths, rarely reflecting in the urgency of their need on how they profited from the grievous loss of others. It was a fact, if an awkward one, that onshore winds had long since come to signal harvest in the minds of these landsmen.

But the white maid was wooden too. And something had caused them to spare her.

I examined her closely. The intervening years had taken their toll. Rust seeped from her right thigh and mildew had gathered about her armpits. The uppermost part of her shield was missing, leaving it flat-topped along an original join. Where it had cracked, the cutlass blade had been bound with white tape that had long since discolored. Snails with whorled shells, black and beige, clung to the maid. The weathering had set about her face, eroding the features toward blankness. But the figure-head remained recognizably human—which, I guessed, was what had saved her all those years ago.

Somebody must have hauled the figurehead from the shoreline swill and been prompted to lay her aside, at a distance from the gathering pile of wreck timbers, so that she should not burn on some winter hearth; then shouldered her up the cliff and brought her to the graveyard so she might serve as a headstone to the men who had once shipped with her. She had survived all those years, but in the course of them become some-thing more complex and resonant than a simple memorial. As she aged, so the world around her changed until she was from an earlier time. She had become an artifact (and as such it seemed miraculous that she had not been carted off to a museum, where a display case would have become her like a coffin). Instead, she had been left amidst the stirring surround of wreck-littered cliffs, graveyard, and vicarage, singing siren songs of the past to those who happened upon her, songs that had spooked my dog but captivated me completely.

There are ships all down my father's line. My father commanded everything from warships to the family dinghy. His own father had boats, and his before him. And although my great-great-grandfather gave his business as a commercial traveler, his own father had been master of a merchant ship back in the mid-nineteenth century.

Perhaps this was why I stood beside the white maid for many minutes and wondered what might be known of the ship she had failed and of her passage to this final resting place. In the distance, the ocean showed in a vee where the valley delivered up its busy stream to the sea. And just for a moment it was as if a tall ship from another time stood there, clos-ing on a night shore in a frenzied cloud of shredded canvas.

Before leaving, I carefully removed a snail from the remains of the

maid's nose and threw it among the celandines. I was making for the path
that diagonally dissected the graveyard when I tripped. A piece of old
planking, painted in a shade of flaking olive, lay hidden among prim-
roses. It had been laboriously inscribed in a white-painted Gothic hand:
*The figurehead of the Caledonia which marks the graves of the captain and
crew . . . was wrecked in 1843.* A ship's name—one quite as Scottish as her
figurehead—and a date, I mused, to add to the place where she had been
lost.

I set the sign straight and made for the church.

Chapter ∞ 2

In 1843, the British government convened a select committee to address the causes of shipwreck.

For decades, shipping losses recorded along Britain's coasts had been averaging almost two vessels a day, with "no less than 1,000 persons in each year" perishing as a result. Moreover, the statistics for a single storm in November 1824—400 vessels and 350 lives lost—suggest that the true figures were sure to have been much higher.

The committee considered the incidence of shipwreck along the north coasts of Cornwall and Devon. Among the witnesses was Goldsworthy Gurney, a resident of Millook, four miles south of Bude. Gurney described the shore between Trevose Head and Lundy, the high-sided granite island lying ten miles northwest of Hartland Point, as "a most dangerous coast." He also submitted three lists of local shipwrecks: those that had happened "within the last 10 years," a list given him "by a clergyman residing on the coast, amounting to 37," and another of forty or fifty ships wrecked in or near Bude Bay. In all, some two hundred vessels had been lost on just forty miles of coast within living memory.

That Gurney had seen frequent shipwrecks, "and most distressing ones, upon the coast," should have surprised nobody. Most British harbors were poorly lit and marked and offered such limited protection that they were commonly dismissed as "wrecking pools" or "ship traps." They were also pitifully few, and nowhere was more inadequately served in this respect than the north coasts of Cornwall and Devon.

"Foul and rocky cliff," a maritime history of Cornwall described this coast as late as 1906. "Grim and testing under the most favourable conditions... Almost certain destruction when, as frequently happens, it is a lee shore in gales." Hydrographer J. W. Norie's *The New British Channel Pilot* (1835) describes a generally perilous world, but northeast of Land's End the volume's tone shifts resignedly toward damage limitation, as if safe passage became an unreasonable expectation once the Longships Light fell astern to the west. Of St. Ives, the most westerly haven along this coast, lit by a single "small lantern on the pier-head," Norie observed, "It ought to be generally known that vessels driven into St Ives Bay by violent north-westerly winds, may escape destruction by running upon the beach.... It is to be remarked, that so often as accident or local knowledge has thrown a vessel upon this beach, the lives and cargo have uniformly been saved, and the ship but little damaged." Farther northeast there was the harbor at Newquay, which recently had been improved, where there were even heartening instances of ships being saved from destruction by kindly locals who, alerted to their distress, "exhibited lights, tar barrels," to guide them to safety. Norie's *Pilot* mentions (though hardly endorses) Port Isaac, where "ships of 200 tons go in at high water, and run on the sandy shore, where they lie safe from the power of the sea." There were similar, last-resort beaches at Bude. But north of Bude, where the cliffs loom high around Morwenstow and run almost unbroken for twelve miles to Hartland Point, the only possible refuges were the tiny, often inaccessible haven at Hartland Quay and the anchorage at the east end of Lundy Island.

The mariners' rhyme cautioned:

> *From Padstow Point to Lundy Light*
> *Is a Watery Grave by Day and Night.*

It was a shifting verse; "Padstow Point" was interchangeable with Pentire Head, as it was also known, or even with Trevose Head just to the south, and "Lundy Light" increasingly tended to give way to Hartland Light with the building of that lighthouse on the mainland opposite in 1875. But the second line, where the couplet's dark message resides, remained firmly fixed. Sailors rounding Land's End and making northeast for the major ports of Bristol or Gloucester feared Padstow and Hartland as protuberances at either end of a great bay forty miles across that was considered a deathtrap for shipping when the winds got up in the west.

As the north coast leaves Cornwall for Devon, converging on the Bristol Channel, it largely follows a northeasterly direction. From Bude, however, the lie of the coast swings almost directly north, fashioning at the bay's northern extremity a final obstacle for shipping in the form of a vicious semipeninsula, a snag that regularly proved impossible to weather, or to round, in the prevailing westerly winds. "If an unfortunate vessel is driven by a north-west or a south-west gale within the Horns of Hartland and Padstow Points," a correspondent wrote in 1852, "God help her hapless crew! for she is doomed to certain destruction. Along the whole coast there is no harbour of refuge—nothing but iron rocks."

That sea conditions often moderated beyond Hartland Point, where the lie of the coast swung east, only compounded the coastline's notoriety. Here, the Bristol Channel could be said to first begin, offering at least some sea room and calm in the comparative shelter of Bideford Bay. Charlotte Chanter, an amateur botanist who knew these shores well, was walking westward, from calm into tumult, when she described the transformation in 1856. She noted "how the coast and sea alter as you pass Hartland Point! No gentle wavelets . . . but sturdy Atlantic billows rolling in from the Far West . . . leap high into the air as they strike against the projecting mass of rock."

A previous shipwreck committee, of 1836, had found British shipping to be in an appalling state. Crews were riddled with incompetents, both masters and men, who were subject neither to examination, qualification, nor even, in some cases, to the attainment of adulthood. One ship, the *Headleys*, was captained on a voyage from Belfast to Quebec by a fourteen-year-old boy named Storey. Masters, moreover, were commonly unacquainted with the workings of nautical instruments. They were often incapable of ascertaining latitude or tracing a ship's course on a chart. Even those who properly counted themselves able navigators could not necessarily rely on such charts. These tended to be the cheapest and least reliable available because it fell to the master, not the shipowner, to provide them out of his own pay. Drunkenness was habitual.

Ships often suffered from defective construction and regularly embarked fatally overladen. One ship's captain, Henry Woodruffe, recalled the *Princess Victoria* as she made her first return voyage from Archangel, Russia, in 1833: "Returning laden, through the White Sea, with grain, coming down on a very fine day, carrying royals [strictly fair-weather sails]," he said, "the ship absolutely burst to pieces."

The insurance industry, which habitually charged premiums of 10 percent or more of the combined value of the vessel and cargo for every voyage made, only made matters worse by allowing vessels to be insured at exaggerated values. The effect of this oversight, as a witness to the 1836 committee acknowledged, was that "the increased value at which she [the vessel] was insured beyond the real value operated as a temptation to the owner rather to be pleased with her being lost than otherwise." Put more brutally, unscrupulous owners were encouraged to run their vessels into advanced states of dereliction. In what was famously called "murder for gain," owners speculated on the profitable loss of their property quite without consideration for their crews.

You might even believe that the *Caledonia* and her crew had it coming to them.

Chapter ∽ *3*

I had walked to Morwenstow from Hartland Quay. The quay lay ten miles to the north, in a brief break in the Devon cliffs, and survived only in name. It had required constant repair for much of the nineteenth century and finally succumbed to a storm of particular savagery in the autumn of 1896. Two short terraces of whitewashed cottages remained, squared up to each other across a shadowed lane that concluded abruptly on a platform of shoreline Atlantic rocks.

The terraces seemed without purpose now that the settlement had been deprived of its original function, serving the vessels that put in here—which were an intrepid few by all accounts. "The pier at Hartland," wrote Henry Mangles Denham, a naval lieutenant in 1832, "is seldom sought as a refuge . . . for a terrific sea from the westward recoils in a destructive undertow round the inner margin of the pier. . . . Nothing better, however, offers between Bude and Clovelly." The place had at least retained its striking looks. A steady stream of sightseers, increasingly representing the commerce of the modern age, visited Hartland Quay's small museum, gift shop, and pub, which went by the name of the Wreckers' Retreat. They arrived by the land route these days, following the narrow high-banked road that bent to circumvent the church tower at the village of Stoke, a high gray beacon half a mile inland. The road then ran straight between sloping fields before switchbacking down a steep incline, which was flanked by ramparts of sea cliffs, with views of Lundy

Island to the northwest, to finish in a car park just above the sea where seagulls loitered.

The red earth path, rutted with boot-buffed stones, climbed steeply, following the cliff top as it rose from the gully where the quay lay. The wind tugged at the dog's ears as it led the way through the gorse. Rusty bracken, brittle as parchment, powdered between my fingers. Early sea pinks, like tiny pompons, clustered among the rocky outcrops. Rollers unfurled at the foot of the cliff, booming and spitting spray skyward. I looked ahead to a succession of high sandstone headlands that stretched into a gray distance where the last stood out distinctly—a face in profile, lying flat and staring upward, the chiseled nose protuberant.

At Spekes Mill Mouth, a worn path led down to the beach. Local people had once filled the panniers of their donkeys here with the beach sand that they then sold inland, where it served as an effective fertilizer for the fields. But beyond Spekes Mill, the cliffs rose higher still, severing all contact with the sea until the shoreline was as inaccessible as these headlands would seem to wish it. From this distance, the black shale rocks appeared embossed on the water. They ran seaward in parallel broken scabs. Furious breakers funneled between them before retreating in foaming disorder. I peered over the edge; the cliff fell away in an eroded jumble of precarious bluffs and protruding boulders, with gray screes gullying between them. At my back, buzzards' shadows passed over the coarse moorland. On the cliff top, a rusting pile of riveted hull plates, bolted engine sections, and the spiky severed cables of a pulley arrangement marked a salvage attempt long since abandoned.

By and by the moorland gave way to grassier pasture, then to arable land. The flat fields, freshly ploughed, were expanses of sheeny sods. The tractor, I noticed, had repeatedly come close to the cliff edge before wheeling sharply away, as if the end of the earth had caught its driver unaware. The landscape had a prairie confidence; the proximity of an ocean unto Labrador was almost inconceivable. Unlike the approach to Devon and Cornwall's south coasts, with their steadily receding contours and widening river valleys that are typical of most seascapes—a carefully scripted, step-by-step handover to the sea—the north coasts charged lemming-like to their magnificent, abrupt conclusions.

Only, the buildings held back. Nor, I guessed, was it merely shelter from the prevailing west wind that had led the people of Stoke and Elmscott, Hardisworthy, Southole, and Welcombe to consistently build their houses, barns, and churches a few significant fields inland. It was as if these scattered communities had long since turned their backs on the sea, which, for all its proximity, played no part in their lives. Routes to the shore were rare indeed. So steep were the valleys that fissured this coastal plateau that there were almost no natural inlets or harbors to have given rise to fishing villages or trading ports. Geography had played a trick upon these people, ensuring that even as the flying spray tasted as salt upon their lips, they remained landsmen. They knew nothing of the ways of the sea, nor of seafaring, and held these traditions in no affection. They regarded the sea's presence as an accident, as if they lived alongside a closed border and had come, by and by, to lose interest in the world that lay beyond it.

Occasional events of note might, of course, revive their curiosity about the unfamiliar shore. They might even be lured down to the water. These cliffs were certainly hazardous, difficult and steep, but they were rarely sheer, like the white chalk cliffs of Dover or the limestone precipices of Moher in County Clare, Ireland. And when an onshore gale arose to embay a passing ship, they would scramble down the screes or risk themselves on such paths as existed, knowing it might pay to be there when ships broke their backs upon these rocks. Charles Kingsley, writer, clergyman, and father of the botanist Charlotte Chanter, grew up at nearby Clovelly and developed a lifelong association with North Devon. Kingsley provides an intriguing glimpse of the excitement that shipwrecks generated in his account of following a stricken ship along this coast, "a great barque, that came drifting and rolling in before the western gale," during the 1840s. Kingsley detailed the crowd that followed the barque's broken progress. But the "parsons and sportsmen, farmers and Preventive men," the local agents of Lloyd's, the marine insurers, were either his natural peers or officials, here for duty or diversion. His account seems strangely incomplete, lacking the hard-up farmhands, the laborers, the milkmaids, urchins, layabouts, opportunists, and part-timers upon which other contemporary accounts insist. "Whilst in other parts of the English coast persons may assemble by hundreds for plunder on the occasion of a wreck," as an official report of 1839 stated, "on the Cornish coast they assemble in thousands."

True though it was that the people of this coast accounted seafarers an alien breed and their stricken vessels fair game, they could also rise to expressions of condolence. The figureheads of shipwrecks such as that witnessed by Kingsley, marker memorials to the lost ships they had formerly adorned, were once a common feature of this coastal landscape. Many of them survived well into the twentieth century. In the absence of the more conventional sea indicators, like fishing nets, or upturned clinker dinghies, their paint peeling, or boatyards heavy with the cheesy musk of fresh timber, they served as powerful reminders of the sea's proximity and destructive power.

One such figurehead, which has since rotted away, stood in the graveyard beneath the great church tower at Stoke. It marked the loss of the *Saltash* on the Hartland rocks in August 1868. Another, of a bearded turbaned Indian warrior, could once be seen in the graveyard at Bude, where it commemorated the fifteen men lost along with the *Bencoolen* in October 1862. I found a photograph of that figurehead in a faded newspaper cutting dated September 1937 that was pasted into an old guidebook to the region. The figurehead was in a sorry state; the cutting contained an appeal for its restoration. "By May 1938," an unknown hand had scribbled across the cutting, "it had fallen to pieces, having only from time to time been repaired with cement."

Another figurehead, that of the *William,* a ship lost in 1894, stood in the graveyard at St. Gennys, near Crackington Haven. In the 1850s, there were some five ships' figureheads at the Morwenstow vicarage. That of the *Jenny Jones,* lost on Brownspear Beach in a ferocious gale of February 1868, could once be found in a garden at Milford, near Speke's Mill.

It has now disappeared, and endures only in a fading black-and-white photograph where it stands alongside a girl, dressed in late-Victorian costume, sitting on a garden bench in the sunshine. Others survive only in brief mentions; one stood on the porch of the vicarage at the nearby village of Bridgerule in the 1950s, another in a garden at Newquay. The figurehead from the *Othello*, wrecked on the Morwenstow rocks in 1808, adorned for many years a new seafront terrace at Bude, one of a rash of developments resulting from that town having "lately become the fashionable Watering Place of the West," as an 1835 map put it. A hundred years of rain and sunshine, however, had eaten away at the cracks that the salt had forced during the figureheads' working days until they were mostly reduced to stumps deep in the dewy grass of gardens and graveyards.

And so to Henna Cliff, where an onshore wind leaned into my shoulder like a pavement drunk to drive me repeatedly from the path. I looked down on a wooded chasm far below and a stream gathering above the shore waterfall where the wind flung a thin spray inland. The way ahead plunged almost to the heaving shore before its reddish-brown seam began

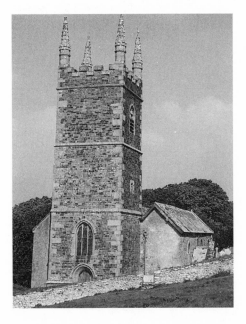

the long climb toward the next headland to the south. I took the inland fork, traversing the valley's northern flank above a slope of impenetrable thorn and blazing gorse, where small speedy birds ranged like pinballs. At the head of the valley I could see a squat church tower facing the sea. On the slopes just below it an imposing vicarage stood, its prominent chimneys crenellated like chess pieces. I followed the edge of a winter beet field,

then shed the clods that clung to my boot treads across a stretch of pastureland, bright as Day-Glo and mottled by pats and molehills, before
dropping into a brief dappled combe in the valley's shallow upper reaches.
I crossed a stream at the footbridge and was climbing the path through
woods into Morwenstow when my dog began to bark.

Chapter ∞ *4*

I brushed at my trousers, passed inside the arched Norman porch, and pushed open the heavy wooden door. The dog clawed at the closing door in protest at its exclusion. The church was larger than I had expected, and unvisited, but something of its silent atmosphere caused me to tiptoe down the stone steps onto the flagged floor. From the seaward end, where braided bell ropes hung from high in the square tower, pillared arches of ornately carved stone marched to the east, forming arcades along either flank of the vaulted nave. There were ranks of dark-stained pews, their ends worked to a primitive beauty. A wooden screen, on which a tall rood crucifix was mounted, concealed the chancel. Light fell through the high stained-glass window on the south wall. At the window's foot ran the caption, in black-stained glass: TO THE GREATER GLORY OF GOD AND IN MEMORY OF ROBERT STEPHEN HAWKER, PRIEST, FORTY YEARS VICAR OF THIS PARISH. FELL ASLEEP 15TH AUGUST 1875, AGED 72, RIP.

I'd never heard of R. S. Hawker until I first came to Morwenstow. In time, I would come to appreciate how his local renown extends almost to cult status, though he never quite seems to have made the grade to a wider audience. It may be that being captivated by Hawker depends upon experiencing his turf at first hand, as if the memorable ensemble of cliffs, vicarage, church, and graveyard, the backdrop to the greater part of his life, acts as a powerful spur to his appeal.

Yet Hawker also boasts a kind of paradoxical universality, providing as he does a classic template for a particular nineteenth-century clerical

stereotype: rural, romantic, literary, and idiosyncratic. Certainly, for a
man better known for foibles than for any concrete corpus of achieve-
ment, he has inspired a disproportionate number of biographies and reminiscences. Hawker of Morwenstow, who spent most of his adult life in
the remote parish with which he is uniquely associated, was parson, poet,
and visionary, favoring yellow ponchos, fishermen's jerseys with the
spear wound that lanced Christ's side stitched blue into the pattern, and
brimless purple hats that apparently derived from his enthusiasm for the
Eastern Orthodox tradition. High Church, a Christian Socialist, and con-
troversial convert to Roman Catholicism on his deathbed, he believed in
demons and mermaids, married a much-loved forty-year-old in his twenties, and, some years after her death, substituted her with a twenty-year-
old when he was in his sixties. He was famously particular, insisting upon
swan's quills for writing, 4B pencils for sketching, Latakia tobacco for his
pipe, and exorbitantly expensive oak shingle tiles for the roof of his
church. He developed a taste for opium and is popularly portrayed in-
dulging the habit, and bending his mind to the composition of romantic
poetry, in the hut that he built on the cliff close to his vicarage. The best
of his verse has been compared to that of Tennyson, with whom he dis-
cussed Arthurian mythology on one of the great poet's visits to Tintagel,
some twenty miles to the south, in 1848. But it is his own description of
his parishioners, as "a mixed multitude of smugglers, wreckers, and dis-
senters of various hue," that best evokes Hawker, placing him in a color-
fully romantic but moody milieu that serves his maverick character well.

The stained-glass window comprised four narrow arched columns.
Within the yellow margin of stylized vine leaves, tonsured and haloed
heads proliferated. The progress of John the Baptist was represented (the
church is dedicated to him and to the local saint, Morwenna), along with
images that I recognized as local: a view of the church itself, with pin-
nacles rising from the tower's four corners; the celebrated Saxon baptismal font that stood by the church door; the graveyard's noted sepulchre
to a local landowner gored to death by a seventeenth-century bull; and
the Celtic cross in commemoration of shipwrecked sailors. Then, in the

top right corner, I noticed her:
the white maid viewed face on,
her eyes rescued from erosion,
above the words FIGUREHEAD
OF THE CALEDONIA. According
to the window caption, Hawker
had been vicar here for forty
years prior to 1875, which put
him at Morwenstow at the time
of the loss of the *Caledonia*. Was
this the man who had buried
captain and crew, and stood the
ship's figurehead over them?

A framed faded photograph
hung on the church's western
wall. It was signed in a brownish
large-lettered scrawl that would
become familiar in the months
ahead, "Yours affectionately,
R. S. Hawker." It was apparently
taken in 1875, a week before
Hawker's death, and showed him in full canonicals, complete with surplice, stole, and biretta, the square hat of the High Church. His imminent
demise might have been inferred from the absence of focus in the old
man's eyes, while the down-turned mouth contributed the faint suggestion of constipation. But it was not an especially telling photograph;
rather, it typically revealed more about the arduous business of being
photographed in the early days than it did of its subject. Its very existence
said something, however, about the span of Hawker's life, one that ended
in the photographic age but began at the very advent of machinery, and
it placed the loss of the *Caledonia* at the heart of that same span.

I stepped outside and wandered among the gravestones. I was looking for verse epitaphs dating from Hawker's incumbency, which have

been described as first drafts of the vicar's poems. Here he was on infant mortality, delivering rhyming comfort to the parents of John Rouse, who had died on January 31, 1840, aged three weeks:

> *Those whom God loves die young*
> *They see no evil days*
> *No falsehood paints their tongue*
> *No sickness their ways.*
>
> *Baptized and so made sure*
> *To gain their blessed abode*
> *What could we pray for more*
> *That they die and are with GOD.*

I was considering the poetic course that Hawker might have charted in the case of shipwrecked dead when I realized I was not alone. On these remote cliffs or along the narrow lanes where grass grew high down the center, Mohican-style, one soon came to expect to be alone. Hawker referred to Morwenstow as "Far Cornwall"; the writer Arthur Mee even managed "the lonely Farthest North of England's Farthest South." The woman was kneeling amongst daffodils before a headstone, scraping at the lichen there.

"Looking for clues?" I asked knowingly, as if the two of us had history's lure in common. I liked to think that I shared her delight as she retrieved the faint characters, one by one, from beneath the lichen, and the old stories began to give themselves up. The woman looked up through owlish spectacles.

"I'm looking for lichens," she explained. "I'm a botanist."

I left by the lych-gate.

Chapter ∞ *5*

The tip of my finger rested against an entry in *Lloyd's Register of Ships* for 1842.

I was looking for a wreck, which was how I'd described my research interest on the application form at the Public Record Office in Kew, West London, and had begun by searching for the ship she had once been. The PRO stood amidst leafy avenues with literary names, lined by Edwardian terraced houses with tiled porches and faux-Tudor gables. But the PRO was an avowedly modern building that resembled the informal campus offices of some high-tech corporation. It was fronted by a paved piazza in which an extensive lake, complete with fountains, was fringed by willows and thickets of bamboo. The lake's sheer sides had been fitted with helpful slipway ramps for swans, ducks, and moorhens that had long since learned to manage without them.

The expanse of water, however, also lent this repository of record an unintended moated impression, as if the old habits of secrecy endured and the building remained protective of its contents. Here, I reminded myself, was where journalists and researchers congregated whenever the building finally bowed to public pressure, coughing up classified documents decades after the political intrigues and scandals, conflicts and crises, that had spawned them.

The interior of the building strove hard, however, to dispel these engrained notions of obstruction. In its bright and spacious hallway a small collection of leafy trees even grew. Though the trees stood indoors, they

C

No.	Ships.	Masters.	Tons.	BUILD.		Owners.	Port belonging to.	Destined Voyage.
				Where.	When.			
26	Caledonia S	Lawson	445	Chestr	1807	Bold&Co.	Liverp'l	Liv. Bmbay
	C.39			PPTSd	s alm	rb.31 ptND&	Srprs40	
7	— Bk	J.Liddell	405	Nwcstl	1836	Macfarlan	Alloa	Lon PPhilip
	F.&C.41			Srprs39	Drp.	41		Lon.Sydney
8	— Bk	M'Cutchn	189	Cringh	1829	M'C'tchn	London	Lon.
	s.&C.40 I.B.			T. Srprs41				
9	— Sk	M'Kenzie	45	Corp'k	1838	Cameron	Corpck	Abn. Coastr
	I. B.			P.&Lh	plk			
30	— Sr	J.M'Leod	130	Invrns	1827	Suter&Co	Invrn'ss	Lon.Invrnss
			101					
1	— Sw	R.Mearns	147	Dndee	1835	M'Gavin	Dundee	Dun. Riga
2	— Bg	Menhinet	227	N.Scot	1840	Ginn	Liverp'l	Liv. Constpl
	YM.&ptr.42		204	BB. S&	RP.			
3	— Bk	P'ckwood	363	Stcktn	1816	Dougall &	K'kaldy	Lth. DStr'ts
	ptr.&ptd.—	J.Kinnaird		ND.&Irp.	32	Srprs43		
4	— Stm	W. Powell	120	Dndee	1838	J. Giro	London	Lon.Coruna
								Built of Iron
5	— Bg	J. Roche	105	Nfndld	1833	Connell &	Cork	Crk. Jmaica
	C.41			E.&P.	Srprs 41			S.S.40—4Yrs
6	— Sw	S. Peter	206	Arbrth	1839	J. Esplin	Arbrth	Lon.Mrsells
Wrecked	C.41		200					
7	— Sw	R. Thew	237	Sndrld	1838	Mid&Lon	Stocktn	Stk. Baltic
	I.B.		227			Sh.Co.		
8	Caledonian	Rchardsn	230	Sndrld	1837	Wake&C.	Sndrlnd	Sld. London
	Sw ptI.B.		222					
9	Calenick Bn	J. Pascoe	110	Llnely	1826	Mitchell	Truro	Fal. Wales
	I. B.			lrp.41				
40	Calista S	T Mauger	208	Jersey	1825	St.Croix	Jersey	LivHondras
	Bk s.M.37		203	ND.TSds	& Srp	rs39		Lon.Hondras
1	Calla Bg	R. Bovey	190	N.Sco.	1839	Hawkins	Exeter	Exr. Nwcstl
	I.B.		203	BB.J.&YP				Exr.Malaga
2	Calthorpe Bg	Bensley	79	Wells	1817	Temple&	Blkney	Shl. Blkney
	I.B.			O.&E.	n.d.38	lrp.41		
3	Calypso S	J. Brown	379	Gr'nck	1825	Eccles&C	Gl'sgow	Cly. Trndad
	F. C.&pts.30 43	Drp.43		PP. TS	ds ND.	&Srprs39 p	NW.&Srp ts42	Gly.Don
4	— Bk	Cromartie	286	Sndrld	1833	Wilk'nson	London	Lon.
	C.36							
5	— Sr	A. Gillis	84	P.E.Isl	1815	Gillis&Co	Liverp'l	Liv. Coaster
	I.B.			BB.&P				
6	— Bk	Millman	266	P.E.Isl	1828	Fogwell &	Drtmth	DrtRchbcto
	s.41			O.J.B.	B&P	Srprs41		
7	— Sw	Punshon	282	Sndrld	1840	J. Burrell	Nwcastl	Liv. Malta
	ptI.B.		299	ptPP.pl	k			
8	Camaieu S	J. Clucus	355	Poole	1841	Clucus&C	Liverp'l	Poo. Liverpl
	C.41		398					
9	Cambria Sr	Lucas	124	Sndrld	1825	W. Beale	Exeter	Exr.
			121	lrp.36	Srprs 39lrp.42			
50	— Sr	R Mahony	73	Cmthn	1803	GN Dunn	Kinsale	Crk. Nwprt
				ND.37Dr	p. 39			

were alluringly suggestive, evoking the dappled glade to which one might retire, book in hand, on a summer afternoon, as if to imbue the acquisition of knowledge with a proper sylvan innocence. There were large circular working tables of blond wood and aluminium. The information desks were manned by smiling assistants. From the banks of user-friendly computer terminals, a vast range of national records—from customs and trade to the foreign office, the health service, and the armed forces—could be requested. Visitors were even supplied with pagers that would sound when items were available for collection.

The visitors, however, seemed to hail from a former researcher's world—of ill-lit corridors and cramped work surfaces, and interminable delays while mislaid items were listlessly pursued in creaking filing cabinets that turned up only the desiccated corpses of gray mice whose diet of cardboard had eventually done for them. They wore gray anoraks with multiple pockets from which bitten Biros thrust, and lingered in doorways, by the lavatory's shiny urinals, or in the cloakrooms, a distant daze playing across their faces. Here to pursue family lineages and obscure histories, to add a few further stitches to their chosen corner of the past's threadbare tapestry, they were evidence that archive research could be a harmfully obsessive habit, but as I carried *Lloyd's Register* for 1842 to a table, it did not cross my mind that I might ever become like them.

I'd grown up among boats. Sepia family-boat portraits by the maritime photographers Beken of Cowes hung on the walls. We'd lived on England's south coast, by a creek in Chichester Harbour, where the retreating tide left a line of weed alive with sand hoppers along the shingle and revealed dark banks of mud that men dug for cockles. The mud sucked noisily at their waders, their heavy footfalls releasing the rank smell of rot. But when the tide was high, my father launched his dinghy there and dreamed of Cape Horn or the Roaring Forties while his sulking son looked up at the little boat's faded brown sail and determined to prove to his father that he did know a halyard from a hamster.

I knew nothing at all, however, about archives or their workings. On this, my first visit to the PRO, I actually felt certain that I was looking in the wrong place. It seemed inconceivable that I should find my ship in these old pages. Wrecks lay elsewhere, barnacle encrustations in the drifting sediment of the seabed, and were truly found by divers directed from the latest scanning equipment installed on high-tech search vessels. The remnants at Morwenstow, soused in atmosphere, seemed too large and resonant to be reducible to the single line of codified detail that I had settled upon.

Shortly after my arrival, however, the PRO information officer directed me to *Lloyd's Register*. It buoyed me to learn that Lloyd's, London's coffeehouse association of shipowners, merchants, and insurance brokers, should have published an index of all UK-registered merchant ships over one hundred tons since 1764. For a moment, I allowed myself to believe that finding my ship might even prove straightforward.

The *Register* listed thousands of abbreviated ship details in an antique black type whose heavy impress had punched an inverted Braille into the backs of bluish brittle pages. The ships' names were arranged alphabetically. Some names were commoner than others; I might have guessed that *Caledonia* would be among the commonest. There were twenty-one in all, hailing from Scottish ports including Inverness, Dundee, Peterhead, Alloa, and Arbroath but also from Guernsey, Chester, Sunderland, Liverpool, Newcastle, and even Newfoundland. I was confounded.

My straying eye then noticed the occasional items that showed in the *Register*'s page margins. These tended to be of a different-colored ink— often red—and of another typeface that regularly overlapped the existing test. They were evidently later additions, and their meaning—Wrecked, Stranded, Lost, Missing, or Sunk—was all too clear. The *Register* not only listed ships, then, but also recorded casualties among them. The word *Wrecked* alongside the entry should lead me to her. There were just two. And the terse obituary on one of them, a *Caledonia* out of Greenock, had been penciled over with a correction.

The abbreviations on the only remaining entry yielded their meaning readily enough. Working from left to right, *Sw* indicated the vessel to be a snow. The snow was in all respects a brig, the common two-masted sailing vessel of the period, except for the distinctive arrangement on the mainmast where a supplementary runner essentially functioning as a separate mast eased the workings of square- and fore-and-aft sails.

The next item of information, which gave the name of the ship's captain or master, was rather more startling. While *St. Peter* achieved a certain canonized exoticism of his own, it was the prosaic company he kept—he was flanked by the likes of "J Roche," "W Powell," and "R Thew"—that tipped the entry toward the surreal. A fishing boat on the Sea of Galilee granted, but the only St. Peter I knew of had no business mastering a mid-nineteenth-century brig. The subsequent facts did, however, return this *Caledonia* to a more plausible mooring. She weighed 206 tons, had been built in Arbroath (which was also her home port) in 1839, and was owned by one J. Esplin. Her "destined voyage" was given as to London and Marseilles. Upon survey, she had been assigned an A1 insurance classification by Lloyd's for ten years, which implied a worthy vessel. *C.41* indicated that she had been copper-bottomed in 1841, and *4 mo* that she had been launched in April, the fourth month, of 1839.

Here, then, were the bones of a ship that bore the right name and had been lost around the time in question. But nothing else in the skeleton linked her with the figurehead at Morwenstow.

"You could check her Certificate of British Registry," suggested the man at the information desk. "That's the ship's basic paperwork, as required by customs. Look in the Board of Trade catalog, under her home port."

It was a battered leather ledger, entitled "Registered Vessels, Montrose and Arbroath, 1839." The ships' certificates it contained were preprinted forms that the local "Comptroller of Customs" had completed in an ornate hand. The certificate I was seeking soon lay before me. The owner of the "*Caledonia, of Arbroath*" was confirmed, in greater detail, as "Joseph Sanderson Esplin of Arbroath in the County of Forfar, Merchant." The rest, however, was a powerful reminder that certificates were not designed to inspire or evoke, not even in the nineteenth century. There were data on tonnage, and "length from the inner part of the Main

THIS is to Certify, that in pursuance of an Act passed in the Fourth Year of the Reign of King WILLIAM the Fourth, intituled, "An Act for the Registering of British Vessels," *Joseph Sanderson Esquire of Arbroath in the County of Forfar, Merchant*

having made and subscribed the Declaration required by the said Act, and having declared that *he is* ~~together with~~

Vessel totally wrecked on the Cornish Coast. See Lloyds List to Sept 1842

Wreckcan 1842

sole Owner (in the proportions specified on the Back hereof) of the Ship or Vessel called the *Caledonia* of *Arbroath, Port of Montrose* which is of the Burthen of *Two Hundred and 3000* Tons, and whereof *Fredrick Mackison*

is Master, and that the said Ship or Vessel was *built at Arbroath aforesaid in this present year, one thousand eight hundred and thirty nine; as appears by the Certificate of Arthur Smith the Builder dated 25th April 1839 (produced) and Declaration of Identity thereon*

and *Robert Libbald Kilgour Tide Surveyor at Arbroath* having certified to us that the said Ship or Vessel has *one* Decks and *two* Masts, that her length from the inner part of the Main Stem to the fore part of the Stern Post aloft is *Eighty two* feet *three* tenths, her breadth in Midships is *Twenty one* feet *seven* tenths, her depth in hold at Midships is *Fourteen* feet *six* tenths, that she is *Brig* rigged, with a *Standing* Bowsprit; is *Square* sterned *carvel* built; has *no* Galleries, and *a female figure* Head; and the said subscribing Owners having consented and agreed to the above Description, and having caused sufficient Security to be given, as is required by the said Act, the said Ship or Vessel called the *Caledonia* has been duly registered at the Port of *Montrose*.

Certified under our Hands, at the Custom-House, in the said Port of *Montrose* this *Twenty ninth* Day of *April* in the Year One Thousand Eight Hundred and *thirty nine*.

Signed   *George Willis* **Collector.**
      John Erskine **Comptroller.**

A true Copy
George Williams

Admeasured under the Act 5 & 6 Will. IV. cap. 56.

Stem to the fore part of the Stern Post aloft," and "breadth in Midships" and "depth in hold at Midships," on rigging, on her bowsprit, and a reference to the ship's builder, one Arthur Smith. And then my ranging eye fell upon a few brief words that sent a pulse of recognition coursing through me: this *Caledonia* had "*a female figure* Head." There was barely time to register this first concrete suggestion that I might have found her before I saw the sentence, scrawled in a hurried hand, as if signing off, which ran across the certificate. "Vessel totally wrecked," it read, "on the Cornish coast per *Lloyd's List* 10th Sept 1842."

God help me! The date was off by a year and two days, but since the Cornish mention far outweighed this as evidence, it now appeared that the graveyard sign must be mistaken. I was out of my seat, weaving my way between the tables toward the information desk, where the officer regarded me warily, as if noting the first signs of obsession. What was *Lloyd's List*? Where was it kept?

"It's Lloyd's shipping news publication," the officer explained patiently. "It provides information about merchant shipping movements and casualties received from ports around the world."

"Where, where?"

"Not here," he replied. "I believe the Guildhall Library keeps it."

I checked my watch; I could just reach the Guildhall before it closed. I left the building in a hurry, stuffing awkward sheafs of paper into my bag. I raced past the lake, alarming a moorhen, which launched itself onto the water with a disgruntled squawk, like a portly matron committing herself to an uncustomary swim. Along the railings that fronted the terraced houses leading to Kew's tube station styrofoam cups had been slammed, the spikes protruding from their upturned bases to resemble Prussian helmets, but unlikely ones featuring the logos of soft-drinks conglomerates. The train lurched with a leisurely gait into a long string of stations, then idled onward, so I reached the Guildhall Library just ten minutes before it closed.

"Five minutes," I told the librarian breathlessly. The librarian, who was busy ushering people out, looked unimpressed.

"Two," I almost shouted my improved offer. The librarian reluctantly allowed me in. The *List* was on microfilm. I dragged the reel from a drawer and speared it onto the spool of a reading machine. Then I put the machine on fast-forward and whirred noisily through the spring and summer of 1842. At my back, the librarian served me a coughed reminder. Then I was at September 10. After several pages detailing arrivals and departures from Archangel to Rio, I saw what I had come for and thumped my fist against the desk.

"You did say two minutes," the aggrieved librarian called out.

"I'm done," I replied, scribbling the last few words from the *List* into my notebook and rewinding the reel through the year until it spun free. I returned it to the drawer, shook the bemused librarian's hand in gratitude, and stepped outside. I sat on a bench and turned to the words I had copied into the notebook: "*Caledonia,* Peter, of Arbroath, from Odessa to Gloucester was totally wrecked near Bude, 7th inst. Only one of the crew saved," it read. "Letter from Morwinston," it concluded, referring to the manner by which word of the ship's loss had reached the *List*.

Morwenstow was misspelt and the master had lost his sainthood. But there was no doubt that I had found my ship.

And there had been a survivor.

Chapter ∞ 6

I returned to Morwenstow three weeks later. I had learned that Robert Hawker had written about the *Caledonia* tragedy. The present owner of the vicarage had copies, which I was welcome to read in the very house where they were originally written.

A drive wound beneath budding sycamores and puddled into a graveled parking area before the vicarage. I climbed from the car and eyed the house. With its slate roof and stepped gables, a castellated porch topped by a cross, and thick freckled walls of gray and brown stone, it seemed made for the crows that wheeled over it. Above its neat fringe of shrub-filled beds rose ecclesiastical windows, tall, arched, and in groups of three or four, with white frames that plunged the leaded panes they housed into darkness. Robert Hawker, who was made vicar of Morwenstow in 1835, had begun building the house in 1837. The origins of the building confounded its singularity—the plans were lifted directly from a popular contemporary architectural volume, Hunt's *Designs for Parsonage Homes*—though Hawker did add idiosyncratic touches of his own by modeling three of the chimneys on the towers of parish churches he knew well: Stratton, near Bude, and North Tamerton and Whitstone, both a few miles inland on the Launceston road. The fourth was modeled on the tomb of his mother.

A kindly middle-aged woman with bright eyes answered the door. Jill Welby led me into the house where Hawker had lived for thirty-eight years until a few weeks before his death. Corridors right-angled with homely Victorian confusion across a tiled floor plan of elegant but moth-eaten rooms. Through black-painted doorframes, I glimpsed the sun falling on old brass, faded prints, and lithographs of Hawker and various members of his family.

"It's not that I particularly like his poetry," shrugged Jill. "It's not even that I particularly like the man." She was striving, it seemed, to arrive by a process of elimination at the reason for her fascination. "It's more to do with his oddness," she concluded. "The contradictions in him." The Welbys had bought the vicarage in 1986; it was as if the spirit of the vicarage's original occupant had since then stolen upon Jill unsolicited, presuming upon their shared experience of residence in this isolated place to forge a kinship that belied the century and a half between them. Though she could not quite say when she had begun to do so, Jill had amassed an impressive collection of Hawker papers over the years. There were letters and postcards, sermons and scribblings, biographies and reminiscences, first editions of his own works, critiques of his poetry, obituaries and other newspaper cuttings, as well as miscellaneous items and even pieces of furniture, like Hawker's pine wardrobe—formerly home to his collection of colorful cassocks—which stood in the vicarage's hallway.

Jill was not alone in being captivated by Hawker's singular life. In time, I would come to understand that a fascination with the man was something of a common local condition. Nicholas Ross, who had lived in nearby Kilkhampton until his death in 1967, had succumbed spectacularly in his later life. He often picnicked on the cliffs at Morwenstow with his wife, Adelaide, reading from Hawker's Arthurian epic poem "The Quest of the Sangraal," or took duck and port to consume at Hawker's cliff top hut on the August anniversary of the vicar's death. Ross, who is buried alongside his wife about fifty feet from the *Caledonia* figurehead, garnered his own extensive collection of papers and memorabilia. He corresponded with other enthusiasts, tracked down descendants of the man, and spent much of his time preparing a book on Hawker that he never completed.

Jill showed me to my room, then led me to the sunlit library. She prowled the shelves, her fingers playing imaginary piano keys on the book spines. She picked out two faded volumes, which she bookmarked and passed to me, then left me to read. I sat on a chair before a low wicker table with a glass top and picked up one of the books. It was an antique mocha-colored hardback with a perishing spine. Its yellowing pages, irregularly cut, snagged my thumb. Though embossed with stylized grapevines and acanthus, like a hymnal, it proved to be a volume of Hawker's poetry, dated 1903 and entitled *Cornish Ballads*. I opened the pages at the bookmark to find a poem entitled "The Figure-Head of the *Caledonia* at her Captain's Grave":

We laid them in their lowly rest,
The strangers of a distant shore;
We smoothed the green turf on their breast,
'Mid baffled Ocean's angry roar;
And there, the relique of the storm,
We fixed fair Scotland's figured form.

She watches by her bold, her brave,
Her shield towards the fatal sea;
Their cherished lady of the wave
Is guardian of their memory.
Stern is her look, but calm, for there
No gale can rend or billow bear.

Stand, silent image! stately stand,
Where sighs shall breathe and tears be shed,
And many a heart of Cornish land,
Will soften for the stranger dead.
They came in paths of storm; they found
This quiet home in Christian ground.

1841

I smiled. The date made the impossible claim that the poem had been written a year before the *Caledonia*'s loss. The error recalled the sign in the graveyard that dated the shipwreck to 1843. Dates seemed to straddle the actual year of the wreck, but never nailed it. These near misses, which suggested facts fading as the *Caledonia* receded into a blurry past, might have served to warn me of the difficulties of my search. But the poem alone had already yielded more than the few scant references I had hoped to glean from the visit, leaving me feeling replete with new material.

So; Hawker *had* been present at the time of the wreck, and had also supervised the recovery of both figurehead and corpses. The experience had clearly left its mark upon him, moving him literally to poetry. The figurehead had touched him most deeply, if the number of euphemisms it had inspired were anything to go by. The poem was a hymn to the figurehead's peculiar capacity to evoke.

All of which reminded me what the poem was not: a conventional dirge for the lost lives of the crew. Hawker seemed less interested in lamenting their deaths, which he hardly mentioned, than in celebrating their proper interment—their "quiet home in Christian ground." There was also the poet's intriguing insistence on his and his associates' part in the process: "We laid them in their lowly rest," "We smoothed the green turf...," and "We fixed" the figurehead above the grave.

I turned to the second volume. Equally aged, it was entitled *Footprints of Former Men in Far Cornwall*. It proved to be a collection of Hawker's prose pieces that had originally appeared in various Victorian periodicals, most notably Charles Dickens's *All the Year Round*, between the 1850s and 1870s. Jill had marked an item called "Remembrances of a Cornish Vicar." I began to read.

Hawker was thirty-nine and had not been long at Morwenstow when, he wrote, he was "plunged all at once into the midst of a fearful scene of the terrors of the sea." He then recounted the events of a stormy September dawn in 1842:

About daybreak of an autumn day I was aroused by a knock at my bedroom-door; it was followed by the agitated voice of a boy, a member of my household, "Oh, sir, there are dead men on vicarage rocks!"

Hawker quickly dressed in gown and slippers, and rushed out to find one of the household, a young lad, "weeping bitterly, and holding out to me in his trembling hands a tortoise alive" that he had found on the shore. The vicar crossed the fields to the cliffs and set off down a steep path to the shore:

It was indeed a scene to be looked on only once in a human life. On a ridge of rock, just left bare by the falling tide, stood a man, my own servant; he had come out to see my flock of ewes, and had found the awful wreck. There he stood, with two dead sailors at his feet which he had just drawn out of the water stiff and stark. The bay was tossing and seething with a tangled mass of rigging, sails, and broken fragments of a ship; the billows rolled up yellow with corn, for the cargo of the vessel had been foreign wheat; and ever and anon there came up out of the water, as though stretched out with life, a human hand and arm.

A survivor was found, "just where a brook of fresh water fell towards the sea." The exhausted man addressed Hawker in French but was in no condition to give details about the ship. They assisted him to the vicarage, where they also bore "the corpses, decently arranged" on "a temporary bier of the broken planks." Later that day, the survivor, "refreshed, and collected, and grateful," told Hawker his story.

The man's name, Hawker wrote, was Le Daine. A native of Jersey, he had joined the *Caledonia* at Malta, where he had been recuperating from illness in the hospital. The *Caledonia*, of Arbroath, had been on a two years' voyage in the Mediterranean trade, last taking on a cargo of grain at the Black Sea port of Odessa. Also engaged at Malta was a

Portuguese cook, who received a grievous wound in a street quarrel the night before the ship departed for Falmouth. To the engagement of the cook, Hawker then claimed, "as one link in a chain of causes . . . the loss of the vessel might be ascribed."

The wounded cook died on the ship's arrival at Falmouth, and while the captain and crew went ashore to attend his funeral there, the cabin boy, "handling in his curiosity the barometer," had broken the instrument. The captain of the *Caledonia* thus had no warning of the "sudden and unexpected hurricane" that was about to befall them when he received orders to make for Gloucester, and to discharge the cargo there. They left Falmouth at dawn, rounded Land's End in fine weather, "and came up the Channel with a fair wind." But about nine at night, "the wind went mad; our canvas burst in bits. We reeved fresh sails; they went also." The captain sent Le Daine forward to look out for Lundy Light, but instead the Jerseyman saw dreaded cliffs on their bow.

Within seconds, they had struck the rocks. As was the practice, the captain sent the crew into the rigging, but a huge wave soon tore away the mast and washed them into the sea. Le Daine remembered the beat of the waves and the sight of a fellow crewman by the name of Alick Kant being swept away, felt a rock under his hand, and finally felt the ground beneath his feet. He climbed a steep, dark cliff and fainted away upon "a kind of platform with grass" where they found him the following morning.

Hawker described the subsequent recovery of all the remaining bodies before concluding his account:

> We placed at the foot of the captain's grave the figurehead of his vessel. It is a carved image, life-size, of his native Caledonia, in the garb of her country, with sword and shield.

I closed the book to a brief puff of dust. History was not supposed to behave like this. Its allure lay in the way it resisted all attempts to know it. The doors of the past should close as the present left it behind, revealing its elusive secrets in grudging glimpses, deceiving those who presumed to master it with the frustrations of false leads, dead ends, apparent illogicalities and contradictions. What amounted to the *Caledonia*'s black box, entirely intact and thoroughly chronicled, had surfaced from the distant past to spoil my sparring with history.

End of story, it seemed.

Chapter ❧ 7

I straightened the books and stepped into the hallway. The high window, with its stained-glass Gothic insets, spilled diamonds of sunlight down the stairs. There was no sign of Jill, and the house was silent except for the chorus of clocks.

I stepped outside and walked through a garden gate into the graveyard. A light wind was ruffling the branches above the figurehead, strobing the white maid in a gentle dapple. I passed the church and left the graveyard by the stone stile for a field of grazing cattle, following Hawker's route to the cliffs that autumn morning in 1842. I entered another field where seagulls strutted upon a terra-cotta expanse of freshly tilled soil whose gentle camber presented a wide view of a shipless ocean and, to my right, the valley that separated me from the great rampart of Henna Cliff. I reached the cliffs and peered over.

The ground fell away in a giddying tangle of briar and thorn, the undergrowth failing as the incline steepened to reveal tufted slabs of rock that slanted precipitously toward the shoreline. Far below, a long bay stretched southward. The tide was low, revealing a strew of glistening boulders amid rafts of black and yellow bladder wrack. Beneath these scattered stones, however, were spines of rock flanked by long aisles of yellow sand that ran seaward in regular order.

I could imagine the sight that had greeted the vicar of Morwenstow more than 150 years before me: the ship broken open and pummeled into parts, her contents scattered among the swell; the snapped timbers spiky

with splinters and tressed in tangles of rigging; the bodies, bundles of torn clothes, sliding down the breaking waves to the rocks; and the shallows yellow with corn. I thought involuntarily of all that spoiled wheat but stopped myself, for its loss seemed insignificant—and the thought improper—in the context of the sailors' deaths. I admonished myself for thinking like a wrecker.

Wheat: I had, I confess, hoped for more from the *Caledonia*'s cargo. It had been a time of fabled sea voyages. Just six years earlier, in 1836, Charles Darwin had returned to England after a five-year voyage around South America and the Galápagos Islands on the *Beagle,* which would inspire his *On the Origin of Species.* In 1841, Herman Melville had gone to sea on the series of voyages that would result in *Moby-Dick.* And in 1845, Sir John Franklin would set out on his ill-fated search for the Northwest Passage. These were journeys of extraordinary scientific, literary, and expeditionary significance, respectively; wheat could not compete. It reduced the crew I had imagined—derring-do explorers, romantic adventurers, questing itinerants—to mere deliverymen. Just as John Masefield's poem "Cargoes" posited the romance of "ivory, apes and peacocks" before resigning itself to the reality of "Tyne coal, Road-rails, pig-lead," this wild wreckers' shore seemed to merit more evocative flotsam than the grain from which sliced white bread was made.

My modern perspective was pampered, of course, and profoundly ignorant. In the mid-nineteenth century, Morwenstow's parish poor habitually scrabbled for scattered grains of wheat among the harvest stubble. Hawker reckoned that a diligent woman could "glean enough to make a bushel of wheat [sixty pounds] and each child, if active, half a bushel." In 1863, "several of the Women" did even better, gathering 120 pounds each—"enough for one person for Three Months of the coming year—and what a help this must be for a poor family." Hawker's late-summer letters, full of anxious references to the harvest, forcibly illustrate the acute privations inflicted by a poor one. "To me it is life or death in the harvest field and to how many more of my poor parishioners," he exclaimed in one letter.

The ancient harvest rituals flourished at Morwenstow throughout the nineteenth century. The last handful of corn, as wheat was commonly known, was cut with great ceremony before being plaited and dressed with cornflowers, poppies, and betony. It was then delivered to the vicar, who hung it from the ceiling above his dining-room table at the vicarage, removing last season's offering to give to the birds. Hawker revived the tradition of making the bread for the harvest Eucharist from the new corn. He first appealed to his parishioners to gather at the church one Sunday in the autumn of 1843 "to receive in the bread of the new corn that blessed sacrament which was ordained to strengthen and refresh our souls." Hawker directed the church to be decorated with fruit, flowers, vegetables, and bread, and is thus credited with pioneering the modern harvest festival.

The early 1840s were a time of profound unrest. The reforms of the 1830s had fostered the illusion that the new decade might herald a better future, but the reality proved continuing poverty and social and political upheaval. The Industrial Revolution had found its stride, driving artisans out of business, stripping them of their pride, and yoking them to low-waged labor at the service of machines. Failed harvests in 1838 and 1839 would usher in the "Hungry Forties," when potato blight compounded food shortages to cause famine in Ireland and misery in Britain. An acute economic depression had held sway since 1839. Trade was slack. Wages fell. The men who broke stones at the quarries on Woolley Moor for the Morwenstow roads were paid just ten pence a day, while weavers in the Midlands would endure daily earnings as low as seven and a half pence. The social conscience of Florence Nightingale, which would one day lead her to service in the dirt and suffering of the Scutari Barracks in Constantinople, was first stirred by the terrible conditions prevailing in England during the summer of 1842, when ignorance and hunger, filth and illness reigned. Nightingale wrote that summer of "the sufferings of man . . . All the people I see are eaten up with care or poverty or disease."

The Corn Laws, which had been restricting wheat imports to inflate the home price since 1805, continued to protect domestic agricultural interests. The predicament of the worker was bad enough in 1835, when the average cost of a sixty-pound bushel of wheat was four shillings and nine pence. This meant, since the average wheat requirement per person daily was one pound by weight, that an Englishman earning a shilling per day expected to spend one twelfth of his income on bread for each and every member of his family; in other words, the average family of four with just one breadwinner—now the term retrieves its original impact—was resigned to spending a third of its income on bread alone. But worse was to follow; the wheat price rose sharply after 1836, almost doubling by 1839, when it cost eight shillings and eight pence a bushel. Now, the the average laborer's entire salary bought him the wheat to feed just seven persons.

The newly founded Anti-Corn Law League, champion of cheap bread, campaigned against the duties levied on imported wheat. The League drew vociferous support from the new industrial heartlands of the North and the Midlands, where beleaguered workers and incensed industrialists alike resented paying artificial subsidies to the prosperous agricultural landowners whenever they bought bread. In January 1839, a petition in Leeds declaiming the Corn Laws attracted more than nine

thousand signatures in just four days. That same month, League meetings at Dundee, Bristol, Leicester, Hawick, Preston, and Aberdeen were
held to petition Parliament for the repeal of the Laws. The *Caledonia*'s
cargo, then, far from being a mundane commodity, was both the vital
staff of life and the defining social issue of the day.

I followed the cliffs to the south, with Florence Nightingale's words
of anguish ringing in my ears. The first of the swallows were swooping
low, flushing insects from the gorse. I could see Hawker's "bluff and broken headland just by the southern boundary of my glebe," where the
Caledonia had struck according to the "Remembrances" account. I immediately recognized it as the same distinctive promontory I had seen from
Hartland, the beaky face with the prominent nose in profile, reposing like
a head on a pillow. I checked its name on my map: Sharpnose Point.

I soon came to a path that descended through thick thorn bushes
laden with globules of ivory blossom, turning back on itself to arrive
after a few yards at a small sturdy structure that had been built into the
cliff face. Hawker's hut had a turfed roof and was fronted by a simple
wooden gable that had weathered to a veined stony gray. A stable door
with a heavy wooden latch gave way to a dark interior, with a continuous
low bench fixed around the walls, like an anchorite's cell.

Over the years, the hut had attracted numerous items of graffiti.
Some of the more rigorously carved ones had acquired something of the
substance and credibility of Egyptian hieroglyph; Derek had evidently
loved Doreen with an enduring passion. It was here Hawker had retreated to reflect on God's sublime surroundings, to entertain Tennyson,
to abandon himself to the Muse and the opium pipe, or even to watch for
basking mermaids (which the pipe's contents may have done much to
conjure).

A light rain had begun to fall. I followed the path inland, which ran
beside a stone wall overgrown with honeysuckle and pink campions,
fringing a tilled field. From the red soil, thinly sprinkled between scattered stones, a green fuzz of tiny wheat shoots showed. The path became
a track that emerged by a green where a few cottages and farm buildings,

a pub, and a red telephone box had congregated. Crosstown, as the place was known, was one of those "clusters of houses," as Hawker had put it, "which would be called, I suppose, in any populous or civilized region, villages." The place, some two hundred yards from the church, barely qualified as a hamlet.

But it did boast the Bush Inn. I pushed open the door of the pub, named after the old tradition of signaling the sale of beer by hanging cut bushes from licensed premises, and found myself in a dark, agreeably old-fashioned parlor, with thick walls, sturdy beams, stone-flagged floors, dark benches, and hot embers in the hearth. A white-haired landlady, dressed in slippers, drew me a pint and took my order for a meat pie in silence. I looked around me. On the windowsills were ornamental horse-drawn carts in brass, and porcelain sheaves of wheat. The walls were hung with horseshoes, corn bouquets, old muskets, a hunting horn, and a stuffed fox head, bucolic trinkets that spoke of the surrounding fields. To the sea there were no such references; there were none of the lobster pots, seashells, dried starfish, or glass buoys artfully arranged in fishing nets and suspended from the smoke-stained ceiling. There was that sense, again, of the community denying the sea's very existence.

The pub was empty, save for two elderly men at the bar, Ken and Peter, who had been walking the cliffs. They walked the cliffs a fair amount these days, they explained, ever since being made redundant by their factory near Bideford, which had turned out electrical terminals until the Estonians began producing them more cheaply. Not, Ken observed resignedly, that you could blame the Estonians. Besides, it was good to walk the cliffs and revisit his father-in-law's old haunts. I wondered what business his father-in-law might have had on the cliffs.

"He was a wrecker," said Ken.

I spluttered, causing the disc of foam to skitter off my beer and fold itself down the side of the glass. I thought of *Jamaica Inn*, and Daphne du Maurier's memorable evocations of brigands descending on this coast whenever storms blew from the northwest, their steeds greased to escape the clutches of the revenue men; of lights on the cliffs and the rending of ships' timbers; of booty rolling in the breakers; of hatchets and muskets and the despairing cries of wretched seamen, their outstretched hands ignored.

"A wrecker, you say," I repeated. Ken guffawed.

"Call it wreck salvage," he explained. "All aboveboard, you know. Heaps of wrecks there were along this coast, especially after the last war. You could get a fair price for scrap in those days, and salvage rights only cost you a few quid. Mind you, it was hard work lugging the scrap up these cliffs. Of course, there was always war stuff washed up that they never declared, I don't mind telling you; tins of Senior Service cigarettes and corned beef, and packs of chewing gum that they found on the shore. Father-in-law would keep it all under the chest of drawers, he would, in case the revenue man showed up."

When Peter and Ken left, a profound silence fell upon the Bush.

"You here for the walking?" asked the landlady.

She nodded when I told her.

"The old figurehead. Stolen it was, back in 1968. Some kids wanted it for a Halloween prank. Found it months later, they did, abandoned in some field near Abbotsham. They say as you shouldn't go near her at midnight; she'll bring her sword down on you, she will."

Things were turning irredeemably gloomy. I tried to rescue the mood by quizzing the landlady about the four black bags of perished leather that hung from the wall behind me. Fist-sized and tied with draw-strings, they had pricked my curiosity. She regarded the objects for a while.

"Shoes for horses," she replied, shuffling out of the bar. "Or slippers more like. To silence the hooves on solemn occasions. Like funerals."

I drank up, brushed the pie crumbs from my hands, and stepped out into the afternoon.

Chapter ∽ 8

I returned to the vicarage along the unpaved road. It was overhung by oaks, ashes, and thorns that the west wind had back-combed until the branches resembled waves, permanently crested. A wicker basket stood by the flower bed below the library window. It was piled high with freshly pulled weeds, their trailing roots beaded with hems of granular soil.

"Did the books help?" Jill's head rose from the shrubs.

"Oh yes," I replied, failing to disguise my low spirits. I had found more than I had cared to find. I had dared hope for no more than the odd tantalizing lead, and had so feared drawing a complete blank that I had not even considered the prospect that now confronted me: that I'd found no less than the final word on the *Caledonia*. That the circumstances surrounding one distant wreck, one of uncounted wrecks to have foundered on this coast, should have been chronicled in such detail left me with a depressing sense that all was known that could be known, and that the past held no secrets. But Jill was gardening, and was unlikely to be in the mood for such rarefied grievances.

"I just hadn't expected to get all the facts in half an hour's reading," I explained lamely.

"The facts?" Jill snorted. "Facts are one thing I don't much associate with Hawker."

"What do you mean?"

"Hawker is a fascinating, even bewildering man," Jill explained, tossing a weed into the wicker basket. "But much of what he says is best taken with a large pinch of salt."

"You mean . . . ?"

"The vicar has a reputation," Jill offered. "For reworking material, for invention. You could even say for lying."

Soon afterward I was back in the library, rapidly working through the Hawker prefaces, introductions, forewords, and commentaries as Jill had suggested. They were soon proving her right. *Footprints*, wrote Thurston Peter in his 1906 *History of Cornwall*, was "quite unreliable as an authority for details owing to the author's unfortunate habit of forging any documents required for picturesque effect." In 1909, a writer named Charles Harper described Hawker as "a man—and a not very scrupulous man—of imagination." Even Hawker's main biographer, Charles Byles, a bespectacled man whose essential milieu is evoked in a single photograph showing him seated in his garden at Golders Green in 1932 surrounded by teetering piles of review copies, acknowledged that his admired father-in-law tended toward fabrication. Byles admitted in his preface to *Footprints* to "an element of fiction in Hawker's biographical studies. . . . He never let facts, or the absence of them, stand in the way of his imagination." And in his biography of Hawker, he wrote that "Hawker's antiquarian studies are remarkable rather for beauty of thought than for historical accuracy." Nor, it seems, did Hawker limit such flights of fancy to his writings. Margaret Jeune, visiting with her husband in 1846, wrote of Hawker in her diary how "another drawback to the effect of his powers of amusement is that he exerts them at the entire expense of truth," and referred to his "tendency to palm off falsehood for the dear honest truth."

This changed things, of course. A single lie, even the rumor of one, is a contagion that casts doubts upon the health of the whole. And if "Remembrances" were riddled with falsehoods, it was not that Hawker's memory had failed him—though the account had been written all of twenty-three years after the loss of the *Caledonia*—but that he had willfully disregarded the truth. I had paid Hawker's writings undue respect, taking them for reliable testimony when it now seemed they might be something else entirely. Armed with a skepticism I had not expected to require—I was, after all, dealing with a man of the cloth—I returned to Hawker's wreck account.

The effect was almost immediate. The text now seemed too . . . wondrous. I considered the possibility that nineteenth-century truths might naturally strike a late-twentieth-century observer so; from the familiar present, the past often tends to appear fabulous. But it was rather that the visual details, which had initially struck me as resonant original observations, now seemed like images borrowed from stock early-Victorian myths. There was the hand and arm of a dead crewman from the *Caledonia,* which "came out of the water, as though stretched out with life." Those words recalled another poetic arm, one rising from the lake to clutch Arthur's Excalibur in *Morte D'Arthur,* especially since Tennyson's poem had been published just four months before the *Caledonia* was lost. Had Hawker filched the image from a poet he greatly admired?

I was also troubled by Hawker's subsequent account of the search for the missing crewmen's bodies. I could credit that the searchers "gathered together one poor fellow in five parts; his limbs had been wrenched off, and his body rent"; such mutilations were repeatedly witnessed along this coast, and even twentieth-century beachcombers had come across severed human feet and other body parts. Still, I was suspicious of the following cameo:

> During our search for his remains, a man came up to me with something in his hand, inquiring, "Can you tell me, sir, what is this? Is it a part of a man?" It was the mangled seaman's heart, and we restored it reverently to its place, where it had once beat high with life and courage, with thrilling hope and sickening fear.

That a heart might physically be rent from its place, remain recognizable through the process, and then be "restored" seemed most improbable, evoking as it did unseemly fiddling about beneath the wretched man's shattered rib cage. It was hard to resist the idea that Hawker had manufactured a confusion of hearts actual and symbolic, so as to justify the cameo's pulsing, poetic payoff: life and courage, hope and fear.

Now the doubts flooded in. I even wondered whether Hawker might have tampered with Le Daine's story. In the light of what I now knew, I began to suspect that the survivor's account was a plot-driven fiction, brimful with the tragic cause-and-effect on which narratives thrive: the wounding of the Portuguese cook in a brawl and his subsequent death, causing captain and crew to attend his funeral in Falmouth and leaving the cabin boy to break the all-important barometer, which left them unaware of the impending storm, and so led directly to their deaths.

I also sensed invention in other aspects of the account: the poignant fact that "captain, and mate, and another of the crew, were to be married on their return to their native town," the cup of matrimonial love dashed cruelly from their lips by death; the storybook valor of the captain, whose body was found with each hand grasping "a small bag or pouch. One contained his pistols; the other held two little log-reckoners of brass; so that his last thoughts were full of duty to his owners and his ship"; the remarkable claim that Le Daine would be shipwrecked twice more in his life; and, finally, that surreal tortoise. Hawker of Morwenstow? Hawker of lies, more likely.

Byles would actually admit that Hawker had embellished the facts in "Remembrances," though he was not specific. "In one or two minor details," he conceded, "he alters the facts to suit his artistic purpose.... This was quite natural as he was writing for a London magazine." Though I could not prove—at least not yet—where and how Hawker had deviated from the truth, Byles's defense of his father-in-law seemed unconvincing, asking as it did that we disregard as motive Hawker's documented fondness for fabrication and swallow instead the proposition that he had reluctantly sacrificed the truth to satisfy the metropolitan appetites of his readership.

Whatever the details, all now seemed changed. "Remembrances" might prove to bear only the faintest resemblance to the truth. It might prove absolute fancy or even active disinformation, masking another story entirely. Certainly, it could no longer be regarded as reliable. What had really happened to the *Caledonia*? I began by returning to the flower bed and, recalling the remarkable longevity of tortoises, asked Jill whether they had by any chance inherited such a creature when they moved here.

Chapter ∞ 9

Jill knew of no tortoise. She could help me, however, with the whereabouts of the Morwenstow parish burial registers, where I might learn something of the crew of the *Caledonia*. Frank Whitehead, who helped out with church matters, kept them on microfiche at his home half a mile inland, at the head of the Morwenstow valley. He met me at the door of his former farmstead and ushered me into a small room where he had prepared the microfiche reader. He brought me a cup of tea and two biscuits, neatly stacked on the saucer, before gently closing the door on his way out.

I inserted a fiche, a passport-sized sheet of plastic, into the machine, restoring the register pages to their original dimensions. The pages and their antique column headings—"Name," "Abode," "When buried," "Age," and "By whom the Ceremony was performed"—were bathed in a blue light as cold as a coffin's interior. As I ranged among these burials for the first time, I felt a novice's sense of intrusion, even of desecration, as if, dressed in clinical white overalls, I were conducting clandestine nighttime exhumations under arc lights.

The Morwenstow burial records are an extended lament to the unknown sailor. Entries such as "the body of a shipwrecked sailor, name unknown," "a Mariner cast ashore," and "A Corpse cast ashore, name only known in Heaven," with references to identifying tattooes, often anchors and initials, exert a powerful poetic effect. Strangely, however, the burials do not occur with any regularity. They positively abound between the 1840s and 1860s, but are relatively infrequent prior to Hawker's incumbency here. Sailors are intermittently recorded as having been singly buried in 1823, 1827, and 1829, and not one is registered as having made it to the graveyard during the 1830s.

It was not until 1808, with the passing of a bill "for providing suitable interment in churchyards or parochial burying grounds in England, for such dead human bodies as may be cast on shore from the sea, in cases of wreck or otherwise," that the sea dead on the British coast had the right to anything better than a makeshift grave above the tidemark. Local man Sam Cleverdon, born in 1792, remembered how his father "would thrust the bodies into the clefts and fissures of the cliffs and make mounds near to point out the place."

The 1808 bill insisted that each coastal parish be responsible for the proper interment of any corpses discovered upon its shoreline. It is most unlikely, however, that the bill had an immediate impact in Morwenstow. Before Hawker's arrival in 1835, the parish had not had a resident vicar for a century; religious instruction on the parishioners' new obligations under the law would have been sporadic. Burying drowned strangers in the graveyard had always been accounted a low priority. The process was extremely unpleasant, not least because it was rare that the dead were found immediately, and the combined effects of decay and rocks often reduced them to pieces, or "gobbets" as they were commonly known. The considerable time and effort required to raise such remains up the cliff, and the expense of burial, were further discouragements. It was easier by far to embrace the conscience-salving suspicion that the foreigner might not be a Christian, and was therefore unsuitable for burial in the hallowed ground of the graveyard.

Hawker, who regarded the burial of the dead as an absolute duty— "one of the seven acts of mercy that God will surely requite"—was quick to crusade against such barbarities. He posted men on the cliffs in the aftermath of storms to report washed-up bodies and even offered payment to those prepared to deliver the bodies to the vicarage.

Many guises are attributed to Hawker in his excellently chronicled life. But of them all—mystic and symbolist, poet, eccentric, Christian

Socialist, prankster, local benefactor, scourge of Methodists, champion of the harvest festival—it is his role as mariner's undertaker that is most vividly and memorably rendered.

When the *Bencoolen* was lost at Bude in November 1862, the tide washed one of the bodies north onto Hawker's glebe. Hawker described its discovery in a letter, betraying a fascination with his own role in the ensuing rituals, which is almost unseemly in its breathlessness: "... the message came at Night, 'A Corpse ashore, Sir, at Stanbury Mouth,' a Creek a Mile South. . . . my Lych House cleared and a plank or two laid to receive the dead. A message—they are nearly come—I go out into the moonlight bareheaded and when I come near I greet the nameless Dead with the Sentences 'I am the Resurrection and the Life,' &c.—They lay down their burthen at my feet—I look upon the Dead—Tall—Stout—wellgrown—Boots on, Elastic, and Socks . . ."

Another vividly observed cameo, which appeared in an obituary of Hawker, confirms him in this mournful but irresistibly heroic role. "It was on a solemn occasion that we first saw Morwenstow," the writer begins. "The sea was still surly and troubled, with wild lights breaking over it, and torn clouds driving through the sky. Up from the shore, along a narrow path between jagged rocks and steep banks tufted with thrift, came the vicar, wearing a cassock and surplice, and conducting a sad procession, which bore along with it the bodies of two seamen flung up the same morning on the sands."

The recovery of sea dead becomes a constant refrain in Hawker's letters. As early as 1837, he writes that "pieces of ships have washed on shore, and a part of a man and a stocking with a human foot in it." In another letter he writes: "The sea is casting up her dead on my shore. . . . We are looking for bodies every tide." Yet another letter reads, "Two bodies thus far on shore one at Poughill one at Kilkhampton . . . We are on the watch all day—mournful work." And: "The search for bodies still goes on. Limbs are cast ashore every now and then, arms, and legs, and at Hartland joining Wellcombe, lumps of flesh have floated above High Water, and been buried in the ground. Five out of Seven corpses had no heads—cut off by the jagged rocks!!" "This is my dread every winter," he observes elsewhere; "—a Wreck, with a large crew—drowned corpses and late Burial—God shield us!" And: "Next morning the Watchers found the Body of one of the Sailors clothed only in a Red Jersey and belt. He was as usual jammed in between the rocks. He was carried to my Premises and placed in the Room up in my yard which we always use as a Deadhouse."

Hawker has acquired an enviable reputation in this regard. N. H. Lawrence Martyn of Tonacombe, the manor house a few hundred yards south of the Bush Inn at Morwenstow, recalled Hawker's "treatment of the drowned—which I suspect you will know as it is proverbial in these parts. . . ." in a letter to Charles Byles, who was busy preparing his biography of his father-in-law in 1903: "When Mr Hawker was told of any bodies being washed in he himself—in surplice etc, used to head the procession of villagers bearing the body or bodies to the mortuary by the lychgate—where the bodies were tenderly laid to await burial. . . ."

Hawker readily cultivated this darkly romantic and elemental tag. Reverend William Haslam, an acquaintance, recalled how Hawker "used to tell thrilling stories of shipwreck; how he saved the lives of some of the sailors, and how he recovered the bodies of others he could not save." And in one undated letter, Hawker writes of his own achievements including "the rescue from the rocks there of 40 dead sailors and the several burial of their bodies."

But it is a scribbled, occasionally illegible note of Hawker's, an apparently private observation pitched somewhere between wistful and bitter, that betrays his peculiar yearning for a particular recognition. It observes how "a man writing about wrecks might have recorded that the Vicar of Morwenstow rescued with his own hands some at his cost all 33 corpses from the sea and laid them at rest. But fatal jealousy so obvious in all such things forbade—So I am d———d with the faint praise of ballad monger." It was as if he wished to be known, above all, for his services to the sea dead.

Which brought me to the burial entries for the *Caledonia*. These entries, by which Hawker set such apparent store, detailed the first seamen that he had had occasion to bury at Morwenstow. They were made in the vicar's large and distinctive hand. The first read "Captain of the *Caledonia* of Arbroath North Britain wrecked here." The captain's name was given as Stevenson Peter. So much for St. Peter, then. It remained an odd appellation, nevertheless, for Stevenson seemed a thoroughly uncommon forename. It was almost as if the two names had been transposed, each seeming less likely in its own place than in that of the other. Captain Peter, whose age was given as "about 28," was buried on September 10, 1842—two days after the *Caledonia*'s loss.

Buried with him, a "Seaman of the *Caledonia* of Arbroath," also aged "about 28," was one Alexander Kent. I knew of Kent from the passing mention in "Remembrances," where he appears in the moments prior to his death in the tumult of shipwreck: "Just then," Hawker has Le Daine tell us as he clings to a sea-swept rock, "I saw Alick Kant, one of our crew, swimming past. I saw him lay his hand on a rock, and I sung out, 'Hold on, Alick!' but a wave rolled and swept him away, and I never saw his face more." Though Le Daine's last sighting of Kent might have been a Hawker fiction, the faulty rendering of the man's name, as though half-remembered, does have the ring of truth about it.

The next was plain David MacDonald. MacDonald, also described as
a seaman and aged "about 18," was the last of the crewmen to have been
buried on September 10. In this detail, at least, Hawker was proved right;
"the three bodies first found," he wrote, "were buried at the same time."

David Macdonald	Seaman of the Caledonia of Arbroath	Septr 10th ·	18	Rt Hawker Vicar
No. 490.				

The fourth crewman to be recovered, William Tasker, seaman, aged seventeen, had been buried two days later, on September 12. But the fifth,

William Tasker	Seaman of the Caledonia of Arbroath	Septr 12th	17	Rt Hawker Vicar
No. 491.				

David Wallace, also given as a seaman and aged "about 30," had not been
buried until October 7, a day short of a month after the *Caledonia* was

David Wallace	Seaman of the Caledonia of Arbroath	Octr 7th	abt 30	Rt Hawker Vicar
No. 494.				

lost. From this bare entry, I could almost smell human putrefaction in autumn's late warmth. I read on, expecting further entries, but October
turned chill and became November. Christmas came and went, and only
locals were registered. By the time I had worked my way into the spring
of the following year, it was clear that the register was through with the
crew of the *Caledonia*. Something was wrong.

I remembered Hawker's unequivocal statement in "Remembrances" that he had buried all of the *Caledonia*'s perished crew. Le Daine, he had written, had "remained as my guest six weeks, and during the whole of this time we sought diligently, and at last we found the whole crew, nine in number." I took Hawker's total to include the ship's sole survivor, Le Daine; the cook, supposedly buried at Falmouth sometime earlier, would have brought the original complement to ten. All of which had prepared me for eight bodies in the burial register. But there were only five.

"And at last," Hawker reconfirmed the burial claim, "the good ship's company—captain, mate and crew—were laid at rest, side by side, beneath our churchyard trees." Hawker had concluded the story as befitted it—the brave crew reunited in death, to the vicar's considerable credit—but not, it now appeared, as it had actually happened. It was possible, of course, that Hawker had merely omitted to enter the details of subsequent burials. Given, however, his apparent preoccupation with his sea-dead tally, his tendency to fabricate, and the fastidiousness with which he appears to have kept the register, this did not seem likely. Which left the possibility that the vicar was racking up burial ceremonies he had not performed, and claiming for his tally sea dead he had not recovered.

I had begun the day by looking for a story and ended it looking for discrepancies, which was where the true story now appeared to reside. I turned off the fiche reader and carried my teacup to the kitchen, where Frank was washing dishes. I thanked him, and we stepped outside into the twilight together.

"We saw a big cat among the trees a few days ago," said Frank, sending me on my way. Such sightings, which had tended to be concentrated on the moors but had recently begun to proliferate along the coast, were thought to be of pumas that had escaped from zoos or private collections.

"I'll keep my eyes open," I replied. I set out along the path that supposedly led down the valley to the vicarage but soon petered out. I clambered through hedgerows of thorn blossom, and picked my way across a stream that watering livestock had turned into a mudhole. I could hear the mew of distant seagulls. Curious ewes and their lambs, pink numbers sprayed on their flanks, gathered at my approach, then bolted into the gathering gloom. I could see the lights of the vicarage ahead of me.

Hours ago, I'd had mere hunches. Now I had missing bodies.

Chapter ⚬ *10*

All night I dreamed of missing bodies, and I awoke to unsavory thoughts. I might have regarded Hawker's lies as merely cavalier or even creative—the writer's license—except that lies tended to have darker meaning along this coast. Later that morning, I drove over to the Wreckers' Retreat at Hartland Quay.

A stiff northwesterly wind funneled along the lane between the whitewashed terraces. There were hikers in the bar who wore bright yellow gaiters and woolly hats and black anoraks, which caused them to resemble bees. Their walking sticks were styled like ski poles. Plastic map holders were slung around their ruddy necks. The outfits brought chortles from the covey of locals who were gathered in a smoky redoubt behind a tabletop pile of ketchup-smeared crockery. The hikers sought refuge in their maps or the paraphernalia on the pub's walls.

Wreckers' Retreat caps and T-shirts proclaiming "I got wrecked at Hartland Quay" were displayed on the shelf above the bar. On a map of the coastline, a rash of red stars marking lost ships ran south toward Morwenstow. A facsimile nineteenth-century handbill advertised a "Wreck Sale," detailing the cargo of a ship that had "recently come to grief in these parts": pieces of fir timber, cases of white lead, barrels of tar, oak handspikes, deerskins, linseed oil, cotton yarn, and bales of wool.

Even the beer was called Wreckers' Ale. Its hand pump was illustrated with a print, suitably monochrome, showing shadowy nineteenth-century figures hurrying down a rock-strewn beach toward a vessel foundering in the breakers of a night sea, masts shattered and tattered sails streaming in the gale.

"I'll have a pint of that," I motioned. I took my glass to a window table where the place mats and beer coasters repeated that classic West Country cameo of storm and clandestine plunder. It was an evocative representation, eliciting lurid speculation regarding the landsmen's intentions, but a coy one in that it never actually confirmed them.

Wrecking had always been a conspicuously nebulous term. Only the day before, at the Bush Inn, I'd heard it used to describe licensed wreck salvage. Equally innocuous, the term could apply to beachcombing. As a local commentator put it: "When . . . a man or woman in a north-coast village talks of 'going wrecking,' it merely means they are going to the beach to gather firewood." The wording was significant, of course, for there had always been other kinds of wrecking that one spoke of less readily.

The First Report of the Constabulary Force Commissioners (1839) cited numerous instances of pillaging from wrecks all along the coasts of England and Wales. "Almost all the inhabitants along the coast are decidedly wreckers," said the Commissioner of the Liverpool police. "If a decided wreck takes place . . . the accumulation of wreckers is the most instantaneous thing you can imagine." But, as the report confirmed, it was the Cornish who had "long been notorious as addicted to this species of plunder." A writer named John Robeson even wrote in 1825 that the Cornish were "taught from infancy to old age to look upon the fatalities of the sea as the most fortunate occurrence that they can possibly witness . . . the shrieks of the sufferers excite no painful emotion, but become like music to the ears of the human vultures who wait their evening prey, and often deprive of life the supplicating wretches whom the fury of the ocean has spared."

When a French brig, *Les Landois*, was wrecked near Sennen, West Cornwall, in October 1838, the cargo of "pipes of wine, casks of brandy, tobacco, cotton, liqueurs etc" littered a mile of beach. Eyewitness Alexander Shairp reported, "There were four or five thousand people of all classes staving in the casks, drinking the liquor and wine, and plundering the property of every description,—hundreds of women with pails, pots, jars and other vessels, carrying it into the country in all directions." The coast guard, "in preservation of our lives," shot over the heads of the plunderers and beat them with their swords.

Nor was plunder always the worst of it. Wreckers were even alleged to ignore the plight of surviving passengers and crewmen. George Borlase, steward of the Manor of Lanisley, near Penzance, wrote to his landlord on March 15, 1753: "My situation in life hath oblig'd me sometimes to be a spectator of things in it which shock humanity . . . the bill [an anti-wrecking legislation then being mooted] does not sufficiently provide against the monstrous barbarity practised by these savages upon the poor sufferers. I have seen many a poor man, half dead, cast ashore and crawling out of the reach of the waves, fallen upon and in a manner stripp'd naked by those villains, and if afterwards he has saved his chest or any more cloaths, they have been taken from him."

A century later, a witness to the Constabulary Force Commissioners stated that "the bodies of the drowned persons are almost invariably stripped of every thing valuable, money, watches etc. It was also asserted that the finger of a drowned captain was 'cut off to secure his ring' in the 1830s while a woman was proved to have 'bitten off the ears' of a drowned female 'to obtain the earrings.'" A Reverend Charles Crump, incensed by the prevalence of wrecking in the 1850s, published a pamphlet poem called "The Morte Stone" after the notorious rock lying off Ilfracombe to the northeast of Hartland. "The daring outrages of these lawless people," wrote Crump, "have long been a source of just complaint, and they still continue unrepressed. The receiver of Droits of the Admiralty, invested with high authority . . . finds it impracticable to secure vessels, wrecked on the coast, from the plundering propensities of the country people, who collect in bodies, frequently of some hundreds, and set at defiance the constituted authorities. . . . Acts of robbery and personal violence on the shipwrecked are attributed to these marauders."

I made to leave. As I drained my pint, I found myself staring at the old image again; the beer coaster had clung to the wet base of my glass. The Wreckers' Retreat on a shore commonly known as the Wreckers' Coast, Wreckers' Ale, and wreckers on the bottom of the glass. Was somebody trying to tell me something?

In the parking lot, I could see the hikers making their way up the cliffs in a yellow straggle. Beyond them loomed the profile of Sharpnose.

Chapter ∞ *11*

Mark Myers lived out at Woolley, three miles east of Morwenstow. He was a marine artist, originally from San Francisco, which was improbably exotic for that windswept farm hamlet. Woolley was snared in a web of narrow lanes on the edge of marshy moorland where the West Country's rivers, the Tamar and the Torridge, rose within yards of each other before following their respective courses to the sea at Plymouth and Bideford.

Mark, who had lived in Cornwall since the early 1970s, turned out to be the archetype of his adopted land: short, with dark features, and a raffish roll-up sticking to his lip. He lived for square-rigged sailing ships and even now, stranded high and dry in the book-strewn confines of his studio, could be effortlessly imagined swarming through rigging, gathering billowing sails on a heaving foredeck, or straining against the wheel in a buffeting sea.

Mark had come to Britain in the 1960s to work on the last few square-riggers, mainly sail-training vessels out of Appledore and Plymouth. He married the daughter of a maritime historian (whose abiding interest had been square-riggers) and settled in Woolley to make a career painting ships' portraits, which were accurate to the last block and tackle. Mark had spent his life researching maritime documents, texts, and images to re-create old ships; I hoped he could help me do the same for the *Caledonia*.

Mark had cabinets crammed with drawings, cuttings, and photographs. His shelves were stacked with nautical titles. Nor did his knowledge stop at square-riggers. He also knew as much as anybody about the local coastline and took time away from his canvases to walk the shore, filling notebooks with detailed sketches of the wreck debris that he found there. Mark knew about the *Caledonia*. Years before, he had noticed a barnacle-encrusted wooden windlass on the shore beneath the cliff at Morwenstow that might have come off the *Caledonia*. He'd even had a go at painting her—or what might have remained of her the morning after the storm—but that was twenty-five years ago, and the painting was not at hand.

I showed Mark a document I had recently traced. He fell upon the "survey held at Arbroath on the Snow *Caledonia*," noting that the ship was eighty feet long, twenty-one feet in the beam, with a hold fourteen feet in depth. But where Mark nodded eagerly at the measurements of "bilge planks," the size of copper bolts in the "lower pintle of the rudder," and the English and African oak in her construction, my ignorance prevented me from following.

The survey was dated April 23, 1839; it had evidently taken place at the time of the *Caledonia*'s completion, which was a trigger to my imagination. It transported me back to a dockyard at the linen-producing port of Arbroath, beyond Dundee on Scotland's east coast. The "excellent and commodious" yard occupied the shelving shore between the harbor and the shore station, a crenellated tower in the Gothic Revival style that had traded signals with Robert Stevenson's remarkable Bell Rock lighthouse eleven miles out to sea. To this scene clung the redolent smells of paint, pitch, and wood shavings; the din of bellows, hammers, and anvils, and the buzz of saws; boilers and stoves, buckets of nails and wedges, and perhaps even the calloused hands of Mr. Arthur Smith, the yard owner, resting contentedly against the fine lines of the hull's smooth flank. With the *Caledonia*'s beginnings a note of optimism was sounded. The survey transformed the requiem perspective of epitaph verses, a moldering figurehead, and entries in a burial register, evoking prosperity for the owner and experience for the crew; the things these men would see before the ship returned them safely to the port of her beginnings!

M 5, 84/94

430

No. 430 **Survey held at** Arbroath **Date** April 23d 1839

on the Snow Caledonia **Master** Fredrick Mickoon

Tonnage 200 703/3500 **Built at** Arbroath **When built** April 1839

By whom built Arthur Smith **Owners** J. S. Coplin

Port belonging to Arbroath **Destined Voyage** Baltic

If Surveyed Afloat or in Dry Dock Sundry Periods building and Finished Afloat

	Feet	Inches		Feet	Inches		Feet	Inches
Length aloft	78	3/10	Extreme Breadth	21	3/10	Depth of Hold	14	6/10

Scantlings of Timber.

		Inches		Inches Middle	Inches Ends
Timber and Space	each	12½			
Floors	sided	11	Moulded	13	9½
1st Foothooks	"	9½	"	9½	9
2nd Ditto	"	9	"	8½	8
3rd Ditto	"	—	"	—	—
Top Timbers	"	8	"	7½	4½
Deck Beams . Number of 17	"	10	"	8¼	5
Hold Beams . Do. do. 7	"	10	"	10½	6½
Keel	"	11	"	14½	
Kelsons	"	11½	"	20	

Thickness of Plank.

Outside	Inches	Inside	Inches
Keel to Bilge	3	Foot Waling	2½
Bilge Planks	4	Bilge Planks	4
Bilge to Wales	3	Ceiling in Flat	2½
Wales	4½	Ditto Bilge to Clamp	2
Topsides	2	Hold Beam Clamps	3
Sheer Strakes	3	Deck Beam Ditto	3
Plank Sheers	3	Ceiling 'twixt Decks	2
Water-ways	7	Hold Beam Shelfs	4
Upper Deck	3	Deck Beam ditto	4

Size of Bolts in Fastenings.

Copper	Inches	Copper	Inches	Iron	Inches
Heel-Knee, and Dead Wood abaft	1	Bolts thro' the Bilge ~~and Foot Waling~~	3/4	Hold Beam	3/4
Scarphs of Keel No. 4	3/4	Butt End Bolts	5/8	Deck Beam	3/4
Floor Timber Bolts	1	Lower Pintle of the Rudder	2¼		
Kelson ditto	1				
Transoms and throats of Hooks	1			same in Iron above the Copper	—
Arms of Hooks	3/4 7/8				—

Entirely copper fastened below the Wales

Timbering.—The Space between the Floor Timbers and Lower Foothooks in this Vessel is 3 Inches. The Space between the Top-timbers is 6 Inches. The Stem, Stern Post, Transoms, Aprons, Knight Heads, Hawse Timbers, are composed of English and African oak and are all free from all defects.

Her Floors and first Foothooks are composed of English oak Timber.

Her other Foothooks and Top Timbers of English and some African oak

Her Shifts of the first and second Foothooks are not less than 3 feet 9 Inches *N.B. When reported by you less than the prescribed Rule, then state how many.*

The rest of the Shifts of the Frame are 4 feet

The Frame is fairly squared from the first Foothook Heads upwards, and not free from sap, and from thence downwards, the frame is Fairly Squared

The alternate Frames are all bolted together.

The Butts of the Timbers are all close together; their thickness not less than 1/3 of the entire moulding at that place. in general

The Frame is Well chocked with no Butt at each end of the chock. partial Bells in Midships

The Main Kelson is composed of African Oak and the False Kelson of English Oak

The Scarphs of the Kelsons are not less than 10 feet — inches.

The Deck and Hold Beams are composed of English and African oak

Planking Outside.—This Vessel's Plank from the Keel to the first Foothook Heads is composed of Elm

From the first Foothook Heads to the Light Water Mark of English and African oak

From the Light Water Mark to the Wales of English and African oak

The Wales and Black-strakes are of African oak and English Woods

The Topsides of English

The Sheer-strakes of African oak Decks, and state of, Yellow pine

The Gunwales of English oak Water-ways of Pitch pine

The Shifts of the Planking are not less than 5 Feet — Inches. *N.B. If reported less than the prescribed Rule, state whether general or partial, and if partial, in what part of the Ship.* The Planking is wrought Long three between.

Planking Inside.—The Clamps are composed of African oak the Stringers of French oak

The Bilge Planks of English and French oak and the remainder of the Ceiling of English oak

Fastenings.—To Hold Beams Double wood Lodging knees of English & Shelf piece

Deck Beams Double wood Lodging knees of English and Shelf piece

Number of Breasthooks Four Pointers none Crutches one

Butts End Bolts are of Copper in the Bottom, and one Bolt in each Butt End through and clenched. except some butts in Midships

Bilge ~~and Footwaling~~ Copper bolted through and clenched.

General Quality of Workmanship Fair

We certify that the preceding is a correct description of the above-named Vessel.

Builder's Name Arthur Smith

Surveyor's Name David Tayster

Her Masts, Yards, &c. are in *Best* condition, and sufficient in size and length.

She has SAILS.		CABLES, &c.			ANCHORS.
N°.	**Fathoms.**		**Inches.**	**N°.**	
2 Fore Suils,	180	Chain	1/8	3	Bower
1 Fore Top Sails,	80	Hempen Stream Cable	8½	1	Stream,
2 Fore Topmast Stay Sails,	70	Hawser	6½	2	Kedge,
1 Main Sails,	70	Towlines	4½		All of proper weight.
2 Main Top Sails,	70	Warp	3¾		
and *Well found with Best Sails*		All of *Best* quality.			

Her Standing and Running Rigging is *all* sufficient in size and *of Best* ~~in~~ quality.

She has *One* Long Boat and *One Jolly Boat*

The present state of the Windlass is *Wright...* ~~Capstan~~ *Wrench* and Rudder *Will hung* with *Bow & Hawser patent*

General Remarks—Statement and Date of Repairs.

This is a Vessel of very good Material, excellent out and inside plank. The Material and being all of the quality required for a 12 years Ship: the workmanship however is inferior and the Frame indifferently squared, and the Chocks not properly nor regularly butted. She is very abundantly fitted with the best Stores and remarkably well equipped in all her fittings & rigging and well adapted for the safe Conveyance of Dry & Perishable Cargoes —

If Sheathed, Doubled, or Felted, *Single Bottom*

and Date when last done _____

And *I am* of opinion this Vessel should be Classed 10 A I

The Amount of the Fee .... £ 3 : 3 : — is received by me, *David Ryhter*

Committee Minute _____ *21 May* 1836

Character assigned _____ *A 1 for 10 Years*

Much of the document was a pre-printed form in which space re-
stricted the surveyor's contributions to the likes of measurements, quantities, and timber types. At the section entitled "concluding remarks,"
however, a comparative expanse was provided that allowed him to indulge his opinion and judgment. "This is a vessel of very good material,
excellent out and inside plank," he declared, before introducing significant qualifiers: "the workmanship, however, is inferior and the frame indifferently squared, nor entirely free from sap." The tone then rose
again. "She is very abundantly fitted," he continued, ". . . and remarkably
well-equipped in all the fittings of riggings and well adapted for the safe
conveyance of dry and perishable cargoes."

I detected a disinclination to sign off on a downward note. Indeed,
there could be glimpsed in the surveyor's conclusion an enthusiasm about
this vessel that exceeded his brief. Phrases like "very good," "excellent,"
"very abundantly fitted," and "remarkably well-equipped" had the cu-
mulative effect of suggesting that the surveyor had temporarily let his
heart get the better of him. I imagined an old soul, a little crabbed, as sur-
veyors are supposed to be, surprised to find himself surrendering to the
sight of this ship, newborn in the Arbroath spring, as the yardsmen finished her afloat and the crew prepared for her maiden voyage, so that his
high praise turned momentarily to something approaching rapture.

That there had been something impressive, even lovely, about the
Caledonia was an appealing hunch that a clipping from the *Arbroath Guide*
soon compounded. It was true, of course, that people rarely spoke ill of
the recently departed, a courtesy that was probably extended to lost ships.
But when the local newspaper wrote, a week after the ship's loss, of "the
beautiful brig the *Caledonia*" and, a few lines later, called her "a splendid
brig," I was tempted to believe it.

The surveyor, getting back to business, had signed off by awarding
the *Caledonia* an AI classification, valid for ten years.

"Good," said Mark. "The best she could possibly have got would
have been an AI for twelve years." Which only prejudice might have prevented. The Select Committee on Shipwreck of 1836 had noted how

builders in Scotland commonly resented that it seemed to be "a fixed principle ... not to class ships as of the highest and best class, twelve years, that were built out of [beyond] the River Thames."

Mark's studio was on the first floor, overlooking fields that stretched away, sloping into wooded gulleys that gathered on their approach to the sea. Closely packed shelves of nautical volumes, periodicals, and registers were piled to the ceiling. A current commission, almost completed, stood on an easel in the center of the room: a square-rigger making to the west, with the Devon hills near Salcombe in the background. She was heeling to port, to expose the arrangement of the deck beyond the high gunwales.

"A brig in the Mediterranean fruit trade in the 1860s," Mark explained, "but the deck arrangement would pass for the *Caledonia*'s." She carried the immense bowsprit of the age, which angled upward like a great bayonet planted against the onrushing sky, the figurehead fixed to the bow beneath it. On the deck, right forward, I could see the windlass where the anchor chain was wound; then, working aft, the hatch to the forecastle, that airless, dark triangle in the bows that constituted the crew's living space, followed by the foremast; then, a small cook's galley, the only housing to stand proud of the deck; the hold hatch where the up-turned longboat was lashed; the main mast; the companionway to the cabins of captain and mate; right aft, the ship's wheel; and hanging above the stern windows, which looked in on the officers' cabins, davits from which the twelve-foot jollyboat hung.

Now for the ship's general appearance. Mark lay aloft into the upper reaches of his library for books containing images approximating that of the *Caledonia*. He hauled down a succession of volumes before laying two early photographs before me. "These would be close to her," he murmured. One photograph, dated 1856, showed the brig *Lyra* grounded on the tidal river at Wisbech; the other, undated, was of an unidentified brig in dry dock at Aberwyswyth, with timber support props, showing chalky white, angled against her hull. Hemp rigging—some latticed to form "ratlines" or rope-ladders—ran in tapering wedges from the gun-wales to the mastheads to create, with yards and sprits, a collage of airy overlapping triangles. In each case, the rigging's mazy geometry gave way to a heavy dark hull, with the fashionable white-painted strip, the port band, running below the gunwale.

The images dated from photography's very infancy; the discovery of the daguerreotype had only been announced in the summer of 1839. The photographs seemed like stolen glimpses of an earlier world that should have been rendered in ink or oil paint, just as it had been for hundreds of years. The fens at Wisbech and the dock at Aberwyswyth seemed unprepared for photography's unforgiving objectivity. Nor were the ships seen at their best. In photography's early days, movement still eluded the medium's capabilities. Far from hammering along under a press of canvas in a big sea, these brigs had been photographed clear of the water and thus out of their element: vulnerable, tubby, their weed-festooned, copper-plated posteriors exposed.

Mark then began passing down books of paintings, each opened to a ship's portrait. These portraits had a quite different effect. Although they made no claim to mimic eyesight (the admittedly blurred, mottled, and monochrome eyesight of the photographs), they succeeded in presenting their subjects in a far more favorable light, at sea and under sail, with a splendid grace and buoyancy. Here, then, were close approximations to

the *Caledonia:* the *John Scott* of Whitehaven, 225 tons and built in 1835; the 180-ton *Circassian,* built at Aberdeen in 1836; and the *Wave,* built at Yarmouth just three months after the *Caledonia* and of almost exactly the same tonnage.

Now a working image of the *Caledonia,* a composite derived from photographs and paintings of comparable contemporary vessels, was beginning to emerge: a handsome, well-maintained vessel, with four rectangular but wind-scalloped sails arranged on each mast, each fractionally smaller than the one below, with triangles of canvas—her jib and staysail—slung from the bowsprit to the foremast, and the spanker, a fore and aft sail, on the main boom. Mark, who had ransacked the library to his satisfaction, sat back and rolled himself a cigarette.

"You won't get any closer than that," he declared. "Unless, of course, a painting of the ship herself was commissioned."

"A painting of her," I murmured. Might there, hanging in the home of some oblivious descendant, perhaps, or begrimed by smoke on the wall of an Arbroath pub, even be a portrait of the *Caledonia* herself?

The *Caledonia*'s short life happened to coincide with a blossoming in the tradition of ship portraiture. Proud owners, masters, and even long-serving mates commissioned portraits of their vessels from artists who, depending on their reputation, worked from well-appointed studios or advertised, cut-rate, for business from visiting mariners in bars and along quaysides. They worked from ports all over the world, but notably in London and Liverpool, Copenhagen, Marseilles, Livorno, Venice, Malta, and Smyrna, now Izmir, in Turkey.

The ships' portraitists, working in oil and occasionally in watercolor, mostly favored broadside views, sometimes redepicting the ship in the background of the same portrait, stern-on. Some painted stock backdrops, amassing half-finished canvases to which they would add ships when the commissions came in. But they knew their market well, which insisted on absolute accuracy, with artistic expression a distant consideration. No master mariner would accept a portrait that misrepresented his ship's rig, or failed to replicate the rake of her masts. This insistence on accuracy might have been expected to rob the paintings of life and reduce them to technical curiosities. The truth was that these ships, though accurately rendered, were invariably framed in the irresistible poetry of big seas and streaming canvas, and it was in their skies and seas—beyond the control of the portrait's commissioner—that the artists expressed themselves. The effect in these paintings was one of exhilaration barely restrained, struggling to get out.

The *Caledonia* might have been painted by any number of contemporary marine artists. These included the highly regarded William John Huggins, whose beat was London; the Roux brothers, who ran a chandler's ship on the quayside at Marseilles near the Hotel de Ville; William Clark at Glasgow; F. T. Albinus at Hamburg; and Jacob Petersen at Copenhagen.

But for now, I could not even say whether the *Caledonia* had visited any of these places.

Chapter ◎ *12*

I made a point of returning to Hawker's hut before I left for home that evening. It struck me, just as my rereading of the vicar's wreck account had yielded startling new meanings, that I might gain something from a second visit.

And this time, as I lifted the latch and pushed open the door, I saw not the graffiti but the timber from which the hut was made. The interior was neatly paneled with planks; some were strictly functional but others, with their scrolled or corniced edges, had evidently done decorative service in seaborne interiors. In the arched roof beams and the uprights were neat round holes from which rusted iron treenails poked. The hut had been assembled entirely from old ships' timbers.

Wreck timber commonly went into the repair or construction of buildings in the area. In many of the older farmhouses and cottages were the same telltale holes in joists and inglenook or ceiling beams. Kitchen cupboards boasted tarnished brass fittings or revealed distinctive cabin lines. Short stair runs were originally ladders from ships' companionways. Elsewhere, it was the cargoes of wrecks that were recovered and used, like the pit props employed in cottages at Millook or the slates from the *Robert,* wrecked at Stanbury in 1894, which roofed a house in Kilkhampton.

These interior details spoke mournfully of another world, but they were merely the result of fastidious Morwenstow beachcombing—or so Hawker would have it. He described the worst type of wrecker known to his parish as a "watcher of the sea and rocks for flotsam and jetsam, and other unconsidered trifles which the waves might turn up to reward the zeal and vigilance of a patient man." He wrote of the *Caledonia* that:

> The people of the shore, after having done their best to search for survivors and to discover the lost bodies, gathered up fragments of the wreck for fuel, and shouldered them away,—not perhaps a lawful spoil, but a venal transgression when compared with the remembered cruelties of the Cornish wreckers.

At least, that's what he wrote in "Remembrances." It was not entirely convincing; Hawker's credibility was already shot, and there was also the reception accorded the wrecked *Les Landois* just four years earlier to consider. Certainly, others did not hold Morwenstow folk in such high repute. A local commentator wrote, upon Hawker's death in 1875, how the people "eked out a precarious existence in the winter, and watched eagerly and expectantly for the shipwrecks that were certain to happen, and upon the plunder of which they surely calculated for the scant provision of their families . . . the Morwenstow wreckers allowed a fainting brother to perish in the sea before their eyes without extending a hand of safety." Charles Kingsley described the people of this coast as "wild folk . . . and merciless to wrecked vessels which they consider as their own by immemorial usage, or rather right divine."

These allegations cast such a shadow that the hut no longer seemed so suited to the composition of poetry or the espying of mermaids. Today, its wreck timbers and seaward aspect prompted another thought entirely: the hut was excellently placed for notice of wrecks.

Hawker may have established a reputation as the savior of the shipwrecked and sea dead, but popular lore tends to place West Country coastal vicars squarely among the worst of the region's wreckers. An old Cornish prayer, attributed to various Scilly Island parsons, beseeches God "not that wrecks should happen, but that if they should happen, that thou wilt guide them into the Scillies for the benefit of the poore inhabitants." Sabine Baring-Gould, the author of the hymn "Onward, Chris-

tian Soldiers" and the man responsible for one of Hawker's more colorful biographies, recounted the yarn of a parson at Poughill, near Bude,
who, happening to hear of a wreck during the Sunday service:

> [he] proceeded down the nave, in his surplice, as far as the font, and
> the people, supposing there was to be a christening, did not stir. But
> when he was near the door he shouted: "My Christian brethren,
> there's a ship wrecked in the cove; let us all start fair!" and, flinging
> off his surplice, led the way to the scene of spoliation.

When Daphne du Maurier made the vicar of Altarnun, on Bodmin
Moor, the leader of the vicious wreckers in *Jamaica Inn* who descended
upon this same stretch of coast to commit their dark deeds, she was
merely confirming a popular view of a clandestine priestly predilection.

Indeed, even Hawker's reputation has not entirely protected him
from allegations that he too was an enthusiastic wrecker. In 1934, a writer
named Stanley Baron attributed Baring-Gould's Poughill story to the
vicar of Morwenstow. "There are men in Morwenstow who still remember Hawker," he wrote. "They will tell you how wrecks would occur
while a service was in progress—how the vicar would walk to the door
and bawl—'Ship's ashore—and I'll be there the first o' ye.'" A historical
brochure from the 1960s even alleged that Hawker was "frequently the
leader of the wreckers who used to profit considerably from the misfortunes of the mariners wrecked upon that treacherous coast."

But why was this of relevance to me?

Because the darkest notions had a natural force along this suggestive
shore; they pushed to the fore. And because Hawker had lied, and his lies
were leading me to presume that he must have been hiding something of
that stormy night.

Chapter ∽ 13

Not a vestige of the vessel was to be seen next day, with the exception of the figurehead, which was thrown ashore in the morning, and is, we understand, to be erected near the graves of those of the unfortunate seamen whose bodies have been found. We subjoin a list of those belonging to Arbroath who perished on this truly melancholy occasion;—Stevenson Peter, commander; James Wallace, mate; Stephen Jones, carpenter; David Wallace, Alexander Kent, and —— Storrier, seamen; David McDonald and William Tasker, apprentices.

—*Arbroath Guide*, September 17, 1842

"Edward's surname was Le D*a*in," said Nicholas Jouault, pronouncing the vowel sound in the French manner, hard like "hat." "He was born in Jersey in 1821. And Hawker got some of his facts confused. For example, Edward did not join the *Caledonia* at Malta, but at Rio de Janeiro where he'd been left by his previous ship to recover from smallpox and where the *Caledonia* was loading a cargo of coffee."

When Nicholas Jouault of St. Martin, Jersey, began tracing his family tree in 1996, he did not expect to uncover a great-great-grandfather who had been the only survivor of a wreck on the coast of Cornwall in a late summer storm of 1842; this information was a gem of the kind that the flinty labor of genealogy always promised, but rarely uncovered. The discovery also unsettled him with the vertiginous sense that all who had followed Edward, himself included, might so easily not have been. That his forebear should by all rights have died in a Cornish sea storm, unmarried and without issue, revealed as a miracle the fact of his own descent. For a moment, family history frightened Nicholas Jouault with glimpses of the void.

Nicholas happened to write to the Morwenstow parish council, whom I was subsequently to contact, in search of further detail about his shipwrecked forebear's six-week convalescence in the parish in the autumn of 1842. Thus it was that I, working from the past toward the present, heard word of Nicholas going in the opposite direction. I wrote to him in Jersey. He promptly replied, saying I was welcome to call any night except for Wednesday, which was his chess evening.

Nicholas emphasized that Le Dain had never forgotten Hawker. Fully ten years after the loss of the *Caledonia,* he had christened his first son Edward Robert Hawker Le Dain. And, 150 years later still, Nicholas would make a similar tribute to his ancestor's savior by renaming his fishing boat the *Robert Hawker.*

So it was that Nicholas Jouault supplied the initial image—of a twenty-year-old Jerseyman, pale from the bout of smallpox he had lately endured, walking the quays at Rio in the last months of 1841, looking to work a passage home. But if this was the moment the story properly started, some nine months before the ship's loss at Morwenstow, I had to be sure of its beginnings. To match man and ship, and bring them homeward together, I had to prove that the *Caledonia* had been at Rio in late 1841. Which led me to a large cardboard document box at the PRO, looking for evidence.

Luck looked to be on my side. Since 1835—just four years before the launch of the *Caledonia*—masters of British ships had been required to submit crew lists for all voyages undertaken. The new crew lists, which replaced a thoroughly haphazard and scant system of muster rolls, revealed where and when ships had called, crew names, and much else besides. Moreover, the bulk had apparently survived and were stacked in boxes at the PRO.

British sea traffic was phenomenally heavy during the mid-nineteenth century. "Within ten years of the peace [of 1815]," as one writer described it, "the British seas had become a veritable forest of sails, and a telescope from such a vantage point as Beachy Head or Plymouth Hoe showed such a panorama of our Mercantile Marine ... a West Indian sugar drogher from Jamaica, a Straits vintager from Malaga, and in her wake a Geordie collier ... then a handsome barque with bright spars—a west-country copper-oreman, being overtaken by a low snaky craft with long skysail poles—a West African oil and ivory trader this last." The coast of North Cornwall, where shipping is sparse today, was almost unimaginably busy. "The number of vessels that pass and repass are very great," said Goldsworthy Gurney. "The last time I was down I counted 90 sail within the headlands at one time."

It astonished me that such crew lists should have existed in the first place. It was as if the every movement of today's road traffic—countless juggernauts, trucks and transit vans carrying potatoes to Faversham, computers to Stranraer, or beer to Exeter, along with personal details of drivers and passengers—were even now being minutely recorded for the benefit of researchers in the twenty-second century. It also amazed me that the lists should have survived, not least because the Board of Trade discarded the majority of the ones submitted after 1860. 1835–1860: a twenty-five-year window of unparalleled maritime archive in which the *Caledonia*'s short life was safely contained. The crew lists should afford me rare glimpses of the lost ship and, showing me the way toward Rio in December 1841, begin to reveal her true story.

I lifted the lid from the cardboard box, and the tightly packed documents stirred as if at the light, their old folds yawning open like dawn blossoms. I reached gingerly within, as if the elusive contents might slip from my fingers even now, and caused a dust cloud to rise above the table and envelop the man opposite, who merely flapped a preoccupied wrist and delved deeper still into his own obsession.

The box was full of Arbroath crew lists. They were a thick sheaf of large sheets of poor-quality fibrous paper, folded in two. The sheets had curled together along the edges where they had grown brittle, then frag-ile, and begun to disintegrate into a mouse litter that had gathered at the bottom of the box. I selected one at random and freed it gently from the sheaf. It came away with a reluctant crackle, as if it had lain undisturbed for decades.

The crew list had acquired a parched brown patina beneath which I could make out a pre-printed form set in various antique typefaces. The form, which solicited details on the voyage of an Arbroath ship called the *Circe*, had been completed and submitted to the port authorities on the ship's return from Memel in the summer of 1839. The form also sought crew details in columns headed "name," "age," "place of birth," "quality or rank," "Ship in which he last served," "Date of joining the ship" and "Time of Death, or leaving the Ship," whose advised word-ing, as if precedence had been given to the more likely eventuality, struck me as a memorable comment on the hazards of the nineteenth-century life at sea.

I began working my way through the sheaf. The lists were arranged in a slovenly alphabetical order, as if by a sullen clerk who adjudged him-self to have been assigned more rewarding tasks. Lists from the same ship had, however, tended to end up batched together, as if the clerk had at least taken a jigsaw pleasure in extending each ship's working history, the

Names.	Age.	Place of Birth.	Quality.	Ship in which he last served.	Date of joining the Ship.	Place where.
Stevenson Peter	27	Arbroath	Master	Susan & Ann	4 March 1841	London
James Wallace	33	Innerkeillor	Mate	Arab	do	do
Alexander Kent	22	Montrose	Seaman	Royal Archer	do	do
David McDonald	16	Arbroath	Ord do	Adelaide	do	do
Peter Sturrock	26	do	2nd Mate	Susan & Ann	18 March	Shields
Stephen Jones	22	do	Carpenter	Leipzig	do	do
David Wallace	27	Innerkeillor	Seaman	Addian	do	do
Charles Webster	19	Arbroath	Apprentice	Caledonia	4 March	London
William Tasker	17	do	do	do	do	do
Thomas Watson	18	London	do	do	do	do

places she had been, and the crewmen who had sailed with her. The past had begun to seduce even him.

Suddenly, a crew list from the "Ship *Caledonia* of *Arbroath*" was lying before me. "Whereof," I read, "*Frederick Meekison* was Master. A LIST OF THE CREW (including the Master and Apprentices) at the period of sailing from the Port of *Arbroath* in the United Kingdom, from which she took her first departure on her voyage to *Copenhagen* and of the Men who joined the Ship subsequent to such Departure and until her Return to the Port of *London*." At the foot of the page, the ship's broker had signed off the document with the words "*Ship Reported 10th Aug 1839, Laying at Church Hole*"—a Thames anchorage where the voyage had concluded.

I knew nothing, however, of a master called Meekison. Nor were the subsequent crewmen's names—Cowan, Ruston, Duncan, and others—the least bit familiar. It was not until I reached the very last name on the list—"William Tasker, aged 14, apprentice, place of birth Arbroath"—that I knew I was not mistaken.

The telling date on the document was April 21, 1839, when most of the men had joined the ship for the voyage—just two days before her Arbroath survey. This crew list had to belong to the *Caledonia*'s maiden voyage. Like the survey, it took me back to the very start of things. It was as if I'd stumbled across a birth certificate or an infant photograph among a mass of memorials from later dates clustering, as memorials are apt to do, around the closure of the life.

There were other crew lists for the *Caledonia*. To work my way through the ship's short life, I set about shuffling them into chronological order. They revealed that she had made repeated summer voyages to the Baltic during her first two years—to Riga, Copenhagen, St. Petersburg, and Memel—and, in the summer of 1840, to Archangel in Russia's White Sea. She might have carried pitch or timber from these chilly northern ports. But the ship's home port was a booming manufacturer of linen, canvas, and sailcloth by the mid-nineteenth century, and her owner, Joseph Esplin, would prove to be one of Arbroath's leading linen manufacturers; the *Caledonia*'s cargo from the Baltic was surely the material from which these products were made, flax.

Lloyd's List confirmed the *Caledonia*'s early voyages: Riga between May and August 1839, St. Petersburg between September and November of the same year, Memel between March and May 1840, Archangel between June and September 1840, and Riga again from October to December. But it was the following spring that interested me, when the *Caledonia* had been assigned a new master. The last of the crew lists was headed "Stevenson Peter, 27, of Arbroath."

New beginnings were in the air in the spring of 1841. The *Caledonia* was headed south for the first time, to Marseilles, for the Baltic ports remained ice-bound until later in the spring. Peter had joined the ship at London in March 1841 along with a largely new crew. I read down the list of names, and a shudder ran through me as I recognized them, one after another; it was a virtual roll call of those who would die with the *Caledonia* eighteen months later.

Several of them I knew from the Morwenstow burial register; evidently, they had signed on for another voyage following the return from Marseilles. There was "Alexander Kent, aged 22, from Montrose, seaman, last ship *Royal Anchor*." From Arbroath there was "David McDonald, aged 16, ordinary seaman, last ship the *Adelaide*," "David Wallace, aged 22, seaman, last ship *Assian*," and "William Tasker, apprentice," of no previous ship.

Two other names tallied with the list of the perished that the *Arbroath Guide* would publish on September 17, 1842: James Wallace, the mate, aged thirty-three, and Stephen Jones, ship's carpenter, aged twenty-two, both from Arbroath. Which, with Le Dain and the brawling cook, who were to join up after the Marseilles trip, left one more crew member whose identity was not quite so clear.

The Marseilles crew list gave him as "Peter Sturrock, 26, 2nd mate, of Arbroath." Sturrock did not appear in the *Guide*'s list of the dead, but the one name outstanding there, "——— Storrier," did suggest a strong if

distorted echo of that name. The absence, moreover, of a Christian name
could imply a certain latitude over his precise surname. Were the Peter
Sturrock who had sailed to Marseilles in March 1841 and the Storrier
whom the *Arbroath Guide* listed as dying at Morwenstow one and the
same man? Probably, especially since further scrutiny of the crew list revealed that Sturrock and Stevenson Peter had their previous ship, the
Susan and Ann, in common. That the second mate had previously
worked for Stevenson Peter shortened the odds on his working for Peter
again. But that did not explain the uncertainties surrounding his name. It
was conceivable that the information received by the *Guide* had been partially illegible (although it was a fact that every other name was correctly
given). Or perhaps the name had been but partially known by the
provider of the lost men's details.

The broker had signed off the Marseilles crew list with the words
"All on Board" and "Ship Laying London Dock, 21st July 1841." From
now on, only *Lloyd's List* could help trace the ship's progress toward Rio.
I delved into the editions of late July 1841 and, sure enough, the *Caledo-
nia* was recorded as having left Gravesend on July 31, heading south past
Dover and west down the English Channel to reach Torbay on August 5.
She had sailed for Rio on August 8.

Lloyd's List was so comprehensive that even the *Caledonia*'s progress
across the ocean was noted. It was the custom of returning vessels to report any sightings or "speakings"—when ships would haul to and draw
alongside each other to exchange news and provisions. Thus the *Forager,*
Thompson, placed the "*Caledonia,* bound to Rio de Janeiro"at 20N 27W,
just north of the Cape Verde Islands. No date was given, but it must
have been sometime before September 4, when she was again spotted,
at 10N 23W—well south of the Cape Verdes—by the *Royal Tar.* Now,
for the autumn Rio arrivals. A few minutes later, almost two months of
crossing the Atlantic behind her, my finger was skewering the ship to the
page. The entry actually read "*Caledonia,* Stevenson, from London, arrived October 1st," but Rio's port clerk would not be the last person to be

confused by the master of the *Caledonia*'s singular name. I had confirmed the *Caledonia*'s visit to Rio. I had fixed Le Dain's passage home.

These facts I could add to those I had already gleaned: the ship's measurements and the dates of her launch, of various port visits, and of her loss. I knew her final year's cargoes: coffee, then wheat. I had her movements as far as Rio, which, on the basis of my fruitful experience of *Lloyd's List*, I could be pretty sure of extending onward, concluding finally at Morwenstow. And I had a reasonable image of the ship.

Then there were Le Dain's reminiscences, primarily a wreck statement signed two weeks after the *Caledonia*'s loss, on September 22, 1842. Le Dain would state that the brawling cook, whom Hawker had had as Portuguese, was an Argentinian named Thomas Samuel. Which completed my set of the men's names, save for the uncertainties about the second mate's.

Beyond their names, I knew most by far about the man from Jersey who would make survival—first of disease, then of shipwreck—his specialty. Le Dain, by virtue of being alive in 1844, when the system was first introduced, was issued a registration ticket which included his physical description. I found his "ticket" deep within reels of microfiche at the PRO. The facts, though spare, yet evoked him: five feet five inches tall, with light-brown hair, light-brown eyes, and a ruddy complexion, and possessed of the ability to write. Here, in the preservation of a few facts among the thousand that make up a man, Edward Le Dain had truly survived his shipmates.

We also have Le Dain to thank for much of what we know of the others, little though it is. Of the master he would remember only two things: his habit of reading "the Bible in his cabin on Sundays" and his marked silence at the ship's end. At the foot of the ship's hierarchy were the two apprentices. One was David McDonald, whom Le Dain would describe as "a good quiet lad as could be in a ship." Le Dain would also recall McDonald's anguish as the ship struck at Morwenstow; the apprentice reportedly took Le Dain by the hand and, much moved, asked the Jerseyman where they might be.

The other apprentice, William Tasker, had been fourteen when he joined the *Caledonia* in the latter months of her building. Le Dain was silent about Tasker, but there were revelations elsewhere. The first crew list was revealing. Not only had Tasker been with the ship from the beginning and remained with her to the end, but the words "1st Voyage" had been scribbled under his name on the crew list; the *Caledonia*'s first time at sea was also Tasker's.

Nor had that maiden voyage been without incident. As an interest develops into a preoccupation, so the physical shape of the word or phrase is impressed upon the mind. I'd become adept at spotting *Caledonia* in dense text. So it was that the word leapt out at me as from the *List* of July 8, 1839. "Elsinore, 2 July," the entry read, "The *Caledonia*, Meekson, from Riga to London, got on shore yesterday on the Saltholmes, but was assisted off and into Copenhagen, leaky."

Saltholm Island lies east of Copenhagen, among the notorious sandbanks that nineteenth-century mariners knew as the Grounds. The Grounds, at the southern end of the Sound separating the Baltic from the Cattegat, were littered with wrecked warships and merchant vessels. One deep-water passage ran between the Middle Bank and Saltholm; this is the route Meekison must have taken in July 1839. *The Seaman's Guide* advised against approaching too near to Saltholm, whose shores shelve so steeply that "you may get aground in thirteen feet of water and yet have seven fathoms [42 feet] under the stern of your ship." The *Caledonia* had nearly been lost, then, on a short Baltic night just three months into her maiden voyage, and William Tasker sent to an even earlier grave.

That the Saltholm incident happened was perhaps no surprise. The crew list also revealed that they were a thoroughly inexperienced lot on that maiden voyage. Three of the men—the two apprentices and the carpenter—had not even been to sea before. The crew of the *Caledonia* under Stevenson Peter were old hands by comparison. Even the apprentice Tasker had two full years' experience by the time the *Caledonia* left Torbay for Rio in the summer of 1841. Not, of course, that all their experience would save them.

When it came to the core of the crew, the pickings were much poorer. There was the assumption that the two Wallaces—the mate, James, and the seaman, David—might be kin, not least because the crew boasted a conspicuous Arbroath core. The rest, however, was speculative hunches and associations or unsubstantiated Hawker claims of the sort I should have disallowed. But they were all I had. I had suggestions of a splendid ship and a ship's portrait, a cook's death at Falmouth, and a broken barometer; marriages never made, a notorious shore, and a vicar's lies; those log-reckoners of brass in a drowned captain's hands; and, finally, a tortoise. These were hardly the usual ingredients of the maritime yarn.

Even so, by confirming the *Caledonia* at Rio in late 1841, I had brought ship and survivor together. I must put the ship to sea. The story, for all its holes, must now begin, with a brown-haired stranger on the harbor mole at Rio looking to fix a passage home.

Chapter ❧ 14

The sailor wore a faded blue calico jacket and striped gun-mouthed trousers that flapped at his ankles. He carried a wooden sea chest on his shoulder. A wide-brimmed straw hat covered his light-brown hair and shadowed his pale face. He might have been quite lost in the giddying bustle of Rio's waterfront, where stevedores bent their backs to bales, crates, and sea chests amidst a din of instructions, queries, and imprecations. Top-hatted merchants from Portugal paused in their negotiations with their brokers to lash out with silver-tipped canes at skulking dogs, whose low-slung udders brushed the dirt. Shawled Spanish ladies stirred the treacly air with their fans and nodded low-lidded acquaintance at cockaded naval men. Hollering hawkers squatted behind raffia baskets of bananas, pineapples, and corn cobs, and trays of small silver fish whose tails were curling in the heat. Behind the human swarm arose a backdrop of whitewashed warehouses and shipping offices, chapels, and glistening palaces, which the mole-side vessels—brigs, snows, and barques—criss-crossed with a web of masts, yards, and stays, like the lacquer cracks over an aged painting.

But Edward Le Dain did catch the eye of a sturdy figure who had emerged from a vessel's hold hatch. Well though Mr. James Wallace knew the sights of sea and quayside, being an experienced hand and the ship's first mate to boot, something of that sailor's progress had surprised him. Certainly, there were few sights rarer on the Rio quayside, which was a brutish sort of place in the 1840s, than that of a sailor so luminously happy to be alive. Or, astonished that he was not dead, as Edward Le Dain would rather have described himself back in the early stages of his recovery, when he'd had time to dwell on such things. But that was then. As he had regained his health, he had discovered himself less astonished by the day until the time came when he began to take his recovery for granted.

The mate dropped back into the hold, directing a parting shot at the galley.

"Cook! More of your cursed coffee before we expire here!"

The mate's broadside swept the quarterdeck, where it encountered the entrenched frown of the ship's master, which it further deepened. Stevenson Peter stood by the taffrail, leafing through a thick sheaf of papers: dockets, bills, receipts, and certificates lately pressed upon him by brokers, carters, exporters, and insurers. It was the usual story, with figures rounded upward, services and surcharges invented, and taxes snatched plain from the Brazilian ether. Not content with such injury, these godless parasites of Rio's coffee trade had mostly mistaken his name on the paperwork. As if Stevenson Peter were to the Portuguese ear some unfathomable conundrum!

And now such concentration as he had brought to bear upon those vexing bills had been wrecked by yet another of Wallace's appeals for coffee. The master of the *Caledonia* was beginning to experience the stirrings of what he would come to recognize as regret—for regret, rarely having occasion to visit the shores of his cautious and ordered mind, was largely unfamiliar to him—that he had ever thought to allow the crew a free hand with the cargo. It had initially seemed an excellent notion, it being his conviction that coffee, though an evil in its own right, constituted by several degrees a lesser evil than grog. It was, besides, only a few years ago that the government had officially advised against the daily supply of spirits, and suggested "substituting the more nutritious and wholesome beverages of coffee, cocoa, chocolate or tea." The coffee was designed to bring other advantages. It should have done away with those instances of pilfering so burdensome to the officers that they sometimes felt themselves to be offshore members of the new police force, as well as fostered an appreciation among the crew that had to pay dividends over the lengthy voyage ahead. And all for a shallow dent in a single sack of the stuff.

Or so he had estimated. But since that recent morning when hunched negro shoulders and a cajoling percussion announced the arrival from the warehouse of the first sacks of green arabica beans, his men had demonstrated a gargantuan appetite for the beverage. The coffee being a costly luxury in Arbroath, the preserve of fine merchants and manufacturers in rooms with tall windows and high ceilings, these sailors would have all that they could of it, and nobody more so than the first mate. It harried the cook to meet the demand, roasting the beans and grinding them with such utensils as he had adapted to the unfamiliar purpose.

Le Dain passed mule carts heavy with hides, and zigzagged like a tacking ship between high piles of plump tobacco bales, stacked balks of mahogany, and sacks of brown sugar, tapioca, and flour. But the smell of roasted coffee, which relieved the prevailing stench of sewage and sweat, drew him on. For an instant Le Dain closed his eyes to inhale the fine aroma, then followed it to the gunwales of the ship lying alongside the far end of the mole. From the hold, where sacks of coffee were fast disappearing, arose a stridently theatrical voice, touched with surliness, which Le Dain recognized from his acquaintance with previous shipmates as Scottish. "Coffee, coffee everywhere," the voice proclaimed, "and all the boards did shrink..."

Le Dain examined the ship with an approving eye. A young vessel, the *Caledonia*, and evidently tight of hull (it being commonly acknowledged that the slightest ingress of moisture could spoil an entire cargo of coffee). And a willing crew, the rigging boys repairing chafings in the hemp and tarring the whole in a protective daub with a cheer that the chore did not normally awake while others holystoned the decks, stitched at sails, swabbed and scrubbed, greased and varnished with an uncommon energy.

He approached the hold hatch. From deep within the ship arose a medley of labored grunts and the rank smell of working men. Le Dain looked down on a sea of bulging hessian where a crush of bodies was cajoling a sack into a corner of the hold with the help of timber levers, curses, and the sharp shoves of sailors' boots.

"Coffee, coffee everywhere," the same voice began again, "and nary a fucking drop to drink."

The hold rumbled with laughter, then fell silent to the voice of the first mate.

"Enough of your fancy verse, Kent," growled Wallace as his head appeared above the hatch to shake itself free of sweat beads, then noticed Le Dain as if for the first time. "Can I assist ye?"

"I was looking for the master." Le Dain spoke with traces of a French accent that caused the mate to bridle.

"You've found the mate. Wallace."

"I'm a spare hand, Mr. Wallace; I'm looking to ship."

"Then you'll speak to the master." Wallace hauled himself from the hold, casting an involuntary squint at the sky for signs of weather. "And where did you mislay your own vessel?"

Le Dain lifted a finger to his pitted face, where depressed white scars showed on his cheeks and neck. But they were as nothing to him, not compared to the pustules that had formed them, pea-sized and filled with a clear liquid that gradually turned turbid, then yellow, before bursting with a foul smell. These covered the skin but also gathered within the throat and the nostrils, so that there were times in the fortnight that the illness had raged when he had wished he might die in Rio's isolation hospital at Jurujuba. But he had endured it; the itching had left him, and he was ready for home.

"Ah, the pox." Wallace nodded. He recognized the type from his years at sea: the survivor, sold on his own charmed invulnerability. Wallace had shared ships with men who had variously overcome illness or injury, shipwreck or piracy, and he knew the uncommon shapes their minds could take. They were the sort to be pitched overboard in a gale—night-time, winter—only to buck the odds and be hauled from a heaving sea to lie on the deck, teeth chattering with the cold but eyes wide with laughter, as if the miracle of recovery had merely been inevitable. On board, it could be a volatile quality, breeding confidence and complacency in equal measures. But the ship, soon to depart, was shorthanded; they could use him. "You'll come to see Mr. Peter," he said.

Le Dain coughed a polite objection. "I'd prefer to address him by his surname, Mr. Wallace."

"That *is* his surname, man," said Wallace. "You bethought a liberal command, did you?" The mate chuckled at the notion, and led the way past the upturned longboat and the lashed water butts to the quarterdeck. The master was on his knees, scrutinizing a repaired deck cleat. He rose to his feet, brushing the whorls of shaved wood from his trousers.

"I'll have this deck swept," he commanded a nearby sailor before turning to the new arrivals.

"The man wants to ship, skip," said the mate, returning directly to the hold.

As the master looked the new man up and down, Le Dain pocketed his own impressions; the master was in his late twenties, with dark hair plastered close to the skull in an ordered clerical fashion, and was dressed in a black smock, with a sheaf of folded papers protruding from the pocket.

"Where're ye from?"

"Jersey, sir," Le Dain replied.

"Not France, then. Last ship?"

"The *Mary Ann*, of that port," said Le Dain. "She sailed in September for Trieste, leaving me here with the illness."

"But you're strong now, are you, Jerseyman?"

"Oh, I was always strong, sir. The illness made me itch, not fail."

The master nodded. "You'll have been at sea some years?"

"I joined at eighteen, sir, in '39. Always out of Jersey, the *Swift*, the *Rollo*, the *Jane & Louise* . . ."

But Stevenson Peter had heard enough. "I'll take you as a seaman. I pay two pounds and ten shillings a month. Two pounds of beef a day, and as much bread as you can use without waste. The same for the cargo—if you must. We're orderly Scots, every one of us, from Arbroath or thereabouts. All except the cook, that is. A Latino with a temper you'll do well to heed, and no dab hand with the coffee either if Mr. Wallace is to be credited. We leave tomorrow at first light. For Corfu and the Lord knows thereafter. Sling your chest and report to the hold. And you'll do well to keep your island sweat off my cargo."

The new crewman was making his way forward when a half utterance—and a whispered warning from within—stopped him in his tracks even as a clasp knife embedded itself in the decking between his feet with the vibration of an impacting arrow. He looked into the rigging, where a young sailor, mouth agape, was staring at him.

"I'm dead sorry," said the sailor, who had been repairing a chafed shroud.

But Le Dain, who felt far from the threat of a dropped blade, merely smiled. He yanked the knife from the decking, which it had penetrated by the better part of an inch, folded it away, and tossed it unerringly back to the sailor, pressing the wounded plank flat with his heel as he passed.

"Ah, the cratered Jerseyman," said Wallace as Le Dain lowered himself into the hold. "No oil painting, I grant, but you'll not catch anything from him now."

The men gave Le Dain cursory glances before returning to their work. All morning they hauled coffee across a rising tide of hessian, squeezing and shouldering the sacks into unlikely gaps until they were drum-tight in their confinement. The work was hot and close, and before he had learned their names Le Dain became acquainted with the magnified smells of his new crewmates—the odors of hot goats and inland August fish stalls, and the metallic stench of black-toothed breath. They worked in silence, pausing to drink from the water butt on the deck, passing the chained ladle between them, wiping brow sweat against their sleeves.

"You in hold! Is dinner!"

The accented shout brought them to the noon foredeck, where the cook had placed a large tray. They scooped the beef and bread into their mouths; the pineapple they mostly slung overboard amidst dismissive comments regarding the scurvy.

"Le Dane, is it?" asked the one called Kent.

"Le Dain," Edward corrected him gently.

"Even so," said Kent, smiling. "Hamlet."

"Hamlet?" the mate inquired roughly through a mashed mouthful of bread.

"Hamlet Le Dane," explained Kent.

"That will be something literary, will it?" Wallace frowned dismissively, and he turned his attention to a steaming pan on the tray, calling out even as the cook disappeared into the galley. "Tomaso."

"Señor Wallace?"

"I thought we were due some coffee. If it's that you can't put your hands on it, you'll find a few tons discreetly stored in the main hold."

The crew sniggered. Tomaso Samuel drew near. He was a thin man with flaming dark eyes, his face glazed with galley sweat. He pointed at the pan.

"Is coffee, Señor Wallace," he replied.

The mate stirred the pan with an unflinching finger. "That's tar," the mate pronounced patiently, as if to a backward child. "That's what you put on the rigging, Tomaso. The boys already did that this morning."

The crew laughed, safe in the mate's presence.

"Is coffee," the cook insisted.

"But not as I know it," said the mate, pouring the steaming treacly beverage into a drinking pot. "An Argentine," he explained, apparently for the new man's benefit, waving the cook away, which was when Le Dain noticed Tomaso's fists contract into tight clenches.

They were stowing the last of the coffee when a small man with thinning hair appeared on the quayside in the late afternoon, a mule cart and emboldened street urchins trailing behind him. The cart was laden with limes and bananas, tomatoes, onions, and cabbages, flagons of vinegar, sides of jerked beef, biscuits, and bags of brown sugar. There were wicker boxes containing live chickens and, hitched to the cart on frayed nooses, a small flock of apprehensive goats.

The *Caledonia*'s second mate announced his arrival with a cough so mild it might merely have been the air parted by a passing flock of parrots. He coughed again. Le Dain left the foredeck and made his way down the gangway to assist, where he introduced himself as the new man. But the second mate replied with a muted mumble. Le Dain was about to ask the man to repeat himself when Tomaso Samuel strode down the gangplank. The Argentine looked over the delivery with a proprietorial eye; his manner might have passed in Rio though it was sure to have raised eyebrows, hackles, even fists back in Arbroath. The cook squeezed the lemons and prodded the cabbages with long interrogative fingers. He uncorked the flagons and sniffed at the contents like a champion vintner, dug into the sugar and ran the fine grains through his fingers, knocked at the jerked beef like a bailiff at a debtor's door, and slapped a goat rump or two, which caused the creatures to kick out, slewing sideways. He suddenly froze, his hands splayed in midair above the provisions. He bent forward to take hold of a small object, which he held up for general inspection.

"What this for?"

The second mate shuffled his feet and delivered an inaudible answer. So unlike a second mate, thought Le Dain, who was yet to arrive at that thankless rank, which sailors bore scant respect, one that held no inherent authority save what its occupant brought to it—which was minimal in this case.

"For cooking, you say?" The cook weighed the object in his cupped palm, exposing the symmetrical yellows and blacks of its waxy underside. "For cooking," he repeated. He turned to the crew, who had gathered at the head of the gangplank. "So cook that," he said, swinging an arm in their direction.

"Less of your skylarking." It was the first mate. "If you've your hearts set on fond farewells tonight, you'll ready this ship for sea."

As the crew returned to work, one of the apprentices found himself holding the cook's strange object in his hand.

The light was fading as clouds of feathers and steam, grunts and gurgles, and Spanish songs and oaths engulfed the galley. Tomaso Samuel emerged with plates of boiled fowl and yams with onions, then plantains fried in molasses. From the gunwale, the cook feigned a studied disinterest while the crew fell upon the food in an awed silence, as if the slightest sound might scatter the vision before them, revealing the usual old beef and biscuit. Le Dain merely stared in astonishment; these weren't ship's victuals.

"Hamlet," Kent grinned. He gestured at the Jerseyman's untouched bowl. "You're prevaricating again."

It had actually occurred to Le Dain that there was meaning in the meal; the outsider was up to something, his fellow outsider. For neither was Le Dain one of them—a Scot from a small Scottish town—which might have been how he understood that Tomaso Samuel was playing his strongest card, his victualing, which alone could make up for the eternal verity that he was not from Arbroath. Which also made sense of his treatment of the second mate, whom Samuel had identified as the weak rivet in the crew's clannishness; cause the crew to laugh at Tomaso Samuel's treatment of the second mate's silent ways, and they laughed with him. It was by such means that Tomaso Samuel sought acceptance, most especially from Mr. Wallace, whence a wider acceptance was sure to follow.

So it was that Le Dain drew further meaning from the evening coffee. It arrived black, strong, and sweet, and although to have described it as finely ground would have constituted a misdescription, for shards were suspended in it, Le Dain noticed that these were significantly smaller than at lunchtime. But Mr. Wallace was not about to concede any such improvements.

"Ah, the familiar infusion," he proclaimed. "An affront to the stomach flavored with the wood shavings from Stephen Jones's tool chest." He was examining a scrap of coffee bean that sat on the tip of his dipped

forefinger, large as a ladybug. "There is a beverage I once had the pleasure of tasting in Marseilles," he reminisced. "Coffee they called it. Curse
me for my wild seafarer's imagination, but I am distantly reminded of it
by this muddy mawkish rubbish."

As the cook turned away, slamming down his heel as if to grind the
mate beneath it, the crew bellowed with laughter.

"Shore leave," pronounced the mate, scarcely containing his triumph. "But we sail in the early hours, and God help the poor devils still
to withdraw from their sweetheart's embrace."

The pox had left Le Dain with little affection for the city; he barely
knew it beyond the fetid ward where he had itched. His crewmates being
new to him besides, he chose to remain on board and retired to the foredeck. He looked to the bowsprit and peered over the gunwale. The figurehead was a fine white maid full of fight, with something of the cook
about her. He perched on the windlass and took pleasure in the ship's fine
lines and neat appearance, the coiled sheets and halyards, the decks
tightly caulked with oakum. From the hatch to the fo'c'sle, that airless
hole he must share with seven others, not to mention slimy hawsers, coils
of rigging, blocks, tackles, and buckets, the rank stench of sweat, food,
and bilge arose. He stared beyond the fo'c'sle to the foremast and, just aft
of it, the ship's upturned longboat, eighteen feet from bow to stern,
which had been lashed over the hold hatch. There, the goats were tethered. In the gloaming, their green eyes peered at Le Dain from beneath
the longboat's bows.

By and by, Le Dain noticed that another pair of eyes were examining
him from among the shrouds. Le Dain beckoned the slight figure
forward.

"Like Mr. Wallace said, I'm not catching," Le Dain reassured it.

"They say you're from Jersey," came the reply. It was the young
sailor who had dropped the knife but caught Samuel's thrown offering;
he had it with him even now. He sported the thin beginnings of a red
beard and pronounced Le Dain's island with a breathy exoticism that
only an Arbroath man could feel. "Do they have these there?"

"It's called a tortoise," said Le Dain, shaking his head.

"I was only wondering what it feeds on."

"Not coffee," Le Dain offered, fearing for the creature's future. "What's your name?"

"McDonald," replied the man inside McDonald. "David," the boy added.

"And tell me, David McDonald, what kind of man is our master?"

"Fair," said David. He smiled. "Since he has a respect for the Bible, Kent knows him as St. Peter."

"So he's a fondness for names, has Kent," murmured Le Dain. "And the second mate?"

"You might rather ask what the second mate calls himself," replied David. "With all that whispering it's hard to know—even after all this time."

A companionable silence fell. Le Dain followed David's gaze across the water, beyond the harbor and the sea lanterns, toward the ocean.

"You're thinking of home," said the Jerseyman.

An eager smile broke over David's face. But trepidation soon eclipsed it, and David hugged the tortoise to his chest. It seemed that David was not durable like the world that had claimed him; the Arbroath streets of his boyhood and the cliff caves north of the town where he had played, and the smell of the hearth at home when there was peat to burn, still filled his dreams. After several years on ships, the sea still seemed strange and cold to him, and he could not believe that this ship had it in her to bring him home, not across all those waves, from this, their farthest point of travel.

"You are all right," murmured Le Dain, who had once had such feelings of his own. "We'll bring you back to England."

"It's Scotland I'm interested in. And I've dishes to swill," he added, turning away.

"Leaves," Le Dain called after him, pointing at the tortoise. "See if le chef, the cook, can let you have some green leaves."

"The cook?" exclaimed David. "The cook don't much care for tortoises."

They called all hands early, when the dark was thick, a single lantern's gleam showing from the custom house. The men had mostly abandoned the fo'c'sle, preferring to pass the tropical nights on mats slung across the cool foredeck. They rose sluggishly, as if their time in port or the evening's excesses had temporarily deprived them of their mariners' instincts, but they had readied themselves by the time the pilot arrived, a smoldering cigar stub protuding from a fleshy mouth. They cast off the bow rope and the *Caledonia* swung gently seaward. Suddenly, amid a fusillade of instructions, there were sailors in the ratlines; sails were loosed, billowing out in ivory-colored clouds, and yards were braced. The light had begun to increase, revealing shuttered shoreline mansions with red-tiled roofs, domed churches, soft green expanses of jungle where scarlet parrots flew, and, high above, the granite crags of Corcovado, the soaring cone of Tijuca, and flat-topped Gavea, their upper reaches gilded with sunlight. As the sails filled, fat with a following wind, the *Caledonia* began to awaken, tentatively at first, as if sensing the burden with which she had been entrusted. She glided down the great harbor, past the suburbs of Catete to starboard and, to port, Jurujuba, where Le Dain had recently lain in a shuttered ward and calmed himself against the mutterings of the dying.

A launch took the pilot off, and Le Dain was ordered to the helm. He was accounted a fine helmsman but had not held a wheel between his hands for months, and he hauled at it to gauge its response. The ship passed between the forts of São Joao and Santa Cruz that guarded the harbor's entrance and emerged onto the ocean swell. She came toward the northeast, with a stiff wind on her port bow. The mate divided the crew into watches, then made his way to the quarterdeck.

"All as it should be, skip," he said. Stevenson Peter nodded, confident in his mate's considerable abilities, and gestured over the ocean.

"God and good sailing, Jim," he remarked, then coughed to signal graver concerns. "I hear of a tortoise on board."

"The tortoise." James Wallace cursed himself for his uncharacteristic forgetfulness. He had meant to deal with the tortoise, which had no place on any vessel commanded by Stevenson Peter. The master progressed through life by absolute adherence to routines, and expected the same of his crew, which meant keeping the Sabbath, refraining from drinking on board, and fulfilling duties to the letter and with a will. It did not mean tortoises. "I entrusted the second mate with the victualing duties," offered Wallace.

"Ah, the second mate," said the master, who knew that silent man's ways from previous ships. "And so?" The partial explanation had not satisfied him.

"The tortoise seems to have been included in the provisions," Wallace continued. "It seems he had the example of the Galápagos tortoises in mind."

"You refer to the tortoises the whalers take from those islands for provisions?"

"The same. The ones they store in the holds, on their backs, for fresh meat."

"The larger tortoises? The giant ones, in fact?"

"The giants," confirmed Wallace. He scrutinized the master's face, and was mightily relieved to see affronted bewilderment finally give way to a faint smile.

Although the tortoise offended the sense of order by which he lived his life, the master was prepared to concede that it alone did not constitute a threat to the well-being of his ship. It was even the custom of some vessels, he understood, to carry tortoises as mascots. And though it was true that the second mate had actually thought to eat this one, Stevenson Peter needed no reminding that wholly intact minds were in short supply throughout the service. Most merchant vessels suffered from follies legion as hold rats, which soon reduced them to rudderless tubs quite beyond command or discipline. In this respect, the *Caledonia* could be said to have exhausted her fair quota of sense and reliability in James Wallace alone, who was a capital first mate by any standards. The *Caledonia* could bear a tortoise and the second mate's occasional delusions.

"And the whereabouts of the tortoise?" the master inquired.

"In the capable charge of one of the apprentices," replied Wallace solemnly.

Stevenson Peter nodded. "See that it's fed, watered, and respected. All God's creatures and all that." The master saw that all was as it should be, slapped the taffrail with one hand and the mate's shoulder with the other, then headed for his cabin with a final pronouncement. "Stand her off to the east, Mr. Wallace. I'd like to be well clear of the shore before we make to the north. It's not my intention to land this cargo prematurely."

The master's words were lightly delivered, but it did not pass the helmsman's attention that they caused David McDonald to blanch, so that the apprentice's head lolled momentarily between the shrouds.

"You heard the master," Mr. Wallace boomed. "Is that what they call east in Jersey?"

Le Dain brought the ship to starboard so that the wind came off her port bow and sidled toward her beam, and for the two hours of his turn at the wheel he held his course steady across the blue ocean.

Chapter ⌘ 15

I rang my sister Clare, who had lately embroiled herself in our own family genealogy, where she'd uncovered a great-great-great-grandfather who was a master mariner around the time of the *Caledonia*.

"This wreck account I've been going on about," I said. "It's full of holes."

"Most wrecks are full of holes."

"The account, I mean."

I hoped Clare might help furnish the crew of the *Caledonia* with family backgrounds of their own, and had rung her to arrange a visit to the Bristol branch of the Family History Centre of the Mormon Church of Latter-Day Saints. The Mormons stress lineage, encouraging members to trace their forebears with a view to redeeming them by proxy conversion to the faith. Their exhaustive research in old parish records and registry archives has been collated as the International Genealogical Index (IGI), a computerized database covering civil registrations worldwide including a comprehensive coverage of christenings and marriages across the UK. The IGI is an excellent tool for Mormons pursuing the obligations of their faith, and researchers of all persuasions have come to rely on it as the undisputed first port of call in any journey of genealogical discovery.

The Family History Centre was contained in a church that stood on the outer fringes of the encroaching conurbation. The fields had a condemned air, serving out their final seasons as pastureland before surrendering to housing estates, gas stations, shopping arcades, theme pubs, and discount carpet stores, and the sheep already appeared like creatures from some arcadian idyll. The church squatted in an extensive surround of tarmac parking lot, and was flanked by avenues of cypress trees that shielded it from prying eyes on adjacent playing fields. It was a large, low-built complex of functional yellow brick, which lent it the impression less of a place of worship than that of a polymer research establishment.

A long corridor carpeted in a gray industrial weave led to the Family History Centre. There were filing cabinets, shelves of lever-arch files, and a portrait of Christ, rendered in disquietingly bright colors, his long wheaten hair parted down the middle. Researchers sat before rows of microfilm and microfiche readers. They leaned forward as if they were zombies nourishing themselves on the weak washes of screen light. Beside each of them lay a pad of paper where family trees grew, but lopsidedly. Some branches were so laden with the scribbled fruit of baptism or burial dates that they were squeezed into the corner of the page like some hothouse plant pushing against glass. Others remained bare and blasted, refusing to bud.

I wondered what these people wanted from this place. What might they achieve by tracing themselves into the past? Did they hope for illustrious antecedents to transform their idea of themselves? Or was genealogy a refuge from the mundane present? Did customer service officers and telephone executives come to the Family History Centre to discover they were descended from flax weavers or shepherds, missionaries or master mariners, people with the smell of the world on their hands?

In one corner, a black-and-white television flashed the security camera's various views of the parking lot. Clare made straight for the computer.

"Right," she said, fingers poised above the keys like a concert pianist. "What county is Arbroath in?"

"Angus."

"And a name?"

"Stevenson Peter," I replied.

"What kind of weird name is that?" she said, tapping keys. There was a pause. "Nothing," she added.

"Oh."

"There's no Stevenson Peter listed," she confirmed. "Not anywhere in Angus. Not anywhere in the UK. Never. You sure he wasn't Peter Stevenson? Much more likely. I've lots of those."

I shook my head.

"Moving swiftly on," I muttered. "James Wallace?"

"Your first mate," she murmured. "James Wallace I can do. In spades. So many of them it would help to know exactly when he was born."

I consulted my copy of the *Caledonia* crew list. "The oldest of the lot," I said. "Wallace was thirty-three in 1841, so born in . . . 1808."

"Then that would seem to be your man," said Clare, highlighting a name upon the screen. "Christened twenty-third July 1808, but in a place called Inverkeilor. Where the hell is that?"

I lifted a forefinger to indicate a solution and left the room; there was a road atlas in the car. I unearthed it in the trunk, among the jumble of empty plastic water bottles, jumper cables, and a chewed children's toy, all lightly downed with dog molt. As I thumbed through the pages, England's central southern counties fell out. They had long since ripped free of the plastic ring-binding; the condition of the M4 corridor, torn and wrinkled, and patterned with coffee circles and my daughter's flattened raisins, reminded me that eastern Scotland, whose contrasting pages lay smooth, sheeny, and totally unexplored, was an unfamiliar beat to me. I laid my finger on Arbroath. The little port lay north of Edinburgh, beyond the peninsular protrusion of Fife and the mouths of the Forth and the Tay that formed it, where the coast beyond Dundee began an unbroken, northeasterly reach to Aberdeen and Rattray Head beyond. Then my eyes fell upon Inverkeilor, just five miles to the north of Arbroath, and I tossed the atlas back into the trunk with a flourish.

"You found it near Arbroath," said Clare.

"But how spooky that you should know."

"Oh, there are ways and means," she replied mysteriously (she'd caught my triumphant gesture on the security camera). She turned back to the keyboard but shook her head at the second mate's name, which was next on the crew list.

"No, no, there was another Wallace, wasn't there?"

"David," I said. "Aged twenty-two on the crew list, so born in 1819."

"There he is," she said shortly. "Born seventeenth February 1819. Inverkeilor again."

"Brothers?" I exclaimed, thumping the desk.

Clare's world-weary grunt indicated that I was getting ahead of myself. Genealogy had disappointed my sister so often that she knew better than to indulge mere hopes, and only celebrated confirmed certainties. "Hmm. Different parents; so they're not brothers. But if we check David's father's parentage" . . . the keys chattered . . . "yes, David's father had the same parents as James." She slapped her hands together. "Which makes James to be David's uncle."

Uncle and nephew. Here was the first indication, then, of the ties that bound the crew of the *Caledonia*. Arbroath was unlike the big ports— London, Newcastle, Glasgow, or Dundee—where the crews tended to be an international crowd. The crew list of an 1840s Dundee ship named the *Arab* typically gave the crew's birthplaces as Aberdeen, Liverpool, London, Limerick, Waterford, Falmouth, Prince Edward Island in Canada, and Dundee itself. Crews hired in Arbroath, however, were much more likely to have been local. By proving a first family connection, Clare confirmed that the grief caused by the *Caledonia*'s loss had fallen undiluted upon a single community.

Clare had soon found baptisms for all the crew, the captain and cook excepted. But while each register entry brought its own brief thrill of discovery—the way the dates fitted with the men's ages on the crew list and the bare facts of their lives began to be revealed—baptisms only confirmed that these men had been born, which we already knew. I was anxious to discover whether any of them had been married, for marriages could mean descendants into the present. Clare fed their names into the marriage database, but came up with only two matches: Stephen Jones, the ship's carpenter, who had married in Arbroath on January 1, 1841, and James Wallace.

"Wallace married in Arbroath in April 1830, when he was twenty-two," said Clare. "But look who he married—a Bathia Watson Peter."

"The captain's sister!"

"Nary a chance," said Clare. I took the faux-Scottish accent to emphasize a steadfast refusal to get excited and nodded reluctantly; it was certainly true that Peter had been a notably common Arbroath surname in the mid-nineteenth century. "But what we might do," Clare continued, "is look up the children of Bathia Peter and James Wallace." She rattled a few keys, sat back as the information scrolled onto the screen, then said, "Well, well, well."

"What is it?"

"Two boys. One, Robert, born sixteenth September 1838. The other, born on nineteenth December 1841 . . ."

"Which is exactly when the *Caledonia* was in Rio . . ."

". . . And named, wait for it, James Stevenson Wallace."

"Stevenson," I repeated.

"Yes. Now that is curious," conceded Clare. But as she pondered the fact that the master's Christian name was echoed in the middle name of the mate's second child, something else was troubling me.

"I'll tell you what else is curious," I exclaimed. "James Stevenson Wallace was born, you said, on nineteenth December 1841, but we know from the crew list that his father, or should I say his mother's husband, joined the *Caledonia* on fourth March of that year, in London."

Clare was silent a moment, pondering the implications. "You're talking gestation."

"I am. And that's two weeks over nine months."

"Which is reasonable. Just about."

"Plus the time taken, assuming the conception took place in Arbroath, for Wallace to have got down to London to join the ship. So add a few days more."

"Unless this Bathia came down to London to see him off—and did so in style."

"To London in those days? At that time of year? When she had a two-year-old to worry about? Unlikely. And tight even if she had."

I left Clare at the computer, tapping out brief flurries of keystrokes like a radio operator transmitting insistent messages to a past in the hope that it might answer her, and I let my mind drift to the dates that crowded round the *Caledonia*'s last voyage. They spoke of a changing world. Steam had been powering ships since 1811, but it was not until 1838 that the *Great Western* crossed the Atlantic in a record fifteen days. The P&O shipping line began a regular steam service to Alexandria, the first leg of the mail delivery to India, in 1840. The first propeller patent, meanwhile, had been taken out in 1836; a screw-propelled steamer towed an Admiralty barge down the Thames to Limehouse at ten knots the following year. A propeller would power the 3,200-ton *Great Britain*, the largest ship that had yet been built, which was under construction at Bristol during 1842. It was not the twilight of the sailing age—the great tea clippers would be raising great clouds of sail to race each other home from India as late as the 1860s—but these revolutionary developments contained the unequivocal message that the *Caledonia* and her like would not be around forever.

One is left to imagine what the *Caledonia*'s crew would have made of such maritime developments. It is hard to believe they could have comprehended that such changes were only the beginning of a transformation that might one day serve not only to render their livings obselete but also to imbue their lives, doubtless hard and brutish in their own judgments, with a marvelous romance—a measure of the enormous distance progress had brought us. These men, who would leave Rio a week before Christmas 1841, knew little more than that they were bound for Corfu with a cargo of coffee.

Historical hindsight might submit as relevant other facts that the crew cannot have appreciated, not least that they shared the seas with two of the century's great writers. Earlier that year, Herman Melville had embarked on a whaler bound for the South Seas. Charles Dickens meanwhile would leave port two weeks after the *Caledonia*'s departure from Rio, crossing the Atlantic by steamer in the opposite direction. He would leave Liverpool on January 3, 1842, for Halifax and Boston on the journey he would recount in his journalistic travelogue *American Notes*.

The tapping of the keys had ceased. My sister, mouthing words to herself, raised a single finger.

"Other children by Bathia's parents," she muttered, and swooped on the keyboard with claw hands. There was a moment of silence before her high-pitched scream raised a row of startled faces, like those of disturbed troughing cattle, from the reading machines. Clare left the computer and began bouncing excitedly around the room. It was a while before she brought herself under control, covered her mouth with her hand and gestured me to the computer.

"I've found your captain," she whispered loudly. "He was doing a me."

I was at her side in seconds. "What are you on about?"

"What was I christened?" she asked me.

"Clare. No you weren't, Frances Clare."

"Exactly. I dropped my first name. I asked the computer to list all children by Bathia's parents, just in case, and there was a John Stevenson Peter, christened seventh October 1813, which fits exactly with Stevenson's age on the crew list. Like me, he had dropped his first Christian name in favor of his second one."

"The deceitful little bastard," I marveled.

"We did say Stevenson was a strange Christian name. We should have guessed it was originally his *second* forename from the fact that his sister Bathia christened her son in the same way. So you were right. Stevenson *was* Bathia's brother. Your captain and mate *were* brothers-in-law. And Bathia named her second son after both of them, her husband and brother respectively."

It is an image loaded with loss; as James Wallace looked out on the Brazilian coast, a long gray welt on the larboard horizon two days out of Rio, he could not know that his distant wife had just given birth to a son—I will not say *his* son—that he would not live to see.

Chapter ❧ 16

The sails shivered. The oily unmoving sea starred like a shattered glass, as if the *Caledonia* had just plummeted from the sky into the ocean's mirrored midst. Sun-stunned limbs stirred and sprawling men blinked. They hastily cleared the foredeck of their surreptitious distractions, lobbing tobacco pipes, playing cards, one of Kent's poetry volumes, coffee pots, nibbled cabbage leaves, tortoise, and all into the depths of a fo'c'sle hammock.

"Trim those yards, Hamlet!"

"Aye, aye," replied Le Dain, whom the crew to a man knew by the nickname Kent had provided (for all that it meant to them), favoring it over the Jerseyman's French-sounding surname. As Le Dain hauled on the sheets, the long-lost wind packed the sails. The ship roused herself as if from sleep, then moved ahead to a cheer from the crew.

Two weeks out of Rio, the doldrums had claimed the *Caledonia*. The fitful head winds failed entirely one morning, the sails hanging limp from the yards so that the ship resembled a laden clotheshorse. The sun tracked across the sky. It cast a brutal heat over the ship, which settled, among stifled yawns and drooping heads, into the glutinous sea. The long swell slapped against the hull; it reminded the master of a horse's tail swishing at the summer flies along her flank. Its lullaby rhythm heralded torpor, which Stevenson Peter feared above all other states of mind—a creeping invader that flourished in the airless heat and inactivity, threatening to sap his ship of its every last ounce of order. He summoned the mate to the cabin and outlined his plan of resistance.

"The routines, Jim," he said, thumping the tabletop so that he set charts and instruments a-jiggle. "The routines must be observed more closely than ever. They are the key to discipline and stability," he stressed, simultaneously reminding himself of his private conviction that they were far more than that, the sacred pattern by which a righteous life was lived.

Thus the men of the *Caledonia* stood their watches on a ship at standstill, vigilant for the briefest breeze. The helmsman felt the wheel shift uselessly beneath his hands as the swell nudged the rudder. Nor was the off-watch permitted to idle. Every morning, they were ordered to rig the pumps and swab the decks yet more thoroughly lest the planks shrink from the heat. They polished the brasses, mopped the floors of the master's and first mate's quarters, and holystoned the decks. They inspected the cargo for moisture and the shrouds, stays, and halyards for chafe. They even read the log.

Every morning a crewman was solemnly summoned aft. He would hold above his head the log-line—a reeled chord, knotted at regular lengths and secured at its seaward end to a wooden float. The line was thrown over the stern, where it usually unwound to the pull of the passing water. The speed of the ship was calculated by counting the knots as they disappeared beyond the taffrail over a period that the master timed with one of his log-reckoners.

These small hourglasses could be regularly seen about the master's person. Each was enclosed in a round brass protective casing about the size of a shotgun cartridge, leaving a window in which the sand's progress through the aperture could be observed. In one, the sands were calibrated to run for fourteen seconds; and for twenty-eight seconds in the other.

In these conditions, however, the sands might have run for eternity quite without purpose. The log-line hung limp from the motionless reel, like an angler's contraption in some fishless sea, and though to persist with the exercise might have brought some moral benefit, as Stevenson

Peter firmly believed, its lack of practical value was not lost on the crew. Indeed, the foredeck, bold with too much coffee, had taken to sniggering over the business most evenings.

"Oh aye," Kent proclaimed in a grave whisper. "A man stands at the taffrail, a wheel above his head, and it's well known that twenty-eight seconds later, when he lowers it, those uninvited boarders called indiscipline and anarchy are sent packing, repelled forever to sink in the wastes of the sea, and so the vessel is restored to perfect order."

Come the morning, the crewman appointed to hold the reel would remember those words and, sensing the silent laughter of the crew at his back and the solemn observation of the officers, would fight for his hide to control the shake of his shoulders.

The sun rose and fell, a stinking slick of sewage and detritus gathered around the ship, and the inventiveness of the officers was tested. By and by, the men found themselves ordered to repair chafings that even their practiced eyes were hard pressed to detect. Serviceable sails were sent down for restitching. One afternoon, languid verse from the foredeck reached Mr. Wallace as he looked out over the steaming rim of his coffee cup, across the hammered disc of water.

"A painted ship," the voice declaimed, "upon a painted ocean."

"So get painting, Kent!" barked the first mate. "The hull if you please. That counts for the lot of you."

For two days the crew took turns in the ship's jollyboat, painting the hull black to the waterline while others gave her port band, figurehead, and masts a fresh coat of white exactly as they had done prior to their departure from Rio. To passing vessels, hypothetical though they must have been in these conditions, the *Caledonia*'s paintwork would have seemed a thing of shimmering brilliance.

Eventually, even these chores could not consume the endless succession of hours, and gaping holes began to appear in the long, hot days. At such times, when the master had stepped below and the watch officer could not summon a single further project from his ransacked mind, the men retired to the shade thrown by the limp sails. Here, they kept the Argentine busy by drinking his coffee, or exchanged drowsy grunts. Sometimes, they collected galley scraps to feed the goats that had not yet succumbed to Samuel's knife, or enticed some movement from McDonald's tortoise, whose daily perambulations had become a focus of lively foredeck interest.

Mostly, however, they retreated into private thoughts, the increasingly arcane ones that bubbled up in their broiled minds. For his part, Edward Le Dain fell to considering the curious question of the second mate's surname. Following the failure of his attempt to make that man's acquaintance, he had maintained an open ear. The master and first mate, however, addressed the second mate as "Mr. Mate," which was unrevealing, while the members of the second mate's watch, compelled by custom to answer him by his surname, seemed to a man to have adopted a singular strategy. Le Dain, who stood watch with Mr. Wallace, often found himself listening from his hammock to the other watch at work beyond the fo'c'sle hatch, where command transformed the second mate, and his orders achieved an unlikely authority. The men pronounced the second mate's name as a truncated grunt, as if it were the natural consequence of physical exertion—running, scrubbing, hauling, or lifting—when the evident truth was that they had only an incomplete idea of it. Even so, that silent presence struck Le Dain as alarmingly incomplete without one: the mate with a mumble by way of a name; that, and Le Dain's sure sense that he would be expected to know it one day.

One afternoon, a gleeful shout had broken the silence.

"Port bow! Mr. Stirrup! Direct the eyes!" Tomaso Samuel had abandoned his coffee duties to point frantically through the galley window. Edward Le Dain, repairing a perfectly seaworthy halyard high in the rigging, looked down on a large leatherback turtle which was passing close to the side of the ship, making progress the *Caledonia* could only dream of.

"Hey, Mr. Stickup! Is your proper tortoise meal!" Samuel guffawed and slapped two flashing galley knives together. The second mate shrank into the shrouds, as if he were inspecting a chafe. James Wallace staggered to his feet.

"You! Dago! More coffee," he bellowed, making a mental note to pronounce the brew filthy. It fell to him to quash Samuel's bravado. Truth to tell, he should long since have adminstered one of his tongue-lashings, and in private, since a public reprimand would further weaken the second mate's position. But he was tired as a dog—he guessed it was the heat—and could summon neither the subtlety nor the authority for the job. Instead he ordered more coffee, which was what he had recently found himself doing in these circumstances. Which, he privately conceded, was hardly an impressive demonstration of leadership.

Truth to tell, James Wallace had not been himself for some days now. He could not account for the growing mental instability that had descended upon him. He slept badly and dreamed of fearful beasts, so his nerves were chafed and tender when he arose from his bunk. He was overcome by indiscriminate irritation and snapped without reason. He was assailed by lethargy, and his eye seemed blunted so that he no longer saw the examples of shoddy seamanship—the ropes poorly coiled, the sails shabbily set, the seaman's surly reply—he would once have swooped upon. And all the time, his thoughts were bearing away into strange reveries, meandering through memories that invariably led him to the Marseilles quayside café of the previous spring where he had drunk creamy coffee and closed his eyes to the morning sun. Blinking his way clear of such daydreams, he would reassert his presence by calling for yet more coffee, which he once was foolish enough to do, on a day of cauldron heat, in the hearing of the master.

"Too much cursed coffee!" exploded Stevenson Peter. "A poison which God made black that it might bear the devil's own color." The master stepped below. In his cabin, he took refuge in the Book of Psalms, but for once he could not lose himself among those blissful pages and, remembering the sprawl of men on the decks and the thick air shorn of the brisk commands that usually lifted his heart, felt the slipping of things. The routines were failing him. Enervation and listlessness had penetrated the ship's seams, like drips between the deck planks, turning his entire crew into slovens. Months later, Stevenson

Peter would reflect that his troubles had begun here, and that he had been losing control ever since.

Thus it was that the wind's sudden return meant more than the promise of mere progress. The crew's cheers alerted the master, who stumbled up the companionway and stared about him.

"God save us if we're not lost yet," he exclaimed. "That's wind of all things, if my memory serves me. Call all hands, Mr. Mate." Within minutes, the ship had begun to buck. The weather rose rapidly, as if to answer for its long desertion. Soon, the sea was shoveling watery diamonds through the scuppers. Within minutes, the wind was threatening the lighter sails that had been left hanging throughout the calm to snare the merest passing breaths.

"All hands aloft at the double," the master ordered. "Royals down. And a reef in the topgallants."

The men swarmed up the ratlines, shedding torpor. Le Dain and David McDonald took the foremast and headed out along the topgallant yard, their boots against the horse-ropes that hung in loops from the yard to provide footholds. The wind was whipping into a squall. It whistled through the shrouds and fretted the sails, and as the ship pitched and the first drops of warm rain splattered against the canvas, the men bent their hands and feet to the rigging and clung on. Then, as a gust drove into the ship, the royal blew out and Le Dain could see Kent far above them, grabbing at flapping shreds of canvas. Above the noise they could hear the mate calling for a reef in the topsails. The two sailors on the topgallant yard set to work on the canvas below them. They hauled it up on the buntlines, then grabbed the reeflines, the ribbon ties that hung from the sail, and hitched them tight round the yard to contain the loose reef. The job completed, Le Dain patted the reefed sailcloth and was making for the mast when instinct caused him to turn. David McDonald had not moved. He was bent over the outer yardarm, making to vomit, his head seized as if by a frenzy of ague. When Le Dain reached him, he noticed that the boy's hands had fixed upon the yard, where they had turned purple from his grip.

"We're done here, David," shouted Le Dain.

But the boy only screwed his eyes shut and cried out, "Oh God help us. I knew we were doomed."

"Not done for, man! Done. Our work is done here."

"She's going down," said McDonald, shaking his head. "Down, down. I can feel it."

A shout of annoyed enquiry arose from the deck. Mr. Wallace was watching them. Le Dain only jabbed frantically at the yard, as if to convey some encountered hitch, and feigned concerted work, his free hand apparently straining at the yard as he turned to McDonald.

"This is no place for you!" he said. "Soon enough they'll see you."

Below them, another wave broke over the bow, and McDonald shuddered. "She won't stand it! She's sinking."

"This ship is not going down," shouted Le Dain. "It's a mere squall, David." Le Dain meant his every word. He truly felt no threat in these winds; they were merely the benevolent force that would bring them home. The Jerseyman's absolute conviction finally seemed to reassure David.

"You're sure of that?" he asked, opening his eyes.

"The ship's not going down," Le Dain reiterated. "You'll return to the deck, David. You've seawater in your eyes. That or tears, which I somehow can't believe." As he spoke, Le Dain saw resolve return to the boy's face. Le Dain prized David's fingers from the rope, then patted him encouragingly before leading the way toward the mast.

Le Dain was right. It proved a passing storm, typical of the latitude. The black clouds disbanded over the horizon, giving way to a dazzle of sun, and the wind from the north softened to a steady breeze. Later, as they were stood down, the mate met Le Dain over the fo'c'sle hatch.

"A word before you step below," he said. He led Le Dain to the quarterdeck, where he dismissed the helmsman.

"The wheel's yours," he said, "while you tell me what kept you on the topgallant yard just now."

"McDonald got a cramp in his hand, Mr. Wallace," replied Le Dain. "He couldn't let go."

"Cramp?" said the mate dismissively. "On my ship? Cramp's for millworkers. Cramp's for clerks. More nonsense about cramp and I'll flay you," he said. Still Le Dain said nothing.

"I'm warning you," said Wallace.

"The boy was scared," muttered Le Dain.

"Scared?" exclaimed Wallace. "Scared of a fresh blow on the open sea, when there's no land within five hundred miles of us? He can keep his fear for a worthy occasion, like a lee shore looming, when he'll have company in his fear, mine included." For a moment, he thought of his own son, Robert, and it occurred to him that McDonald was a mere boy, half his own age. He shrugged, uncertain in his actions. "You might ask Kent to lend him his Falconer," he suggested. "A read it might pay young McDonald to read. If he can read, that is. Not," he added, "that *you* would understand fear, of course."

Later that evening, Le Dain awoke and clambered from his off-watch hammock. He heaved himself onto the foredeck. The ship was sailing through a bright night in a moderate wind. The watch hands were dozing. Phosphorescence flitted around the Jerseyman's arc of piss where it hit the water. Then he heard a noise, rhythmic as a saw. It came from the galley. Curious, Le Dain moved aft and peered inside.

Through the gloom, he could see the sleeping chickens in stacked boxes against the bulwark, and Tomaso Samuel bent over the stove, breathing heavily. As his eyesight adapted to the gloom, he could make out the Argentine's splayed hand lying within an empty saucepan that he was gristing, with circular motions, against a metal tray. It was then that the familiar smell reached Le Dain, and he understood: Samuel had fashioned an improved grinder, which would wring a compliment from the mate, one day, on the quality of the coffee.

As Le Dain returned below, he noticed the shaft of moonlight that fell across David's hammock. The boy was reading the book Kent had lent him and a frown furrowed his brow as he learned what he should truly fear in the world.

Chapter ∽ *17*

According to government records, over six hundred British vessels were confirmed wrecked during 1842, mostly on the kingdom's own shores.

Shipwreck, moreover, was common at a time when other forms of transport were largely regarded as unhazardous. Carriage accidents were common enough but rarely fatal, and William Huskisson's death by collision with a locomotive at the unveiling of George Stephenson's "Rocket" in 1830 had been regarded as a freak incident rather than as a forewarning of train travel's inherent dangers.

By the Romantic period, shipwreck's epic elemental nature, its heroic scope, and the awful privations it often entailed had long since conquered the morbid reaches of Britain's island psyche. Instances of shipwreck found a rapt audience, not least in the "broadsides," the single-sheet fliers of the eighteenth and nineteenth centuries that were the prototypes and, latterly, competitors of the tabloid newspaper. Unabashedly sensationalist in content, the broadsides' stock-in-trade was murder trials, prize fights, and mutant births; wretched women were regularly reported as being "delivered of three living monsters, the heads having the human form and the remainder parts that of the CANINE SPECIES!" But few such stories could match the popular appeal of a DREADFUL SHIPWRECK, as these halfpenny publications were commonly headlined.

The "affecting narrative, melancholy to relate" of the shipwreck broadside was rendered in a stock vocabulary borrowed from the inflated strains of Gothic Romanticism. Hapless seafarers—"wanderers of the foam"—were said to "sink to rise no more" and so met "a watery grave." The sea boasted "insatiate jaws," and the prevailing seascape was invariably evoked by phrases such as "howling tempest," "raging main," and "foaming billows." There were anguished rhetorical appeals—"Who can paint the feelings of the wretched sufferers at that awful moment?"; pathetic details—"the crew subsisted for a whole day on a turnip"; and inappropriate doggerels:

> *Full twenty-one days longer*
> *Our perils did survive*
> *Eating our dead companions*
> *We kept ourselves alive.*

The broadside publishers seem to have been quite as worldly as their tabloid descendants. Their commercial success relied on a familiarity with popular public taste, which favored instances of shipwreck where human suffering was most prolonged. Readers wallowed in the horror of unfortunates clinging lengthily to rocks and wreckage, succumbing gradually to frostbite and exhaustion, or enduring such extremes of hunger and thirst that they eventually resorted to consuming the ship's dog en route to that extreme taboo, consuming each other.

A broadside entitled the "HORRIBLE SHIPWRECK of the *Caledonia*" (it was a common ship's name) was typical of the period. The *Caledonia* had foundered on a voyage from Quebec to Greenock in 1837. When the vessel became waterlogged, the crew took to the shrouds. In time, two men were washed away. After drifting for eleven days, the remaining crew "came to the dreadful resolve to put one of their mates to death (which they did by cutting his throat) for the purpose of drinking his blood." On the thirteenth day, they were preparing to put to death another crewman—"a poor youth now in St Peter's Hospital"—when salvation hove into view in the form of a Russian vessel. There were six survivors, but these were "so dreadfully frost-bitten that nearly all of them will be obliged to lose their limbs."

A gruesome prospect, but James Wallace was right: such things rarely worried the seasoned mariner who knew that he was far less likely to be dispatched by ravenous shipmates than by the rocks of a lee shore. The wind direction defines a lee shore; it blows directly onto it. Modern yachts, rigged fore and aft, can sail close—up to about 35 degrees—to the direction of the wind; lee shores rarely present a real threat to today's yachtsmen, even those without an engine to call upon. It was quite a different matter, however, with square-rigged ships, which could not make headway any closer than 70 degrees from the wind. An embayed square-rigger on a lee shore was always in some degree of trouble. As the *Penzance Gazette* of September 21, 1842 (perhaps prompted by the storms that had battered Cornwall just two weeks earlier), put it:

> But though the situation of a vessel in a heavy gale of wind appears indescribably terrific . . . it is truly said ships seldom or ever founder in deep water. . . . It is not, therefore, from the ocean itself that man has so much to fear; the earth and the water each afford to man a life of considerable security, yet there exists between these two elements an everlasting war, into which no passing vessel can enter with impunity; for of all the terrors of this world, there is surely no one greater than that of being on a lee-shore in a gale of wind, and in shallow water.

Such terrors were the subject of William Falconer's epic poem "The Shipwreck" (1762). Falconer was just one of three survivors from the loss of the *Britannia* on the coast of Greece, which inspired his acclaimed and best-selling poem. "The Shipwreck" achieved a resonance and an audience—not least among mariners—that lasted well into the nineteenth century. Sailors who otherwise knew not a line of literature would commonly be familiar with Falconer; some could even quote him at length. His story seems to have had something of the impact on succeeding generations that the *Titanic* story continues to bear on ours.

It may have been the appallingly arbitrary way in which the lee shore meted out death or salvation that mariners so feared. Unlike the gruesome protracted privations that were the sensational broadsides' stock-in-trade, being wrecked on a lee shore promised an instant resolution, one way or the other. The only question was whether one lived or died. Once all hope of saving the ship was lost—the wind set hard against the land, the shore looming—the sailor was left with the looming breakers, and the tantalizing fact of dry land just beyond them. But the kindly wave that might carry him to the safety of the beach might as easily impale him upon a razored rock, so that "in gaining his point he shall lose its object—that England, with all its virtue, may fade before his eyes," as the *Penzance Gazette* put it.

Falconer had experienced it for himself, as he wrote in the last couplet of "The Shipwreck":

> *Then might I, with unrivalled strains, deplore*
> *The impervious horrors of a leeward shore.*

Chapter ∞ 18

The most recent wreck on the Hartland coast, the stretch "most notorious of all for tales of wreckers," had been that of the *Johanna*. Joe Gifford was apparently the man to see about the *Johanna*; he even had some of her remnants.

Joe came from a family of wreckers, which was something to come from. I set out for Kilkhampton with colorful expectations, imagining an isolated cottage in whose shadowy corners old barrels, chests, and crates might be glimpsed, with dilapidated outhouses where ropes and grappling irons lay beneath mildewed tarpaulins, and a brooding man with a nose for a northwest wind and dark secrets in his eyes.

The reality, needless to say, had not kept pace. In the poverty of his hometown, all peeling facades and unoccupied premises that huddled in the shadow of the impressive church where the remains of Sir Bevil Grenville lay, a few hardy convenience stores had sprouted. The main road ran through the middle of town and seemed in a hurry to leave. Joe lived in a simple terraced home, with a front garden where a bird table perched in a dead cherry tree. He was a big, kindly man, with a thick mop of brown hair and a pronounced Cornish accent that snagged on his shallow, asthmatic breath. He led me into a sparsely furnished kitchen, with three chairs and a table. A jar of coffee, a bottle of Coke, and a half onion wrapped in plastic were on the work surface.

Joe told me his story. He was born during a snowstorm on Christmas Day of 1938. His father, Charlie, had been one of nine children to have been brought up on his own father's farm at Southole, a remote hamlet just north of Welcombe. By his retirement, Charlie's father had somehow installed most of his many children in local farms or small tracts of land of their own. Charlie got Welcombe House, on the slopes above Marsland Water, as well as an adjoining bungalow, seven acres of land, and the local milk route.

When the milk route failed a few years after his marriage, Charlie Gifford turned his hand to wrecking. But the romantic term masked a reality as mundane as the abandoned milk route. Like his father before him, who had recovered the coal cargo from the *Cambalu*, wrecked near Southole in 1933, Charlie bought the salvage rights to wrecked ships from the insurers and removed anything with a scrap value. He was the marine equivalent of the auto wrecker.

The first wreck that Charlie Gifford could call his own was that of the *Sjofna*, a Norwegian freighter wrecked at Welcombe Mouth in 1944. Joe had childhood memories of being taken on board the broken-backed ship, for which his father had paid five pounds—largely for the copper and brass he hoped to remove. Then there was the *Saltburn*, to which Charlie secured the rights in 1947; much of the timber went to restoring a cottage at Milford near Speke's Mill, which still carries the ship's name.

Joe also remembered the war cargoes that came ashore during his childhood: barrels of Guinness (which his father concealed by decanting into milk churns), tins of biscuits and coffee, cigarettes, truck axles, motorbikes, timber, socket sets, spanners, watches, processed cheese, peanuts, pencils, boxes of lard, bales of raw rubber, even cigars, perfume, and condoms for the troops. "It was uncle who had most of them condom boxes," said Joe, "but he never lived long enough to use them."

In the 1950s, the Bristol Channel was awash with war wrecks and there was plenty of work for Charlie Gifford. But by the 1960s, he was having to make salvage bids as far afield as the Scilly Isles; Joe even remembered his straitened father appealing for wrecks, like a farmer praying for rain. By the time of Joe's adulthood, wrecks had become such a rarity that he was forced to take other work. He became a welder, working on the tugs they built in the yards at Appledore. He still kept an eye on the coast, however, and with his own hands carried away several hundredweight of aluminum that washed up at Marsland during the 1970s. The metal came from a shattered sea container in which a few green chunks of stinking beef and bone still hung from weed-draped meat hooks. That was it, except for Joe's last haul—a two-handled saucepan from the *Johanna* containing a spoon embedded in two inches of solidified porridge.

The *Johanna*, traveling from Rotterdam to Barry, hit the rocks at Hartland Point in the early hours of New Year's Eve, 1982. A helicopter lifted off the four crewmen at four A.M. The three Dutch officers—the captain and the mates—were transferred to the Clovelly lifeboat shortly before dawn. The falling tide, however, soon swept away the shallow waters that hem Hartland Point to expose the 960-ton freighter's grimy hull on a wide bed of boulders and dank, weed-fringed rock pools; had they waited, the men could have made their own way ashore in nothing more than a pair of boots. The *Johanna*, carrying grain like the *Caledonia* 140 years earlier, had hit the rocks, in moderate weather, not four hundred yards from the Hartland lighthouse. Since the beam was visible from twenty miles, suspicions were aroused that her loss might have been a prime example of that nineteenth-century scam, the maritime insurance job. But the darker implications of the freighter's resting place—that she could be readily reached by landsmen—were soon to become apparent.

News of the wreck traveled fast. It had occurred on a Friday morning, at the beginning of an unseasonably mild holiday weekend, which made it the indisputable family outing. A first few locals had reached the unguarded ship that morning and removed its wheel and bell as trophies. It was on Saturday morning, however, when the next daytime tide permitted it, that traffic first converged on the lighthouse in such volumes that it blocked the narrow lanes for miles around. Farmers opened their fields as parking lots, charging entrance money. Crowds shouldered ropes and toolboxes down the steep path to the shore. They made their way across the foreshore, positioned ladders and slung grappling irons, and clambered aboard. The ship's prize possessions—her washing machine, deep freezers, microwave, radio equipment, and television—were first to go. The crowd then raided the ship's stores: cases of lager, whisky, and Coke, tins of food, and cans of paint. They next turned their attention to any loose objects that might be of use or value, removing chairs, ropes, tools, the ship's dinghy and life raft, items of clothing, ship's papers, and even her Christmas tree. Afterward, they opened their toolboxes and set about removing windows, doors, navigation lights, portholes, and even the captain's lavatory seat. And when they had picked the ship clean, some ransacked her, firing off extinguishers and signal rockets, and smashing unwanted catering jars to leave a slick of glass and ketchup against the bulkheads. "Sunday was like being in the middle of a flock of starlings," a local man said. "Hacksaws were going. Hammers were crashing and there was a constant sound of splintering wood and breaking crockery." They then left the carcass of the *Johanna* to the ravages of succeeding winters.

The newspapers feasted upon the story. They spoke of the people of Hartland "reviving a tradition of bygone centuries." Some locals spoke out against such press coverage. Just as his Morwenstow counterpart over a century before had done, the vicar of Hartland defended the reputation of his parishioners, considering it "most unfair that our community should come in for so much of the blame for the vandalism committed aboard the *Johanna.* . . . There were far more wreckers and robbers than the entire population of Hartland. There may have been one or two people from Hartland involved. But the overwhelming majority were from elsewhere." Other locals did not, however, deny their actions, but sought merely to justify them. "It isn't as if we caused the ship to be wrecked," a Bude man remarked. "Which is what used to happen in times gone by."

The loss of the *Johanna* seemed less like a modern shipping incident than a wrecking yarn out of another time, one that confirmed all that had been alleged of the past. The modern world, for all its sanitizing effects, had evidently failed to eradicate the atavistic instincts of these coastal people. "There is still very much of the wrecker blood in the inhabitants here," Nicholas Ross wrote from Kilkhampton in 1957. "At the least hint of a wreckage, a reflex is set up in them and they rush for the rocks."

People who could do this to a ship in the 1980s might have been capable of anything 140 years earlier.

Chapter ✷ *19*

Britain was in a deepening depression in the spring of 1842. The strait-ened government introduced income tax for the first time in peacetime and there was widespread unrest over the Corn Laws, which the *Times* of March 8 declared to be "the groundwork, the main-spring of the dread-ful distresses under which the country is suffering."

Sir Robert Peel's government moved to amend the legislation. Dur-ing the introductory debate in the House of Commons on February 9, Peel conceded that wheat prices had been higher than was socially de-sirable, and that the ideal was to achieve a stable price of between fifty-five and sixty shillings per quarter. When it emerged, however, that the prime minister would not countenance the abolition of the Corn Laws, effigies of Peel were burned in Hawick, Bradford-upon-Avon, Hull, and Manchester.

Britain's wheat producers had enjoyed uninterrupted protection since the Napoleonic Wars, when the price of wheat had risen from forty-three shillings a quarter in 1792 to 126 shillings in 1812. Heady profits (and the pressing national need) had encouraged landowners to invest in the cultivation of new arable land, only to face ruin when wheat prices plummeted at war's end—to sixty shillings in January 1815. That year, a law was passed prohibiting the import of foreign wheat until do-mestic prices exceeded eighty shillings. High bread prices subsequently set the consumer, underrepresented, overtaxed, and embittered, firmly against the producer, privileged but prepared to scrap for his every last advantage.

In a bid to encourage moderate wheat prices without ruinously undermining returns to the producers, the government had introduced a sliding scale of duties on wheat imports in 1828. Low domestic prices would mean high import tariffs, but as prices climbed, revealing a shortage in the British market, so tariffs would fall.

The effect of the sliding scale was, however, to introduce a highly speculative cast to the wheat market. The scale was designed so that the higher prices rose, the more dramatically duties plummeted. For every shilling the average price exceeded seventy-one shillings, for example, the duty payable fell by four shillings. It was alleged that unscrupulous importers and their agents submitted fictitious purchases at high prices to inflate the corn returns on which the average wheat price was calculated, and thus reduce the duty payable. Others simply withheld stocks precisely at the time they were most needed in the eventual expectation of increased prices and lower duties. The poor harvest months of 1841 and the succeeding winter had proved a classic case in point. Prices were reported to have reached "famine levels" while more than one million quarters of wheat were reckoned to be in bond waiting for cheaper duty, "when all will suddenly be thrown on the market, just as new English wheat is forthcoming!"

A new bill, which was passed in April 1842 and became law later that summer, did away with the dramatic duty reductions that had proved such a temptation to speculators, and lowered duties overall; importers would pay thirteen shillings duty where they had previously paid twenty-seven on a wheat price of sixty shillings, and seven shillings instead of twenty on a price of sixty-five shillings. It was hoped that the new duties would attract enough foreign wheat to avoid the famine conditions of the previous year.

The *Caledonia* and her cargo of coffee, meanwhile, were crossing the Ionian and Aegean seas. "We discharged at Corfu, and Syra, and Smyrna, and Constantinople," Le Dain would write in the wreck statement that he made at Morwenstow on September 22, 1842. The *Caledonia* is sighted in *Lloyd's List,* arriving at Syra in the Cyclades "from Rio and Corfu" on March 20, 1842, and leaving for Smyrna a few days later.

Gulf of Smyrna, April 3, 1842

From the quarterdeck, Stevenson Peter allowed himself the indulgent observation that his charge must look magnificent, surfing eastward under her full press of sunlit canvas, the topgallants, royals, and even studding sails abloat with a wind that had with great good fortune persisted beyond its customary hour. Though he almost regretted that there were few passing vessels to appreciate her—only distant fishing caiques working the shallows, painted in yellows and turquoises—the better part of him took comfort from an empty sea.

The afternoon had drawn on, and the truncated orange sun, which sat on the high ground of the Cheshme Peninsula, diminished by the instant. Smyrna's magnificent approaches, a wide gulf hemmed by gilded hills from where the scents of pine and Asian herbs wafted, were a dangerous distraction when the idling winds might evaporate at the very next moment and abandon his vessel to the dangers of this coast. On all sides were discreet coves where rapid schooners, heavily armed, awaited the onset of dusk. Only recently had a vessel out of Calymnos, after discharging her cargo of sponges at Smyrna, fallen foul of pirates in these very waters. The ship had been stripped to the bilges, and all but one of her eight crew butchered. So it was that Stevenson Peter had sent a sailor to the masthead and charged him with maintaining a strop-sharp lookout.

The quarterdeck's palpable tension appeared, however, to slacken as it worked its way forward until it seemed entirely absent by the time it reached the foredeck, where the watch was unaccountably a-snigger. The master let the skylarking pass, though it struck him as beyond reason that his formerly sober crew apparently comprehended nothing of their predicament, and from his pockets he withdrew the log-reckoners, which he turned between his fingers like worry beads. Stevenson Peter carried pistols, but he was a godly man who was not inclined to violence. He reckoned, moreover, that the pistols would serve no purpose in his un-practiced hands but incense approaching pirates to greater violence of their own. He preferred to rely on his log-reckoners, for they reminded him of the Atlantic and Mediterranean distances the ship had safely cov-ered. The log-reckoners, which had measured out God's providence over the ocean's vastness, were more than instruments of mere chronology; they were the talismans that kept his ship from harm.

The wind held up and Smyrna gradually took shape through the sea haze. The port lay toward the head of the gulf, where it sprawled along the southern shore. From the low brown city, spiky minarets, blurred cy-presses and plumes of smoke arose. The surrounding plain was patterned with lemon and orange groves and roughly tilled smallholdings with whitewashed windmills and fig trees at the corners. Pink daubs of olean-der marked the brooks that drained the high ground where the old castle stood.

As the master took in the gathering view, he eased his grip upon the log-reckoners. Safety beckoned and, with it, the prospect of unloading another consignment of the cursed cargo. Coffee produced feverish heat and anxiety, palpitations and trembling. It paralyzed the animal and vital functions and crippled the moral faculties. Coffee, he had heard it said, gave one the intelligence and activity of an oyster. He had also heard men speak of its hallucinogenic effects, which caused them to imagine they were plunging down precipices, or being pursued by wild beasts. And he had heard the allegations of women that it rendered their menfolk as un-fruitful as the sandy deserts from where that unhappy berry came, though his own marital state meant that this was no concern of his.

Even though he did not drink the evil potion, coffee kept the master awake at night through fret alone. Coffee made the owner good money, but turned the master gray. It needed nursing. Neglect it one moment, and it spoiled. It was well known how the slightest moisture reduced the coffee to lumps that resembled sheep droppings and acquired a compa-rable flavor. Keeping the cargo dry was an art, entailing constant deck swills and regular checks of the dunnage, the wedged planks that formed a skin between the sacks and the bilge waters. Nor was moisture the whole of it, for coffee seemed to take contagion from anything. It was said that a few bags of peppercorns on board a ship from India had spoiled a whole cargo of coffee, but that was nothing compared to guano. A mere scattering of the stuff, inadvertently left in the hold from a previous voyage, could contribute to the coffee in the course of its carriage an adventitious flavor so loathsome that Albanians alone would take the stuff—at a ruinous discount.

And then there was the crew. Though coffee had no place in a Christian diet, there was no question that it had been effective in maintaining the wakefulness of the watches through the small hours. It now appeared to the master, however, that it had another effect over time: of imparting to the crew an uncharacteristically sour flavor and a demonic energy combined. A constant bickering prevailed between men who had once known better, as if something had exaggerated the natural effects of their enforced proximity. There was fatigue in the afternoon and wild laughter in the small hours. His orderly and reliable men had, it seemed, been invaded by strange spirits whose impetuous moods veered from sullenness to exuberance. The master had learned that one of the apprentices was suffering from a sudden trepidation regarding shipwreck. The cook spent all his time making coffee and was proving a damned impertinence, and the foredeck was rent by endless literary spoutings, which Kent had once had the sense to keep in check; the Lord preserve them when they reached the Hellespont. There'd been untoward nonsense involving the tortoise and repeated eruptions of high spirits, which, even this afternoon, a time that particularly called for vigilance, seemed to be affecting the foredeck.

What most troubled Stevenson Peter, however, were the changes wrought in the ship's mate. His brother-in-law had taken to the coffee like an opium addict, hollering for it at all hours. To Stevenson Peter it seemed that the coffee had unmanned him, stripping the mate of his considerable abilities. He had become moody, distant, and largely disinterested in the business of the ship. The master determined to find a private moment to address him on the subject.

They were approaching Smyrna's bustling harbor under reduced sail, the water spotted by caiques, sponge boats, polaccas, and men-of-war.

"You can relieve the lookout, Mr. Wallace," said the master, pocketing the log-reckoners and stepping below. Wallace cleared his head with a shake and gestured weakly at the masthead as the crew moved to drop anchor.

Rumors of plague around the city confined the crew to the ship that evening. In the gloaming, as the muezzins intoned their call to prayer, Tomaso Samuel butchered the last of the goat kids. He ripped its sucking gums from its mother's udder and, swinging it over the gunwale, pierced its downy throat in a single action so a spurt of blood pissed against the water. As the crew ate, one pair of green eyes watched them from beneath the longboat. The harbormaster's caique drew alongside; David McDonald was dispatched to fetch the ship's papers from the master.

Later, as the crew settled on the foredeck with their pipes and their pots of coffee, McDonald scooped the tortoise from the fo'c'sle. From his pocket, he pulled a stub of old carrot that he had found on the galley floor. He cut the carrot into small pieces, which the crew arranged across the deck in a lengthy loop around the windlass, obliging the hungry creature to entertain them by its perambulations.

"Will you look at the wee pins on him tonight," admired Stephen Jones.

"Faster than a stagecoach," said Kent. "You know we should read his log!" The men laughed. "Hamlet," continued Kent. "You'll fetch a sand-glass from St. Peter, won't you, for our worthy purpose?" And a moment later, as the risen Le Dain made his way aft, Kent added in an awed voice, "Did the daft Frenchie not ken I was joking?"

෧෨

"An unholy mess." Stevenson Peter shook his head like a metronome. He was sitting in his cabin, poring over the journals from London that had been delivered to the ship's side along with the post bag. James Wallace sat opposite, holding the day's seventh pot of coffee in his hand.

"A mess?" asked Wallace, looking about him though not at himself, who, with a stubbly beard, rheumy eyes, and a bloodless pallor, was most certainly one.

"The country, the country," muttered Stevenson Peter, waving the journal at the mate. "The poor, cursed country."

Wallace was still sitting there, mostly oblivious to the observations of the master (an unfixed gaze playing across his face), when David Mc-Donald appeared at the cabin door.

"The harbor master's alongside, sir," he said. "He's asking for the ship's papers."

Stevenson Peter looked up from the journal and passed over a sheaf of documents. "And tell the Turk to get my name right for a blessed change," he shouted as McDonald backed out. "Now, what was I saying?"

Wallace jolted himself awake, vaguely remembering the substance of the master's musings. "The Corn Laws, I believe," he answered.

The apprentice had not long left when another disturbance assailed the cabin.

"What in the devil is that noise?" exclaimed Stevenson Peter.

"Some floating character making a din," said Wallace, stifling a yawn as he peered from the cabin windows. A man in a fez, flourishing a paintbrush, was hailing the ship from a caique. "Seems to want to know if you'll have the ship painted."

"Painted?" cried Stevenson Peter, remembering the doldrums. "How much more painted could she possibly be? Another coat and she'd sink. Is the fellow myopic?"

"I think he means a portrait, skip. He's waving an easel at me."

"Oh, that sort of painting." The notion was immediately appealing, for the master was proud of his ship, but tonight he was in no mood to talk business with a Turk. "Tell him to come back tomorrow and we'll see. Now, where were we?"

"If I remember rightly," Wallace blinked, "you were explaining the sliding scale."

Nor had the master got far with the intricacies of tariff duties when there came another knock on the cabin door. It was the Jerseyman.

"Yes?" said the master. "What the devil is it now?"

"The men were wondering if they might borrow a log-reckoner, sir."

"To what purpose, pray?"

Le Dain did not pause. "They're timing the tortoise, sir. They're racing him round the windlass, sir, eating carrots on the way. He seems to be faster tonight."

"For the love of God get him out of here, Mr. Wallace!"

Wallace gave Le Dain a clout across the head and bellowed at him to "get forward and stay there, you pocked frog," then slammed the door behind him. "He's got this thing about being immortal, him having endured the pox," Wallace explained. "It makes him do stupid things, as if nothing can hurt him. But I think I just did," he added, nursing his fist.

Stevenson Peter only held his head in his hands and shook it gently from side to side. "What on earth is happening to my ship? Never in all my time at sea have I heard such nonsense."

"It may be the men have been away too long, skip."

"Away too long, my shredded foretopsail! A year away, and tortoise races? A year away, and the foredeck giggling like a crowd of dairymaids? It's the coffee. Fancy Regency nonsense it is, with its dreamy misleading vapors, and it does nobody any good. No nutriment whatsoever in a whole shipload of the cursed stuff. Rots the mind and makes for idle coffeehouse banter. It's turning their heads, and yours too. Most of all yours, if you must know. You're losing your faculties. You're not the mate you were. Look at you. You're a shoddy mess. And you've let the ship become a shambles too. Once we unload the last of this cargo at Constantinople, I'll not have a sip of coffee on board, not a bean, do you understand?"

"Sir," said Wallace obediently. There was a pause.

"So," said Stevenson Peter. "That's the sliding scale."

"And can I ask why you're telling me all this?"

"Owners' instructions," Stevenson Peter replied, waving a document. "We're to pick up a cargo of wheat at Odessa. Then Falmouth for further orders." The master's good humor returned even as he spoke. Wheat was an honorable freight, a holy one. The staff of life. Hallowed food for the people's mouths. St. Paul had carried wheat (true though it was that particular voyage had not ended fortuitously), and Stevenson Peter would delight in being entrusted with such a cargo. He turned to a final item in the post pile. "Oh, and I nearly forgot," he said. "A letter for you. From Bathia."

Wallace took the letter and fingered it, aware that his brother-in-law had deliberately withheld it.

"What news from home?" asked Stevenson Peter eventually. He looked up from the journal in a conciliatory manner. But Wallace had slipped his wife's letter into a deep pocket.

"I'll let you know," he said brusquely, and left the cabin.

Chapter ❧ 20

Mark Myers had turned up something on the *Caledonia*.

"I've found the painting," he said, leading me up to his studio. *The Wreck of the Caledonia* stood against a bookshelf. It showed a livid Morwenstow morning, sunshine piercing the lowering clouds above Sharpnose to illuminate a shore seething with rocks and the debris of a broken ship: spars, timber, rigging, shattered masts, and, at the center of the picture, the figurehead staring skyward from the peak of the upturned foundering bow. And the scene had attracted a crowd.

I counted some sixty figures in the painting. Mostly, these were distant clusters silhouetted against the clifftop, some of them on horseback. A few had ventured down to the shore and were perched along the tops of the rocky spines that thrust into the surge. Two of them appeared in the foreground. One was reaching seaward. He may merely have been curious, pointing to some item of wreckage, but the gesture hinted at a declaration of intent or even possession; that's mine, it seemed to say, once the sea has settled.

It was a bold picture. Mark's work usually required him to reproduce the certainties of specific ships—their rigs, their lines, their dimensions and deck arrangements—which made him the natural successor to the nineteenth-century ships' portraitists. But here he had ventured into more speculative territory. The picture hinted at this coast's notoriety, and was particular about time and place in doing so: Morwenstow, North Cornwall, on the morning of September 8, 1842.

The painting recalled an 1805 print by Rowlandson, the London caricaturist, entitled *Clearing a Wreck in Cornwall*. The three same elements—shore, wreck, and humans—dominate both painting and print; crucially, however, the tide is out in the print. The wild postponing sea

that restricts the people of Morwenstow to pointing in the Myers painting is no bar to impulse here. The temptation, moreover, is greater in the print, where the wreck—and its contents—remain intact. The cargo of bales is being removed to bullock-drawn carts, which are disappearing inland in a laden line. Raised sticks suggest that the carters are in a hurry to be gone. The wreck appears to be recent; the authorities are apparently absent from the scene. A body lies on the shore. Two people stand over the corpse, and it is here that the artist abandons the viewer to his own presumptions. That's to say, the two people may be performing the only kindness they can by closing the corpse's eyes—or they may be stripping it of any remaining valuables.

It was time that I too visited the shore. Mark gave me detailed directions, for it was not an easy descent. He was offering to lend me a rope when he suddenly stopped, confronted by an old memory.

"The bottle," he said suddenly. "Wait a minute. What do you know of the *Caledonia* bottle?"

I shrugged blankly.

"An old bottle—and the message they found inside—used to be displayed on the stairs of the hotel at Portledge. That's about twenty miles away, just around the corner beyond Clovelly. We were at dinner there one evening years ago when I noticed it. I wrote the letter details down in one of my notebooks." Myers went straight to a cabinet, and from a file marked *Caledonia* pulled a little black notebook.

His entry, hastily made on a hotel staircase, was scrawled but legible; "The letter," it read, "on a yellowed sheet of paper, has a short, coarsely written message from a very blunt pen which reads to the following effect":

Caledonia. 14 August 1842.

Dear Brother
And it please God I be with y against Michaelmas. Prepare y
search at Lundy for ye Jenny ivories. Adieu
William
Odessa

Mark had then copied the author's sketch of what was recognizably Lundy Island, narrow but thickening to its southern end—and with an *x* on its southwestern coast.

"It's a treasure map!" I exclaimed.

Mark gave a seasoned shrug and rolled a cigarette.

"Looks like it," he agreed. "Not that the letter makes much sense to me."

I slung his rope over my shoulder, thanked him, and left.

∞

It transpired that a local family had picked up the *Caledonia* bottle from the beach at Portledge in the summer of 1967. They handed it in at the hotel in the woods above the beach. There, it was put aside until the summer's end, when a closer examination intrigued the hotel manager sufficiently to send the bottle and its contents to Exeter University. The university staff scrutinized the green bottle and the letter, which was written in brown ink on paper that dated to the period, and were minded to accept it as genuine. The local paper, which ran a story on the discovery in February 1968, declared that the "possibility of a hoax has been considered, but all the evidence is against it and small research emphasises the authenticity of the letter."

The bare facts certainly fitted. A ship by the name of the *Jenny* had indeed been lost on Lundy Island and had been carrying ivory. The wreck had occurred some forty-five years earlier, on January 27, 1797. "We state with extreme concern the loss of the ship Jenny, Captain BUCKLE, of Bristol, on his return from the coast of Africa, with a valuable cargo of ivory, dye-wood, gold-dust and other merchandize," the *Times* reported. "Having for some days experienced very foggy weather, the ship's reckoning could not be accurately kept, and in consequence she unfortunately ran ashore on the Lundy Island, when the ship went to pieces, and the Captain with the crew, except the mate, unhappily perished." The place where she was lost, on the island's southwest coast, has since been known as Jenny's Cove.

So much for the wreck, but what of the letter? There were, as we know, plenty of ships by the name of *Caledonia* at the time, but of them only the *Caledonia* of Arbroath, master Peter, visited Odessa in the summer of 1842. There was, besides, a William on board: Tasker. There is no indication in the records that Tasker had brothers. It seems he must have been addressing a friend or accomplice whom he knew sufficiently well to be confident of seeing on his return at Michaelmas—September 29.

But how had the bottle come to be washed up at Portledge? Though the letter was headed Odessa, it seemed inconceivable that it could have entered the sea there. The odds on it finding its way through three separate narrows—the Bosphorus, the Dardanelles, and the Straits of Gibraltar—before washing up within twenty miles of the *Caledonia*'s final resting place were infinitesimal. *Lloyd's List* discounted the possibility for good when the *Caledonia* was reported in its pages as having "spoken" the brig *Mathew* of Sunderland at Cape St. Vincent, Portugal's southwest corner, on August 15, 1842, which placed her over twenty-five hundred miles from Odessa the day following the date on the letter. What, then, had caused Tasker to write the letter at that time? And why had he headed it *Odessa*?

The apprentice might, I figured, have conceived of the letter in Odessa, or made a first draft of it there, or, writing the letter at sea, have even remembered the place that had inspired its contents. If few nineteenth-century ship's apprentices knew how to write, fewer still would have been acquainted with the conventions of letter writing. The real problem lay not with the letter, but the bottle. Tasker may not have been an accomplished correspondent, but in his three and a half years at sea he was sure to have acquired plenty of common sense. Enough, certainly, to have appreciated that the message in the bottle, being at best a chancy means of delivery, must be directed to its finder, and never to a specific person. Which led me to suppose that Tasker had never intended to dispatch the letter by bottle. The date on the letter indicated that it was written around the time that the *Caledonia* left the Mediterranean for the Atlantic on its final run to Britain. He presumably wrote it with the ship's imminent return in mind, intending to entrust it at the first opportunity to the Penny Post system (just two years old at the time), and only consigned it to the bottle and thence the sea out of necessity.

Still, it was to be wondered how Tasker had learned of the *Jenny*'s treasure. His onboard presence had so far proved a shadowy one. His character, known only for his constancy to the ship—and the nerve-fraying experience of the *Caledonia*'s grounding off Copenhagen in July 1839—had been reluctant to emerge. But by suggesting a private agenda, a youthful obsession, the letter looked set to change all that.

I could start by finding the bottle.

Chapter ∞ *21*

In November 1841 the British Government, which was drafting proposed amendments to the Corn Laws, requested information on grain prices from its overseas consuls. Wheat, it transpired, fetched an average fifty-five shillings per quarter in Rotterdam. It cost forty-nine shillings in Riga, thirty-nine shillings and one penny in St. Petersburg, and thirty-five shillings in Hamburg. It was cheapest, however—at twenty-six shillings and sixpence a quarter—in Odessa.

Entire fleets of British traders, energized by cheap wheat and the recent import-duty reductions on grain, made for Russia's booming grain port in the summer of 1842, with as many as 150 vessels arriving from Constantinople in a single day. One of them was the *Caledonia*. She thus was hauled from her own story into a wider economic history. It was a reminder that the *Caledonia*'s progress was not her own; market prices and distant duty amendments dictated the set of her sails and the direction of her helm.

She had arrived at Constantinople from Smyrna on April 14, 1842, where the crew discharged the last of the coffee. According to Le Dain's statement, they "took in ballast" there—weighting the ship's bilges, typically with local rubble, stone, or sand—to compensate for the absence of cargo on her onward voyage. She did not leave for Odessa, at the Black Sea's northwestern corner, until May 12. Nor was she quick to make her destination. The explanation for her delay may be found in John Purdy's *The New Sailing Directory* of 1834, which describes the prevailing east-northeast and northeast winds, which, "from want of precaution," have caused many vessels to be "carried to the coast of Roumeli [modern Turkey's Black Sea shore], and detained there for a long time."

The *Caledonia* eventually arrived at Odessa on May 30, where she would stay for over a month.

Bay of Odessa, July 3, 1842
"Where is Tasker? I'll crush his balls so I will."

James Wallace spoke with such force that the gulls, which had adopted a hovering pose beyond the low stern, exploded as if from a shotgun to scatter across the sky. From his place in the stern, Wallace was well placed to tally the longboat's contents: the last of the cargo (some thirty sacks of the best South Russian wheat) and the sweat-beaded crewmen perched atop them, where they rowed as best they could, but, plainly, no Tasker.

Wallace swore roundly. He swiveled his awkward bulk to scan the receding shore, and felt the perspiration seep from the cracks and crevices of his person. The heat was fearful. It had risen from the baked steppes of Russia (where ears of wheat were even now turning to gold in their millions) to settle with an immense weight upon the city. It seemed to bow the dusty acacia trees and suspended a monochrome haze over the low cliffs where the city perched, so that the granaries and palaces, the terraces and garden squares, the Italianate cathedral and opera house, the promenade and the Greek church with its gilt spire, appeared whited, like bleached bones. Nor could anything be seen of the city's prize construction, the bold granite steps that would one day connect the harbor and the town above it with such sweeping splendor that some Odessa residents, borne away by their enthusiasm, were already prophesying that the steps would come to be as famous as the waterways of St. Petersburg or the domed mosques of Constantinople.

But the view was clearer toward sea level. There, Wallace could plainly discern two figures on the quayside from which the longboat had recently departed. The two were deep in conversation. So much so that the cursed Tasker—for it was he, he and the old fellow, the deranged fossil who'd been pestering the crew ever since they'd first begun to load the cargo—was even now wholly oblivious to the longboat's departure.

"Oh, damn his foolish bloody eyes," muttered Wallace, waving the crew onward. "Let the wee toad swim."

The *Caledonia* had arrived weeks earlier to the sight of a shorefront seething with the grain ships of every nation. Such was the crush that she had been obliged to drop anchor in the bay. Even from there, however, the crew could see the clouds of locusts that descended to glut themselves upon the grain-laden ox carts whose creaking wheels announced their arrival from the great estates in Podolia and Wolhynia.

The crew spent the first days emptying the ship's bilges of ballast. It was a thankless task, and only the exotic cargoes being offloaded into Russian lighters elsewhere in the bay—the wines and dried fruits, perfumes and attar of roses, shawls and cambrics, tobacco and the amber mouthpieces of smoking pipes—allowed the *Caledonia*'s men the refuge of luxurious daydreams as they shoveled bilge-stinking rubble over the gunwale. Still, they did wonder why the laden lighters that dotted the bay used only oars to land their cargoes and never seemed to seek assistance from the sails.

As the men were soon to learn, the quarantine authorities had been so alarmed by recent outbreaks of plague, cholera, and smallpox that the use of sails was forbidden in the port area lest the cloth should imbibe contagion, and subsequently impart it by some kind of wafting action. The medical men of the day had condemned sailcloth as a "susceptible" product, one capable of harboring pestilence. Other susceptible materials, largely vegetable or animal in origin, included everything from wool and hemp to books and straw bonnets, while mineral products were regarded as safe. So while a raised sail and an onshore wind were considered injurious to the health of the entire city, exposing it to wholesale contagion, no risk apparently attached to sharing a water glass with an infected person.

"Then they can keep their Russian canoes," pronounced a disbelieving Stevenson Peter. "We'll use our very own longboat."

But the longboat was not designed to carry wheat sacks, and the toil proved unsparing. Only Alexander Kent seemed unaffected. Every morning, as the shore party bent their oars toward the quay (and their minds bowed beneath the burdensome prospect before them), Kent would turn toward the city and, if he were not at the oars that morning, would stretch out his hands to embrace the place and the great poet who had been exiled here eighteen years before. Pushkin! Who had seduced the wife of the city's governor-general. Pushkin! Who had begun his masterpiece, *Eugene Onegin*, here. Pushkin! Who had died at the hands of a duelist just five years before. Another port, another writer, some of the crew groaned inwardly, thanking God that this Pushkin character wasn't much translated yet into the English.

The mate soon silenced Kent, however; Mr. Wallace's good humor did not much endure beyond breakfast these days. The heat, the labor, and the acute lack of coffee meant that his mood was invariably brackish by lunchtime. By the evening, returning to the ship, it was decidedly foul, what with added irritations such as the feeble oarsmanship of Tomaso Samuel.

Even as they bent beneath the sacks, however, the crew took solace from the fact that the cargo would at least carry them home. They were confessedly homesick, and withering in the heat. That they had wintered in the tropics caused them to feel like exiles in an eternal summer. They clung to the memory of Arbroath's bracing autumn chill, taking cheer from the homely thoughts it evoked, but its imprint was turning faint and unreliable after all this time, and they craved to experience it again. Thus it was that they noticed the dissidents, dreamers, and poets who walked the promenade or the beaches of their place of exile. These men smoked their pipes and watched the sailors through mournful eyes that too yearned for home, and their presence only whetted the crewmen's wish to be gone.

The Fossil was different. He had a shock of white hair, a seafarer's beard, and glazed eyes. He was dressed in old canvas, rags so greasy as to have been soused in whale oil but exuding a stench that far exceeded the most offensive emissions of that venerable mammal. He arrived on the quayside one day, putting a collective wrinkle in the noses of the *Caledonia*'s crew and setting a bewildered frown upon their brows. He had no apparent purpose there. Certainly, he never broached the subject of a passage home. Nor could the crew guess where his home might be, save that he spoke a passing English.

Every morning, he would shuffle along the quay to his chosen station, which was a bollard. For much of the time he merely observed the crew's labors from that perch, intermittently filling his pipe with dark Turkish tobacco, pulling at his bottle of grog, or declaring repeatedly that his own shouldering days were long since over. In the evening, when the men made for the longboat for the last time, the Fossil would stir himself with a sudden vigor, as if he had appointments to keep and the bollard had afforded him no more than a temporary resting place (while many among the crew had come to believe it might prove his final one).

There was a morning when the Fossil rose from his bollard of a sudden and, apparently knowing something of the ways of ships and the hierarchies that governed them, approached the first mate but in an uncertain zigzag, as if beating against an unfavorable wind. Mr. Wallace was short with him.

"Oh no no," he bellowed, wagging his finger at the man's approach. "Avaunt, ancient mariner! Kent, Kent! Some verse to defend me if you please. How does it run?"

The sack-laden Kent moved to stand beside the mate. "By thy long gray beard and glittering eye," he puffed, "now wherefore stopp'st thou me?"

The Fossil retired to a safe distance but was not to be denied, and shortly turned his attentions on the second mate. It delighted him to discover that that inoffensive man had no intention of rejecting him, but he soon tired of the second mate's wretched whisper.

"It hurts my ears grievous when I try to catch his name," he protested, swigging at his green bottle.

The Fossil sought companionship among the crew with little more success. David Wallace swung a half-hearted kick at him; Tomaso Samuel swore at him in Spanish; Edward Le Dain smiled at him so serenely that the poor man, discerning a devious trap, scuttled back to his bollard; and David McDonald ran away from him. He eventually came to William Tasker, who was his final hope.

Tasker would believe—initially, at least—that it was to his own great misfortune that the Fossil attached to him with the tenacity of a limpet that had just found the sea's very last rock. The crew took pleasure in pointing him in Tasker's direction. So it was that Tasker would repeatedly see his own reflection, bent double beneath a wheat sack, in the glassy eyeballs of the approaching Fossil. Through bilge-foul breath, the man subjected Tasker to gibberish, rambling about the stars, the sea, and the fish therein that knew, he claimed, his every private thought and those of all men, but sprinkled these observations with canny requests for coin or clothing, as if he hoped by these sudden forays into sense to catch Tasker off guard. Then his gaze might lift to the sack on the apprentice's back; his own shouldering days were over, he would say, but the loads he had carried in his time! Gold once, and dye-wood, and the ivories of Africa's elephants.

Tasker could never quite say when he had first become curious, discerning compelling strands of coherence among the gulfs of madness that were the Fossil's monologues. By and by, he came to listen when the Fossil talked of gold and ivories. Then there were the fond mentions of Jenny, whom Tasker initially took to be the lasting object of the Fossil's affection. But the Fossil was clear; he had been this Jenny's mate, not her paramour. Tasker gradually came to understand that the Fossil was referring to a ship.

She had been wrecked back in the last century, en route from Africa to Bristol. On Lundy, if the young man knew the place. And the cargo had never left the island. Only the Fossil had; he was the one survivor. Not that he would ever return there now—his seafaring days were long over—but the young man might find his way there if he knew what was good for him. All of which went some way toward explaining Tasker's distraction. For Mr. Wallace had espied his missing apprentice from the longboat at the very moment that the Fossil was drawing him a treasure map.

The cook's errant oar splashed seawater into the longboat, where it splattered across the mate's boots. James Wallace might have ignored it; he owed a mounting debt of sorts to the Argentine, who had been preparing him occasional discreet coffees from a hidden store in defiance of the master's ban for some weeks now. But it was late in a long day, and Wallace's eyes turned black and narrow.

"Oh to be back in old Marseilles!" he exclaimed. "The girls there dance for a centime, and the coffee! Not black and bitter in the manner of some I know, like the infusion of an old horseman's breeches after too many summers in the saddle, but frothy. Creamy. Like feathers. Oh, what would I give for a *café olé*!" The Spanish flavor that the mate imported to that final word sounded most awry—particularly to a French-speaker's ears.

"*Au lait.*" At the correction, a hush fell over the longboat.

"Did Hamlet say something?"

"I said it's *au lait*, Mr Wallace," said Le Dain. "French for 'with milk.'"

"Si!" shouted Tomaso Samuel, slapping his head so that he almost lost his oars over the side. "*Con leche!*" He uttered the words with a kind of wonder, as if they were the answer to his every problem.

"One thing I don't need from you is coffee lessons," roared Wallace, turning on Samuel. "And learn to row while you're about it, you dago epileptic!"

Tomaso Samuel hacked ineffectually at the water. But this time he allowed himself a smile, one so private you could barely see the triumph between his lips.

℘

The longboat drew alongside the *Caledonia*, and the weary crew hauled the last sacks over the gunwale. Stevenson Peter, who had heard the longboat's return, closed his Bible, squared away his cabin, and strode forward to the hold, where bulging sacks of wheat, neatly stowed, lapped around the hatch.

"An excellent job, Mr. Wallace. Mr. Mate. Men. You deserve a run ashore in Constantinople for this. In the meantime, we sail on the evening tide. Is there something amiss, uh, Hamlet?"

Le Dain was staring over the master's shoulder as if that man did not exist, for he had espied a distant disturbance in the water.

"It's one of the apprentices, I believe, sir. Drowning."

The master had long since accustomed himself to such prankish outbursts from the Jerseyman, most recently regarding the request for the log-reckoners. In his more tolerant moods, he merely attributed them to that man's southerly island nature. And that the new cargo—a godly thing, the food of men's souls in the solemn sacrament of the Gospel— was safely stowed had certainly put him in an excellent humor. His mood was further helped by the fact that the crew were off the pernicious coffee and had apparently regained something of their original stability. It was much as if his old ship had been returned to him. So he merely murmured, "*Très amusant,* sailor."

But Edward Le Dain started forward, as if he had heard nothing of the master's words. Stevenson Peter bethought himself to have heard a passing "With your permission, sir," as the Jerseyman vaulted onto the gunwale and launched himself into the water, his legs braced for the unfamiliar element as if he had just jumped from the top of a garden wall. There was a considerable splash and a brief silence before the mate called out.

"Man overboard! Best oarsmen to the boat, and for the sake of those in the water let that exclude Samuel."

Stevenson Peter turned in the direction of Le Dain's disappearance; the Jerseyman had been right. "Two of my men are in the water, Mr. Wallace," he observed.

"The far one being Tasker, sir, returning to the ship."

"By an unconventional means. Mostly, we use the ship's boat. Did you merely forget him?"

"He must have been preoccupied when we left the shore, sir."

"Careless, Mr. Wallace. I am not in the habit of abandoning my crewmen on quaysides. And the gallant rescuer; is the Jerseyman the least familiar with the swimming?"

"He seems to be learning as we speak, sir."

It was William Tasker who was fast approaching an exhausted end. His crude stroke betrayed his belief that swimming was a miracle that depended on a sustained thrash of the limbs. Stop, and he would sink as surely as a bird, folding its wings, must drop from the sky. In his great gasps he had drunk deep of the Bay of Odessa, and he was on the point of giving himself up to its murky depths when he heard the sudden din and saw the longboat making its way toward him. The Fossil's tale had surely captivated him, so much so that he had known nothing of the longboat's departure. It had been a distant speck by the time the Fossil completed his scribblings, handed over the piece of paper, and pulled from his pocket the green bottle, swigging at its dregs to signal that his business with Tasker was ended.

It was a wonder that Tasker knew how to swim at all, which was a rare talent, not least among Arbroath people, who were suspicious of their chill northerly seas, which took their men and gave them only fish in return. He had first swum three summers since, a few days after the *Caledonia* had grounded off Copenhagen on her maiden voyage. The grounding had taught young Tasker much about the fragility of ships and sailors' lives. He would always remember Mr. Meekison's silence as she struck of a sudden, bow first, in the late afternoon, and the creak of the timbers as the falling tide lowered her onto the seabed and butted her against the shingle shelf. He remembered the view across the moonlit water to the Saltholm shore, where cattle occasionally lifted their grazing heads, mildly curious about the thuds that emanated from the body of the grounded ship. He also remembered the chill current that swirled past the ship's sides, sped on by the squeeze of the Sound of Elsinore thirty miles to the north. And he knew, should a summer storm arise and throw him into the water, that he would flail for his life, but he did not expect to save it.

But the night had stayed calm. The men watched the light muster with the dawn, glinting on the steeples of the city. A passing steamer threw them a line, hauled the vessel off on the rising tide to the cheers of the crew, and towed her, leaky but intact, into Copenhagen. As they approached the port, William Tasker made a resolution. In the early mornings, before the crew were put to work on the repairs to the *Caledonia's* hull, the apprentice could be seen practicing an erratic swimming action in the shallows opposite Copenhagen's custom house. And when they hauled him aboard the *Caledonia's* longboat in the Bay of Odessa three summers later, he had seawater in his belly but a grin across his face quite as wide as the Jerseyman's and, safe in his pocket, the green stoppered bottle, which he had grabbed from the Fossil as that man drained it and that now contained a scribbled scrap of paper.

Tasker made his way to the fo'c'sle to change into his spare trousers and shirt. He found Edward Le Dain there, wringing out his clothes.

"Thanks," said Tasker. "I didn't know ye could swim."

"Nor I."

"Well, thanks," he repeated. "By the way, where's Lundy?"

"Where?" exclaimed Le Dain. "It's Monday. In French."

"No no," replied Tasker. "It's an island I've heard of."

That night, as the *Caledonia* ran south into the Black Sea before a northerly wind, Wallace sent Le Dain forward to keep lookout. He sat astride the windlass, the briny smell of the sea in his nostrils. The Cape Fontane light had fallen astern and given way to occasional pinpricks of Bessarabian light on the starboard bow.

It was then that Le Dain heard another strange noise. It had a rhythmic quality, and was attended by a heavy breathing. Le Dain was a mannerly man, and though the noise persisted and grew louder, he would have been inclined to ignore it but an accompanying bleat of outrage rent the air which propelled him across the foredeck to investigate. To his astonishment, a figure was unmistakably straddling the last surviving goat in the lee of the longboat. The wretched creature, since deprived of her every last offspring, butted her protesting hind legs against the gunwale. Then Le Dain heard a whispered volley of Spanish oaths and made out the bucket between the goat's legs. He frowned even as he understood; it would be some days before Le Dain realized what the cook could possibly want with goat's milk.

Chapter ∞ 22

One day in high summer I parked the car, slung a coiled blue rope over my shoulder, and turned toward the lych-gate. I was making for the shore.

I paused before the small stone hut that adjoined the lych-gate. The door was locked, but beyond the cobwebs at the window a shelf of rusting keys and spark plugs was visible, along with the gloomy outlines of gas canisters, ropes, and a stack of timbers. What had once been Hawker's "Dead House," where drowned sailors were carried and "prepared for Burial by a very motherly woman, my Sexton's wife," was now a garden shed.

I left the graveyard by the stile, a smooth slab of stone set vertically in the wall, and cut diagonally across the fields where Jersey cattle floated in the haze. That bodies were lain in the Dead House reminded me of the fact that corpses were once borne up these cliffs. Talk of "sad processions" and Hawker's mention of a "temporary bier of the broken planks" even suggested a dignified progress; a reasonable path must have existed. But the incursions of the ocean were continually reconfiguring the coast at Morwenstow, and the way to the shore was as inconstant as the lie of the cliffs it passed down. A field geologist named E. A. Newell Arber, writing in 1911, identified the former path as having descended below Hawker's hut, and added how it had "now fallen into disrepair and ends in space." Newell Arber had failed to find any way to the shore here at the time of his visit. Landslides had evidently steepened these cliffs since Hawker's time.

There were always those, however, who would find a way down. Another, more precipitous, descent was duly established a few hundred yards to the north, in the shadow of Henna Cliff. Nicholas Ross described the route in a letter to a fellow Hawker enthusiast, Cyril Wilkinson, vice-provost of Worcester College, Oxford, in August 1957:

> Between Hennacliffe and the path from the Vicarage there is an incline downwards of about thirty degrees at first. It is there I scramble down. But the thirty degrees becomes, at the end of the grass and heather, almost one of sixty degrees... here one gives up climbing and slides instead. The slide on the face of very very smooth rock measures about 20 feet. At the bottom one must have the greatest care, for here there is a drop of about ten feet to the actual shore. I keep on going into that region because Hawker is there.

Mark Myers had assured me that Ross's path survived, and was the only reasonable way down. It branched off the main coast path just south of the Morwenstow stream where the rising cliff, emerging from the cleft of the valley, presented a gently rounded rump to the ocean. At first the path appeared undemanding. On this bulging headland it could even indulge in a few gentle slaloms. Soon, however, it was shouldered into a scree gully, where it straightened and dropped sharply away.

I was apprehensive. I had no head for heights. I comforted myself by suspecting exaggeration in Ross's version of the descent, passing him off as an elderly intellectual who was rather too well acquainted with the armchair. But the path grew more precipitous. As I sought safety in a low hunch, clutching protruding rocks or the gnarled roots of heather and gorse, I increasingly began to recognize the accuracy of Ross's description. My boots put up brief smoke puffs of alarm on the dusty path.

I soon reached Ross's "face of very very smooth rock," which supplanted the scree in an instant. The transition was remarkable for its regularity and typical of this coastline's arresting geology, in which layers of sediment had buckled to create exquisite arches and flying buttresses or snapped entirely to leave canted sea rocks rearing skyward where gulls milled.

The path was well-trodden through the scree. But where it reached the rock, gray as elephant hide and splattered with circular lichens, passing feet left no impression and the way ahead seemed uncertain. Myers, who knew it as "slippery rock," had warned me off the descent if rain threatened. But even though the day was fine, the rock dry and warm to the touch, the route now began to feel perilous. I had obviously misjudged Ross, and had not even the courage to follow his example in sliding down the rock face. I squatted to unshoulder the rope, which I passed around a large boulder that jutted from the scree's hem, then tied it repeatedly until the knot resembled a coughed-up hairball, though a reliable one. I flung the coils into space and watched the snaking rope jerk to a halt far below me so that it lay down the rock straight as a seam. I hauled hard on it, took a deep breath, and then began to let myself down.

I descended backward, holding the rope by both hands and wrapping it around a wrist for good measure. The translucent underwings of gulls passed overhead. I worked my way gradually down the rock, and as I found each new footfall, I burrowed the boot into the security of the shallow fissures, pocked with erosion, that traversed the rock.

When I finally dared look down, I was some three feet above the shore. I was at the northern extent of a bay that a close pair of high shale ramparts by the name of Lucky Hole divided into two scalloped coves. The cliffs, scarred with diagonal screes, the most recent reddish brown, others aging into the dominant grays and greens of the scrub, loomed high above me. At their feet, the screes funneled onto the beach, a chalk-colored shingle that gave way to a broken shelf of drying rocks extending seaward. The day was windless and warm, the surf distant.

They called it Cotton Beach, which evoked striped canvas windbreaks, picnics, and sandcastles. Cove described it better, for there was no human sound here, only the fishy smell of a negligible death in the air. Nicholas Ross had described the place's allure with the assertion,

"Hawker is there." I did not sense the vicar's presence, but the probability that this shore had not seen a visitor for months—only enthusiasts like Nicholas Ross, Mark Myers, or Joe Gifford ever made it here—lent it a forbidding atmosphere.

I began to search beneath the northernmost cliffs, where Mark Myers had once spotted the old wooden windlass. The shore had shifted as dramatically as the cliffs, however, for a crush of great boulders, some taller than men, shoved up against the undercliff. I would not find the windlass, and adjusted my expectations accordingly. Like detectives, who popularly return to crime scenes long since sieved for evidence, I now hoped the place might induce some mental alchemy, causing scraps of information to be recast, shiny with significance.

I began to work the beach. I made my methodical way down to the flat surf, where the low-lying rocks were arranged in parallel furrows that ran seaward, resembling a freshly ploughed field whose turned soil, topped with limpets, barnacles, and seaweed, was drying gray in the sun. Rounded stones had gathered in the clear depths of rock pools. Then I turned, edged a few yards to the south, and headed back up the beach to the muted suck of the sea and the occasional cry of its birds. Far above me, I could make out Hawker's hut.

This shore had seen all kinds of cargoes; its very name was taken from the cotton bales that had washed up with the *Othello* in 1808. Over the centuries, the cargoes cast ashore here had also included copper ore, tree bark and Delabole slates, casks of flour, "fine ollive oyle," "limmons and orringes," tobacco, bayonets and muskets, butter, beeswax, pigments, shellac, sides of bacon, cured leathers, feathers, peat, casks of wine, and salt fish. There had been a live Newfoundland dog, pigs, and geese. There had been the body parts of men—feet, hands, and torsos—and ships' parts, including bollards and stern posts, crankshafts, anchor chains and mast bends, portholes and winch bearings.

Today's pickings proved sparer. There was some rusted ship's cable, which had sunk into the sand to show like the ribs of a partially exhumed skeleton. Shards of ship's iron were scattered about. These had rusted to wafers no larger than beer coasters, acquiring the rounded and shapely contours of viscous spillages on linoleum and the vivid color of flame. And, stuck fast among the rocks that crowded into Lucky Hole, two anchors tall as men and a huge shackle were wedged. The rest was old plastic bottles, a rotted shoe, rusted aerosol cans, a length of black plastic piping with a jubilee clip attached at one end, and a shattered blue crate on which the name of a fishery at Port Isaac, some thirty miles to the southeast, was printed.

I clambered over the ledges and parapets of Lucky Hole. Now Sharpnose Point came into view again, and I could see the reef of rocks that ran seaward at its base. I worked my way along the shore until it petered out at the approaching headland and the water drew close. Soon, I stood directly beneath Sharpnose Point. Its facial resemblance, impressive all the way from Hartland Quay, had dissolved into a shapeless crag looming above me.

I was here, then. From Sharpnose's foot, the rocks on which the *Caledonia* had struck ran a hundred meters into the sea. Even in today's calm conditions, when the tide sucked sonorously at the rocks or slapped

gently against their flanks, these projections gave notice of themselves. Seismic disturbance had levered some of the shales almost to the vertical so that their broken jags, closely packed layers of smooth-sided primordial mud, thrust high out of the water like childishly drawn alpine peaks. Others had remained closer to the horizontal, where they were washed by the swell, their surfaces mottled like the soles of rubber plimsolls or stippled like dried cowpats.

The tide had turned. The sea was making shiny sallies into crannies it had recently abandoned. Tresses of weed were lifted, caressed, then re-deposited on rocks, where anemone winked. I would have to hurry to return by Slippery Rock, and hoped instead to find a more leisurely route from the shore at this end of the bay. I reached the foot of a waterfall, whose desultory summer flow splattered the rocks at my feet. Beyond it, somebody had secured a rope up a scree slope. Heaving on the rope, however, released a posse of falling boulders, and I leapt clear.

Around the headland, however, where the swell broke close to my feet, the cliff was a slope of tufty grass, thick with sea pinks, dandelions, and kidney vetch. It made for a thoroughly attractive scene, which doubtless contributed to my deception. But I could not know how the slope appeared from above, and so I set off without delay. The climb began easily enough, the grassy clumps providing abundant holds for hands and feet. My progress felt comfortable, and I even stopped to admire the view. Beyond the jags and spurs of those murderous rocks, the sea was a gray burnished plate where a single ship sat, a distant tanker, red and white.

The incline increased. At first, my footholds merely became less leisurely—I had to exert a little pressure upon my boots—and I placed my hands with greater care. But the incline increased again, and when I next paused to catch my breath I could feel my holds begin to sag. Grassy outcrops were threatening to pull loose. I had to move again for fear of sliding backward. And I had to keep moving. The incline increased once more.

My fingers were beginning to scrabble. My boots, hacking at the grass, spat out crushed flowers, pebbles, and plumes of dusty soil as I fought for forward momentum. I was breathing heavily now. One of my legs slipped, and I hollered. The three remaining limbs, surging with adrenaline, kicked at the cliff face and succeeded in halting my slide. I hesitated for a moment, then lunged upward in a final effort. One of my flailing arms found the cliff top and hooked over it. I hauled myself up and lay there for a while, panting. When I had recovered, I looked down the giddying cliff and swore at my stupidity.

I had emerged on the slope above the Tidna, the next stream south from Morwenstow, the one that ended in the waterfall I had recently passed on the shore. I clambered down to the stream where it backed up before the precipice and, parting the flag irises, cooled my flushed face in the water. Then I threw myself down, exhausted, on the grassy sward beside the stream, where insects droned. I was dozing in the sun when it struck me that I had ended up in a particular place, and I sat up.

It must have been here, "just where a brook of fresh water fell towards the sea"—the only such brook within a short distance of Sharpnose—that they had found Le Dain. Le Dain had seen "the cliff, steep and dark, above my head" and "had climbed up until I reached a kind of platform with grass, and there I fell down flat upon my face." It seemed I had just replicated Edward Le Dain's own cliff climb, and ended in a heap exactly where he had.

Hawker claimed that he himself had discovered the prostrate Edward Le Dain on the morning of September 8, 1842:

> I made haste . . . and, on turning a rock, just where a brook of fresh water fell towards the sea, there lay the body of a man in a seaman's garb. . . . He opened his eyes at our voices, and as he saw me leaning over him in my cassock-shaped dressing-gown, he sobbed, with a piteous cry, "Oh mon père, mon père!"

> Or so he wrote in "Remembrances."

∽

Some weeks earlier, I had driven down to Dorset to view a particular book. The book, Sabine Baring-Gould's *The Vicar of Morwenstow*, was in the possession of Reverend Richard Adams, but had originally belonged to Adams's great-grandfather, John Adams. It happened that John Adams had also been on the Morwenstow cliffs on the morning of September 8, 1842.

Adams was born in 1822 and brought up at Stanbury, the manor house that stands a mile south of Morwenstow Vicarage. Adams and Hawker were not only neighbors; they had a remarkable amount in common. Like Hawker, Adams became both clergyman and poet. He even won Oxford's prestigious Newdigate Prize for Poetry in 1847, just as Hawker had done twenty years earlier.

But the two men fell out with each other. The initial disagreement stemmed from Hawker's expensive insistence on oak shingles to reroof the church at Morwenstow, where various members of Adams's family served as churchwardens. By 1847, their relationship had deteriorated to the point that Hawker accused Adams of plagiarizing his own work in the prize-winning poem. Adams denied the allegation and suggested Hawker was motivated by the mounting debt that, to his increasing resentment, he owed the Adams family.

The Vicar of Morwenstow was first published in the spring of 1876, just six months after Hawker's death. It was accounted a rushed job; one reviewer sent it on its retitled way as *Stories about Wrecks and Fairies*. Certainly, Baring-Gould's treatment of the *Caledonia* episode was cursory, reprinting much of Hawker's "Remembrances" account verbatim. I knew the latter book well and had a copy of it on my shelves, which might have made the long drive to view another copy of it seem a pointless one except that, at some stage in 1876, John Adams had penciled various comments in the margins of the reprinted "Remembrances" pages.

The inflamed nature of the margin comments, and the accompanying exclamation marks, suggests that Adams knew nothing of his deceased former friend's published version of the events surrounding the *Caledonia* until he came across it, thirty-four years later, in the pages of *The Vicar of Morwenstow*. It was as if he were hearing the lies for the first time. Where Hawker had written, "About daybreak of an autumn day I was aroused by a knock at my bedroom door; it was followed by the agitated voice of a boy, a member of my household, 'Oh sir, there are dead men on Vicarage rocks!'" Adams had scribbled, "False. I was breakfasting at the Vicarage when news of the wreck came. A man brought in a tortoise and said that the beach was covered with wreck but that no bodies had been found."

It was, however, Hawker's claim to the discovery of Le Dain that Adams disputed most hotly. "False again," he had written. "The man was found by me and not by Hawker. I saw him in a deep gully among rushes as I stood on Tonnacombe Cliff and with the help of two men conveyed him to Stanbury where he was attended by a doctor and remained some weeks." And a page later: "Hawker was under the cliff on the beach when Le Daine was found by myself and taken to Stanbury where he was nursed. J. A."

Later that same year, Adams published *St Malo's Quest*, a collection of poems including one entitled "Lines on the Crew of the Caledonia." And at the bottom of the poem, he added a footnote:

> One only of the crew of nine men escaped death. He was thrown on a ledge of rock, and scrambled up a precipice so steep and rugged that no human being would have attempted to climb it in broad daylight. I found him, a few hours after the wreck, speechless and covered in bruises, in a gully a quarter of a mile from the sea, and had him conveyed on a stretcher to my father's house, where he was tenderly nursed for several weeks.

St Malo's Quest would prove to be among the last achievements of John Adams, who, touring America in the spring of 1877, perished in the night fire that consumed the Southern Hotel in St. Louis.

I climbed to my feet. Skylarks were singing as I followed the cliff path back to the church, pondering the vicar of Morwenstow's lies as I went.

Chapter ∞ 23

A few mornings later I fell in behind a tractor where the road swung east beyond Hartland. Zigzags of molded mud from its churning rear treads clattered into the road. Lapwings flocked over the high thorn hedges like flung confetti. The stands of ash, beech, and sycamore were in full leaf. I caught glimpses of Lundy through field gates, steep-sided as a tree stump and monochrome in the sea haze.

I was headed for the big house at Portledge, supposed home of the *Caledonia* letter bottle. The estate entrance gate opened automatically at the approach of my car to reveal a long drive ribbed with the exposed roots of copper beech trees. The handsome house lay in a bowled glade, set about with fields and copses, on a sea-facing slope.

Portledge was the ancestral home of the Pine Coffin family; I'd been smiling all the way from Morwenstow. The original family were apparently called the Coffins—a game lot, then, to have allowed the marital overtures of young Pine. I rang the doorbell, expecting an extravagantly dressed, absentminded aristocrat in a melee of excitable dogs. But it was a perfectly equable housekeeper who came to hear me out.

"Of course I know about the bottle," she exclaimed. "Green, with a yellowing letter. In a box on the windowsill on the first landing. Let me show you." She led me to the foot of the stairs, where the windowsill at the top of the first flight was clearly visible—but no box was on display.

"That's where it was," she said. My heart sank. "But I have no idea what happened to it when the Pine Coffins sold up."

Sold up? That the Pine Coffins might have been separated from their ancestral home seemed a preposterous notion. A character in Charles Kingsley's *Westward Ho!*, speaking from the seasoned depths of the sixteenth century, described Portledge as the place "where the Coffins had lived ever since Noah's Flood (if, indeed, they had not merely returned thither after that temporary displacement)."

But it was true. The Pine Coffins had fought a long battle against dwindling finances. For a time, they had run the house as a hotel. But as vacationers began discovering the attractions of the Spanish sun, the hotel's fortunes declined and the family was eventually compelled to sell. A buyer grown rich in the entertainment sector took possession in 1995, but spent much of his time in tropical locations, while the Pine Coffins regrouped in a modest Bideford bungalow.

"You might try Kathy," said the housekeeper. "I think she was working here when the house sale went through. It's possible she might remember something of the bottle. She works at the BP station outside Barnstaple if you're going that way."

I thanked her and followed a delta of worn paths through woodland to the shore. Tasker's letter had eluded me, but I remained quite confident of finding it. The letter was an established local curiosity that was sure to have been preserved. In the meantime, I could at least visit the beach where it had washed up.

The shoreline stretched into the distance, a rock-strewn strand of pink sand. A few vacationers, mostly guests at the estate's self-catering properties, lay on the beach. A boy emerged from the sea to stand by his parents, his teeth chattering. He held his hands by his sides, affecting a hypothermic helplessness, and allowed his mother to drape a towel around his shivering shoulders. A thin man sat on a towel in new swimming trunks and picked his nose behind a paperback. His dog nudged a plastic football toward him with its muzzle, but a gusting wind from the west repeatedly slung the ball back down the beach. A paunchy man, a hard-boiled egg in his hand, climbed to his feet from a family picnic to retrieve the fleeing plastic bag in which he had been putting his eggshell.

I returned to the car and was driving up the track, where the breeze in the fields stirred the green wheat like chiffon, when something occurred to me: I might have taken more from that brief visit to the beach. I distinctly felt I had missed a clue of sorts; not that I could say what. The frustrating sense persisted, unspecific but forceful, as I drove across the river bridge at Bideford, where the delicate footfalls of wading birds had stitched neat patterns across the mud flats and the wind buffeted the car.

The wind. The breeze in the wheat. The ball and the plastic bag blowing along the beach at Portledge. The exposed thorn trees all along this coast, bent to resemble great breakers tumbling eastward; the prevailing wind was from the west. And when wind and tide worked together, they evidently washed seaborne objects north and east. Like the *Caledonia* bottle, which had ended up around the corner at Portledge. Like the broken Port Isaac fish crate I'd seen on the beach at Morwenstow, which had washed up thirty miles northeast of its home port. Like the body of the seaman from the *Bencoolen,* lost off Bude, which Hawker had found on the shore of his glebe; even the drowned, it seemed, traveled.

The drowned: the three missing bodies from the *Caledonia!* Hawker's discredited claim to the discovery of Le Dain had reminded me of his earlier insistence that James Wallace, Peter Sturrock, and Stephen Jones all lay in the graveyard at Morwenstow. I owed it to the three men that I should learn where they had really ended up. And it was here, northeast of Morwenstow, that I should be looking.

I took the Barnstaple turning and drove into town. At the records office, which was housed on the upper floor of the town's modern library building, opposite the cattle market, I asked to consult the 1842 burial records for the Devon coastal parishes starting from the Cornish county boundary.

"Oh, yes," said the librarian. "Can I ask what you're looking for?"

"Bodies on the beach," I explained.

"Oh, yes," he intoned. As he leaned over the back of his seat to consult a wall map, gray flesh winked at me through a stretched hole in his sleeveless shirt. "Welcombe, Hartland, Clovelly, Parkham, Alwington..."

"Why don't I start with them?" I suggested, and followed him to the microfiche cabinet.

I sat at my reader, between elderly women with wagging pencils, and began my body sweep at Welcombe. Though it had only a brief shoreline, Morwenstow's neighboring parish was clearly the first place to look. Moreover, Hawker had been performing burials here in the curate's absence as early as 1838. But there was no sign of the missing crewmen at Welcombe. Nor at Hartland, the next parish to the north. After Hartland came Clovelly, whose shoreline began several miles east of Hartland Point. The Clovelly fiche gave me pause. Though I wished to find evidence of the missing men's burials, part of me hoped that I would not find them here, not at such a distance from Morwenstow.

I remembered what Hawker had written of the *Caledonia* dead: the "disfigured faces," the bodies jammed under rocks and "loathsome from decay," and the captain "manifestly lifted by a billow and hurled against a rock." One of them, he wrote, had been found in five parts, his limbs "wrenched off" and his body "rent." This shore was brutal to seaborne corpses, and the condition of the missing *Caledonia* corpses was sure to have worsened the farther they were washed from Morwenstow. By Clovelly, beyond Hartland Point, they must have been battered without mercy. Time and again, the surf would have dumped them against the boulders at the top of the beach before the backwash dragged them over the rocks, bludgeoning and scarifying as the current nudged them north. It therefore relieved me to discover that they had not washed up at Clovelly.

The next parish, Parkham, began a mile east of Clovelly village and concluded after three miles at Peppercombe, a wooded valley that ran down to the shore at the western end of the very beach—Portledge— where I had stood just an hour earlier. But the parish seemed inconceivably distant from Morwenstow, and I was disengaged as I slipped the fiche into the reader. Seconds later, however, I had banged my head against the screen as I strained for a better look; there *was* a dead man on the beach there. "A Stranger," the entry read, "found drowned on the

Beach in this Parish." The corpse, abode unknown, had been buried at Parkham church by William Walter, rector of Bideford, on September 25, 1842, some seventeen days after the loss of the *Caledonia*. The only clue to the man's identification was his age, which was given as "about years 22."

A stranger found drowned on the Beach in this Parish — No. 394.	not-known.	Sept. 25	about years 22.	William Walter, Rector of Bideford Officiating Minister.

The next parish, Alwington, yielded a second corpse: "A man. Name unknown." The additional information, "Washed in under Gilscot," referred to a farm perched above the western extent of Portledge beach; this body had washed up hard by Alwington's parish boundary with Parkham. The age column was blank, as if it could not even be guessed at. But the date of the burial at Alwington Church, performed by one J. T. Pine Coffin, was given as September 25—the same day the Parkham corpse had been buried.

A man. name unknown. — No. 171.	Washed in under Gilscot	Sep: 25	—	J T Pine Coffin Rector

Two bodies, both found on the shore, had been buried in neighboring parish graveyards on the same day. That must mean something, for such burials were an uncommon enough event, even in the 1840s. The bodies must have been found at the same time, and therefore at no great distance from each other on or near the shared parish boundary at Peppercombe. That the corpses had ended up in neighboring graveyards was due to the fact, I guessed, that the rectors of Parkham and Alwington, informed of two shoreline corpses on their parish boundary, had agreed to divvy up the burden of burying them.

But were they two of the men I had been looking for? The September 15, 1842, edition of *The North Devon Journal,* a Barnstaple weekly, reported the storm of the night of Wednesday, September 7, and the hurricane of the following day, which "have been felt throughout the kingdom, and particularly along the coast, and have been attended with the loss of a vast deal of property, besides human life." Then, in the edition of September 29, I got very lucky. "The bodies of two men," stated a news item, "were taken up a few days since at Peppercombe, in this bay, and were recognized by the only survivor of that wreck to be two of the unfortunate crew of the barque, 'Caledonia,' lately wrecked between Hartland and Bude."

"That's my boys!" I exclaimed, louder than I had intended, and I smiled apologetically at my neighbors.

"You found something?" an elderly lady asked politely. Glasses hung around her thin neck on a gold chain. She turned away when I told her what I had discovered.

News of the bodies must have been received at Morwenstow on about September 24. Edward Le Dain had probably made the journey to Peppercombe that day, setting out along a rutted version of the same road I had traveled that morning. He may have chosen to walk in the fine autumn weather. Or one of his benefactors, allowing for the Jerseyman's lack of strength or the mental ordeal before him, might have arranged a gig to transport him there. He arrived at the place after about fifteen miles, perhaps at one of the cottages that stand deep in dank, ferny woodland in the lower reaches of the combe, just above the beach, where he somehow identified the two corpses as his sometime crewmates.

So, the lie was nailed. The corpses were not brought back to Morwenstow to be laid "side by side, beneath our churchyard trees," as Hawker had it. But something irked me about the actual circumstances of their burial. Once Le Dain had positively identified the men as his shipmates, it might have been assumed that these two Arbroath men, far from home and family, would at least be accorded the posthuman comfort of being laid to rest alongside each other. But the vicars of Parkham and

Alwington had separated the men, condemning them to solitary graves in the yards of their two gray churches a mile apart.

I wondered to whom the unnamed corpses belonged. There was only one clue of any substance: the age of the body buried at Parkham was given as about twenty-two. It most likely belonged to Stephen Jones, who would have been twenty-three at the time. Of the other two—James Wallace, thirty-four, and Peter Sturrock, twenty-seven—it seems we know only that one was buried at Alwington.

Something else contradicted the fact of their identification: their descriptions as "Name unknown" and "A Stranger." It made no sense that Le Dain's testimony should go unrecorded after he had been called upon to identify the bodies. Unless, of course, Le Dain had not given names but merely confirmed the corpses as his shipmates. Perhaps he had recognized one of the corpses as the man we now know to have been named Peter Sturrock, which he would not admit he had never known. It's a tenuous deduction, but it does lead us to the likelihood that the unrecovered corpse was that of James Wallace.

What was now quite certain, however, was that Tasker's letter bottle had washed up on the very same beach as the bodies of two men from the *Caledonia*. That it had traveled on the same currents, miraculously surviving the rocks, that had brought the two corpses to Portledge, was the strongest evidence yet that the letter bottle was genuine.

I stopped off at the BP gas station, as the housekeeper had suggested. Three women were working the cash registers. I tried to identify them from their name tags but turned away as they caught my eye, for I did not wish it to appear that I was staring at their breasts. In time, however, I managed to make out the name "Kathy." I loaded up with enough sandwiches, water, and crisps to keep Kathy occupied while I quizzed her, and moved smartly in as her register became vacant.

"Kathy," I said. "I was given your name by the woman at Portledge."

"Oh," she replied, running a laser over the bar code on my prawn sandwiches. "The big house."

"She thought you might remember what happened to the bottle, the green bottle with the letter that used to be on the stairs there."

"The green bottle on the stairs. A real talking-point that was. It was on the windowsill on the first landing. Was in a nice box it was, made of wood. Any petrol?"

"No. I know all that. I wonder if you know what happened to it."

"Savercard? The box, you're saying?"

"The box and what was inside it—the letter and the bottle."

"Collect tokens? It's not there, you're saying?"

"It apparently disappeared with the move."

"Six pounds thirty-five. Haven't a clue. You could try the chef who used to work there, though. He knew the family well. Your change, dear."

Chapter ∞ *24*

The homeward-bound *Caledonia* called at Constantinople on July 6, 1842.

Constantinople was a notoriously dangerous city in the nineteenth century. According to an account of 1825, to return a curse received from a Turkish porter in Stamboul, the Imperial City on the south shore of the Golden Horn, "would be to sign one's death warrant." Herman Melville wrote in his notebook of a visit to Constantinople in the 1850s: "Staid in all night. Dangerous going out, owing to footpads and assassins," and "Englishman at dinner . . . Said nothing would tempt him to go by night through Galata. Assassinations every night."

It would be the briefest port visit the *Caledonia* ever made. She left Constantinople the following day—"to Falmouth for orders," as *Lloyd's List* put it.

Constantinople, July 6, 1842
"An impressive aspect, Mr. Wallace," declared Stevenson Peter, challenging the mate to match his own excellent humor. "Though no doubt a godless one."

As the *Caledonia* rode the twinkling sluice of the Bosphorus current, it seemed to her master that all was right with the ship. The reckless laughter, the threadbare respect, the tortoise races, the requests for his log-reckoners, and the swimming now seemed like a contagious fever of the collective brain that had run its course and left his crew as ordered as

he would have wished it, if even a little subdued, though he put this down
to regret as they contemplated their past deportment with shame.

"Whaa," replied Mr. Wallace belatedly. "Very attractive, I'm sure,
skip." He had slipped into a reverie so absorbing that it had blinded him
to the blue-domed mosques and the waterside mansions of the Bosphorus, the castles and burial grounds, the glades of myrtles and cypresses
where the sunlight played on fountains and gilded pavilions, and the por-
poises that rolled over on the bow wave, their white bellies glinting.

At dawn two days earlier, Wallace had hauled himself from his bunk
to assume the watch under a pallid sky. He had just put Le Dain at the
helm and checked the set of the sails when the cook appeared from the
galley, a steaming pot in his clasp. As the Argentine handed over the pot,
he surprised the mate by pressing a surreptitious finger to his lips. Wallace was about to clout the cook for his familiarity when something gave
him cause to sniff the contents of the pot, and he halted. In the middle of
the Black Sea, somewhere west of the Danube's mouth, Tomaso Samuel
had just served him a *café au lait*. The mate glanced over his shoulder to
check against the presence of the master, then raised the mug to quiver-
ing lips.

At the first sip, the mate's throat apple set about a-bobbing as if
awoken to rapture from a long sleep. The coffee was exquisite. Hot but
creamy, faintly perfumed and ground smooth as silk, with a candy sweet-
ness that summoned a saliva to his mouth the instant he swallowed, as if
his body's very mechanisms were greedy for the next mouthful. But the
master had forbidden coffee, and though its outlaw status merely en-
hanced the taste yet further, he had to be discreet. Even as he attempted
outward indifference to the contents of the pot, however, he felt ecstasy
ballooning involuntarily into words between his teeth.

"Oh my precious bloody God that is good that is."

Le Dain raised a single eyebrow and stared straight ahead, the
helmsman's proper bearing, where he caught sight of Tomaso Samuel
standing in the galley, arms folded in satisfaction.

The *Caledonia* berthed in the Golden Horn, the inlet anchorage where the city's shipping clustered, and the master proved true to his promise. The crew were free to go ashore, though it fell to McDonald to stay on board. The apprentice would return for them with the jollyboat once the events of the evening had begrimed the trousers and shirts they had turned out of their sea chests, passably clean now, with sweat and liquor and the mud of inevitable stumbles. As the shore party scrubbed, shaved, and instilled some order in their hair, Tasker turned to Edward Le Dain.

"What's a tusk worth?" he whispered.

"A tusk?"

"An elephant's. What's one cost?"

"What would I pay for one, you mean?"

"Aye."

"I've not had occasion. Why are you asking?"

"Oh. Reasons of my own."

It was dusk when the men clambered into the jollyboat.

"Some caution if you will, Mr. Wallace," murmured the master, who had no interest in visiting the heathen disordered city.

James Wallace raised an obedient arm to the silhouette at the taffrail as hands fell to the oars. They made their way past caiques with carved prows, common barques laden with fruit or a press of humans, and polaccas with their pajama-striped sails. Doves took to the air with a racket of wings and passed over the high domes of the mosques.

"San Pedro—is still looking?" whispered Tomaso Samuel, whose view was obscured by the backs of heaving oarsmen.

William Tasker watched the master disappear down the companionway. "Back with his Bible," he whispered.

The troublesome Samuel, dipping his shoulder, tipped an oarful of seawater into the lap of the second mate. "Sorry, Mr. Stutter," said Samuel without conviction. "Is mistake." The second mate murmured an incomprehensible protest.

"Enough now, Tomaso," said Mr. Wallace, but all fight had left his lips, still soft from the cook's *café au lait*.

They clambered ashore at Galata and watched McDonald row into the gathering dusk. They were quiet as they left the quayside. Though they had been ashore in Constantinople only a few months earlier, they all felt the exotic press of the city. It assailed their every sense, and they climbed the manure-splattered cobbles in a tight phalanx, like an outing of schoolchildren ogling an unfamiliar world. Turkish merchants with clipped mustaches, red fezzes, and long black frock coats perched upon the seats of brightly painted calèches. There were Jews shawled in cloaks and dressed in brown hats, bearded clerics beneath green turbans, and packs of skulking mastiffs, which drew confidence from the encroaching darkness. Hawkers balanced confectionery trays on their heads and hollered at high windows. And above the tottering balconies and carved gables of the timber houses, stiff-legged storks arose from their roof nests to score angular scratches across the failing peach sky.

Turks were installing themselves in the outdoor cafés, where the cooling breezes of evening rattled the foliage of the plane trees. They reposed on divans draped in bright rugs, and hauled hard on their hookah pipes so the contents of the clay bowls—coals and tobacco, or sickly hashish—winked red hot at their exertions, and the air reeked with aromatic exhalations. But the crew of the *Caledonia* felt an Arbroath unease at these displays of oriental luxury, and their footsteps soon carried them back to the district they considered their own, the wretched quarter by the waterfront where the stench of slops arose and the cobbles were slick with glistening fish scales.

They ducked inside an ill-lit doorway from which pipe smoke poured in such volumes it was as if the edifice itself were aflame—the seasonal scourge of the Constantinople summer. It was a simple place, with gaping holes in the floorboards and unpaned windows with views of blinking lights across the Bosphorus in Asia. The room milled with Russians and with Dutchmen, with hulking Finns and with dark-eyed Italians. The

Caledonia men sat themselves on the raised wooden divan that ran along one wall, where the dirt of old hair had left a series of oval stains.

The innkeeper eyed the new arrivals with suspicion, for suspicion was his way, as he brought them glasses, a jug of water, and a bottle of the coarse aniseed that was the region's staple liquor.

"Coffee? You got coffee?" James Wallace shouted over the hubbub.

The innkeeper broke his stride, pushed his fez up his forehead, and said, "Coffee come later."

"As you wish, Pasha," Wallace replied equably. The men drank. "Whoa!" the mate exclaimed at the fiery grog.

"My heart aches," declaimed Kent.

"Ooh." The second mate was choking. He stared at the cloudy substance in his glass and reached hurriedly for the water.

"You OK, Mr. Stomach?" Tomaso Samuel slapped the second mate across the shoulders. And the discreet smile that James Wallace allowed himself was noticed among his men.

Later, when spirits were soaring under the liquor's sustained onslaught, William Tasker nudged Edward Le Dain again.

"So. You know anybody who might want some?"

"Some what?"

"Elephants' tusks."

The bar had grown busy now. The room was a crush of swarthy bodies that smelled of salt, ships, and tobacco. Men shouted to be heard above the foreign babble. Tasker slumped into Le Dain's lap.

"I'm serious, me. I'm going to be very rich."

Le Dain laughed and pulled him upright.

"No, no," the apprentice insisted. "I'm to be wealthy. Might even buy that island of yours if it's truly as fine as you say. Wealthy as . . ."

"Croesus?" Kent ventured.

"Creases, that's me!" said Tasker, banging the divan with his glass. "I'll even have my own fleet of ships, no doubting. You can be one of my masters if you like, Hamlet. You did save me from the Russian brine."

"You're kind, William."

"Kind, nothing," said Tasker magnanimously; then he hiccuped, blanched, and stumbled outside to be sick.

The innkeeper moved through the crowd, his red fez showing among the caps and straw hats. He deposited bottles and glasses, demanded coin, and eventually placed a small, delicate cup encased in a metalwork filigree in front of James Wallace before filling it from a steaming copper pot.

"Is that it?" the mate muttered under his breath.

He could in truth have done without the coffee, for the aniseed was proving an excellent substitute, pulsing through his veins with its blazing energy. But he had allowed an annoyance, however brief, into his query. And Tomaso Samuel had heard it. It led him to remember the wink he had received from the mate in that Black Sea dawn as he had collected his empty coffee pot from him. It was a significant wink. It marked the beginning of an understanding, the promise of eventual acceptance and friendship, and Samuel determined to consolidate it. He leaned forward and grabbed the innkeeper's passing arm.

"Is not how Mr. Wallace he likes his coffee," he pronounced imperiously.

The innkeeper craned his head, as if he had not understood the Argentine.

"The coffee!" Samuel bellowed, waving a dismissive backhand at the cup. "He like it with the milk, creamy, and he like more than a thimble!"

The innkeeper moved his head closer still.

"Steady, Samuel," said Wallace, who suspected that the Turk might not take to foreign instruction in the making of coffee. "It's of no consequence."

"Problem with coffee?" The innkeeper pronounced the words slowly, as if the nature of the grievance had only just dawned upon him. He had stooped low now, so his face was at level with Samuel's, and inches from it.

"No problem, Pasha," began a conciliatory James Wallace, but Tomaso Samuel would not be stopped.

"Take it away!" he yelled, waving his arms. "You bring Mr. Wallace coffee how he like. Not this . . . ship's tar."

It was Le Dain who saw the flaring in the innkeeper's eyes. The Jerseyman rose to his feet, the palms of his hands exposed, a firebreak against the gathering tension. But he was too late. The innkeeper threw a jug of water in Le Dain's face. Incensed, Samuel swore and spat at the innkeeper. A gobbet of saliva, milky with raki, landed on the innkeeper's fez. Then Samuel lurched forward, fists balling, to run onto something that flashed in the air, like a fish. The innkeeper held the blade low and slammed it into the Argentine's belly. It sliced through his canvas shirt, punctured his skin, and sank into the flesh under his ribs, where the innkeeper gave it a brutal twist, heaved it free, and was gone. The door banged at his back as a familiar figure stumbled into the silent inn.

"Where's he off to just when I needed a drink?" It was Tasker, wiping flecks of vomit off his chin. "Rich as bloody Creases," he mumbled, then noticed the silence and joined it.

"Jesus," said Wallace. Samuel had slumped back onto the divan, his mouth wide open in a silent appeal for help. The blood had already left a plate-sized stain on his shirt and trousers. A first drop of blood fell audibly to the floorboards.

They helped Samuel outside, tearing the shirts from their backs to stem the bleeding. Wallace supported Samuel by the shoulder on his uninjured flank and they hurried him down to the quayside, hollering for McDonald. Shutters banged at the clamor, and pigeons abandoned their roosts in the plane trees. The jollyboat soon appeared out of the gloom. An onboard lantern illuminated two rowing figures. With a sinking heart, Wallace realized that their din had roused the master. As the boat drew near the quay, Stevenson Peter rose to his feet.

"What the devil," he hissed, "is all this about?"

"It's Samuel, sir," said Wallace. He was aware of the stench of drink on them. He had never meant the captain to see them like this. "They put a knife in him." Wallace made it sound like Constantinople's general vengeance, not an actual event, recently committed by an identifiable individual.

"Let's get him back to the ship and have a look at him," said Stevenson Peter.

The men rowed hard but ineffectively, for the drink had disrupted their rhythm. Oars clattered against each other, then hastily disentangled themselves. In the risen moon, Samuel's frightened face was white as milk.

"How did it happen?" The master did not address Wallace by name, but it was from the mate that an answer was expected.

"It was an argument. We tried to prevent it."

"An argument over what?"

In the brief silence, the men of the *Caledonia* cowered.

"It was an argument over coffee, sir."

The *Caledonia* left Constantinople at first light.

Chapter ∞ 25

I drove to Falmouth in search of Tomaso Samuel. Holiday traffic choked the roads. Rear windows were collages of inflatable orange armbands and plastic spades, smears of damp sand, and dogs' tongues panting from the centers of misted ovals. Rain showers gave way to sunshine and steaming tarmac. Wheat ripened.

Falmouth was where the *Caledonia*'s cook was said to have died, which was my best fix on that elusive man. Tomaso Samuel had resolutely refused to show up in my researches. His death, which had apparently occurred some two weeks before those of his shipmates, seemed obscured by the deeper shadow of the *Caledonia*'s loss. Samuel alone of the crew was not mentioned in the subsequent newspaper reports. Repeated references to his shipmates in crew lists and burial registers, death certificates, baptismal rolls, and marriage registers had served to substantiate them even as Tomaso Samuel turned into a wraith.

Samuel's name originally appeared only once, in Le Dain's wreck statement, which claimed he was from "Buenos Ayres," and had joined the *Caledonia* at London before her departure for Rio in the summer of 1841. Both Le Dain and Hawker agreed, however, that Samuel had died at Falmouth and that the crew went ashore to bury him "at Falmouth Church." I should therefore be able to corroborate the simple fact of Samuel's existence by the evidence of his death in the burial registers for Falmouth, where the *Caledonia* had arrived on August 24 after a seven-week passage from Constantinople.

I might, in truth, have skirted Samuel, who was fast approaching a premature exit from the story, except that his significance did not necessarily end with his death. Robert Hawker regarded Samuel as a pivotal figure in the story, and actually ascribed the loss of the *Caledonia* to Samuel's death—"as one link in a chain of causes." Besides, I'd often thought of the crew going ashore in a strange port to bury their querulous shipmate, but to be permitted that presentiment of their own ends I needed some confirmation of Samuel's death.

Cornwall's county records were stored in a nondescript building, above a sweep of Victorian terraces on Truro's hilly outskirts. I took the microfilmed burial register to the reader and set to work. But Tomaso Samuel was not there. By midafternoon, I was beginning to despair. He wouldn't give himself up. I had worked my way through a pile of books and papers about mid-nineteenth-century Falmouth. I had checked the newspapers for the period. These were mostly full of gleeful observations regarding marine accidents at Southampton, which had recently ousted Falmouth as the nation's packet port—"The *Montrose*, steamer, on making the new dock at Southampton, the wind blowing fresh against the tide, ran on a mudbank!"—and coverage of everything from the landing at Falmouth of Spanish cattle to the opening of a new Tee-Total Wesleyan Chapel. But no Tomaso Samuel.

I was leafing through *A History and Description of the Town and Harbour of Falmouth* (1828), about to abandon the search, when I read of a small settlement on the harbor called St. Just. "Near the mouth of the creek is the station of the lazaretto," it read. The lazaret, or place of confinement for cases of contagious disease, it continued, was "an old vessel lying aground on the south-east shore: and a little outside, is the anchorage of St Just Pool, where vessels perform quarantine."

Quarantine. A word I remembered seeing recently somewhere in a relevant text.

Quarantine, from the French for "forty days," was an extension of the original *trentina*, the thirty days' confinement first implemented at Venice when the Black Death raged in 1348. Britain's own quarantine laws were originally a response to the London plague outbreak of 1665, but the British duly came to recognize the menace from other contagions, particularly smallpox, yellow fever from the West Indies, and cholera. Cholera first reached Britain from the continent in 1831, when thirty thousand people died, and again in 1847.

Quarantine stations were established at all the major ports. The laws were stringently observed. The lazaret, typically a floating hulk, served as a place of confinement for the sick and often doubled as the quarantine service's administrative office. Persons in good health were confined to their own vessels for the duration of the quarantine. The quarantine laws included detailed procedural directions for both humans and cargoes. Goods considered capable of harboring pestilence were to be cleansed by a daily airing during the quarantine period, or by exposure to dews on deck. Paper was susceptible; any money, letters, or ships' documents received from vessels in quarantine were to be dipped in vinegar, then placed in a fumigating box, before they could be forwarded.

Fears of contagion were certainly abroad in the summer of 1842. A letter to the *Times* hardly a week before the *Caledonia*'s arrival at Falmouth wrote of a brig, newly arrived from overseas, that lay at anchor in the Mersey at Liverpool:

> Sickness to an alarming extent has prevailed . . . so much so, that out of a small crew, seven of the hands have already died of the disease whatever may be its nature . . . the seventh, which was not even stiff, I myself saw brought ashore in a boat, not in a coffin or shell but merely covered with a flag, placed in a cart in the most hurried manner and immediately carted off to the dead-house.

I found the reference I was looking for in Le Dain's wreck statement. The crew, he reported, attended Samuel's funeral, "and the next day we then performed quarantine." No wonder; the *Caledonia* had just returned from the pestilential East, in high summer. And while her grain cargo would not have caused her to be quarantined, the sacks in which it was carried were considered to carry contagion.

I turned up a map of Falmouth Harbor, looking for St. Just. The harbor was enormous, and conspicuously symmetrical. It was composed of a long, wide inland waterway that faced directly north and was called Carrick Roads. Six rivers or creeks, three from either shore, fed into the waterway from the northwest or northeast respectively. These creeks divided neatly into three pairs, facing their opposite numbers across the waterway so that the whole resembled a tree, primitively rendered, with three sets of branches growing upward from it. The lowest branches, just north of the main harbor mouth, were the stoutest. They housed Falmouth town and docks on the west side and the fishing port of St. Mawes on the east. The topmost branches, which seemed to grow from the tree's very crown, were the lengthiest. But it was the middle branches, the smallest pair, that interested me, with the western one housing the marina and boatyard at Mylor, and St. Just on the eastern one. And at St. Just, the map showed a small black square on which a cross was perched: a church.

I called up the burial registers for St. Just. Earlier in my researches, I had felt misgivings at such intrusions, wondering what gave me the right to interfere in the distant deaths of men who had never sought my attention. Sometimes my enquiries even felt like desecrations, as if I were exhuming corpses for clues, like a forensic pathologist looking for telltale stains in the earth or revealingly scored bones. But with Samuel I felt no such thing. Perhaps the process was hardening me. Or perhaps I felt that the man was being unreasonably elusive. It may have been that a part of me even agreed with Hawker that Samuel bore some responsibility by his actions for the death of his shipmates. I would dig him up if it was the last thing I did.

And there he was, clear as day. "Thomas Samulle," of the "Brig *Caledonia* in Quarantine Pool," aged twenty-four, had been buried at St. Just on August 26, 1842, just two days after the ship's arrival at Falmouth. So the crew had gathered around the cook's grave a fortnight before others would collect around their own.

The rector of St. Just, C. W. Carlyon, had evidently had quite an August, for Samuel's burial had been preceded by a double drowning: of William Real Richards, "drowned with George Bideford," and George Bideford, "drowned," who were buried on August 19 and 21. Lavinia Green, aged two, of St. Mawes had also been buried on the nineteenth. Carlyon had thought fit to include the exceptional manner of the little girl's death: cholera.

I left Truro in clearing weather. The sky was flawless by the time I reached St. Just, except for the planes that left high white scratches across the blue canopy above this renowned beauty spot. It was late afternoon, when the last of the coach parties were returning to congregate around their revving vehicles, which sent exhaust clouds scudding across the car park. The tourists spoke of shrubs and cameras, and the troublesome knee of one of their party. One complained of the driver's impatience to leave.

"He's probably here every other day, Marge," her tolerant companion explained. "You know what they say about familiarity."

"Familiarity?" Marge retorted. "The only things that are familiar about him are his driver's seat and that behind of his."

It was a remarkable place. "I have blundered into a Garden of Eden that cannot be described in pen or paint," the celebrated traveler H. V. Morton enthused of St. Just in the 1920s. It was certainly nothing like the exposed coast of North Cornwall. It even seemed less like England than an English ideal, a verdant hollow by the sheltered water, with its thirteenth-century church, its terraced graveyard, and, on the slopes behind it, luxuriant subtropical gardens—the work of a nineteenth-century Cornish traveler. The gardens, set among landscaped streams, were a profusion of tree ferns and bamboo clumps, fan palms, cedars, azaleas, and strawberry trees, which gave the impression that the church was a faithful colonial replica, a piece of England re-created amidst the exotic foliage of Manchuria or New Zealand.

The church stood on the south shore of the creek, where it dog-legged into a natural basin hemmed by sheltering hills. The tide was out, exposing the grimy hulls of two yachts that stood beside each other, draped in old tarpaulins and tethered to shoreline shrubs. Beyond them lay a thick skein of mud, where flesh-colored mooring buoys floundered on their rope ends. Magpies shuttled between the great pines below the church on their jerky flights.

I looked for Samuel's headstone without success. That should not have surprised me. Samuel was not only a foreigner but in all likelihood a Catholic, and had moreover been buried in what had begun to look like questionable circumstances. I turned away, consigning him to an un-marked grave. I left the graveyard and followed the shadowed path be-neath overhanging sycamores and holly trees above the creek's southern shore, stumbling over a gnarled knot of a root. I descended to the shingle and stepped across the dried bladder wrack until I reached the mouth of the creek. A few yachts were anchored in the bay where the old quaran-tine pool had been. It was here, then, that the crew of the *Caledonia* had passed much of their last fortnight.

I looked beyond the yachts. On the far side of Carrick Roads, be-yond the still water, I could see the docks and cranes at Falmouth and the tawny tones of the fields, freshly cut for silage, on the upper slopes of the low hills. Then I followed the shoreline to the north until I saw an indis-tinct thicket of masts before a few low buildings. Mylor.

I had been to Mylor before, with my father in October 1989, and for a long time I had not wished to return. But it was as if the *Caledonia* story had brought me to this view of Mylor by design, and I could not turn my back on the place. The road into Mylor passes through thick stands of trees; on the autumn day that Dad and I arrived here, they had largely shed their foliage, allowing us glimpses of the muddy creek below. The road then passes a farm and turns sharply to the left, where it meets the churchyard, down a brief steep hill to the water's edge. Above the shore a huge anchor lies rusting. Two stone quays arch out from the shore to contain a small harbor that empties to a muddy seabed at low tide. The

view beyond, of the low hills of the Roseland peninsula, is briefly interrupted by the roofs of St. Just. Directly opposite the harbor, on the other
side of the road, the churchyard is screened by ash and sycamore trees,
so the church and its low tower are hardly visible. A boatyard abuts the
church grounds, and beyond it stands a white building that houses a yacht
broker's and a restaurant. Along the back of this building, which faces
cavernous wooden sheds containing masts, spars, booms, and rigging,
a raised wooden walkway runs. Beneath this walkway, the business of
restaurant and boatyard meet in a mess of old generators and empty cans
of cooking oil, and wet suits hang from the decked slats of the walkway
to dry; sometimes, when the wind catches them, the suits resemble a
macabre cocktail party. Wooden steps lead up to this walkway, where
doors give onto a number of sparsely furnished flats. My father rented
one such flat for that week in October.

We had come to work on the *Caillac*, Dad's two-masted gaff ketch,
which he had been refitting for several years. Her Gaelic name, meaning
sea cow, made good sense in the boatyard where she was on blocks, a
beamy thing with the tubby lines of a fishing boat and an odd canoe stern.
But Dad loved her. She had been built in 1930 by a Glasgow yard for a tobacco tycoon and had circumnavigated the globe in her early years. Her
saloon, paneled in walnut, originally carried a piano. It was Dad's dream
that he too would sail her around the world one day.

Now, however, her masts, rigging, and all her fittings had been removed. The floorboards had been lifted to reveal her oak frames and teak
carvel-built hull, which we were to spend the week sanding. A ladder
leaned against the boat's side; as Dad reached the deck and looked her
over, he rubbed his chest with a circular motion and muttered that there
was much to do.

In the evenings, he sat in the flat's small living room, drinking whisky
and making lists. He wondered how the *Caillac* should be rigged and
sketched sail plans. He considered pirates in the Malacca Straits, and even
asked himself whether the ship should carry a cache of hand grenades.
Sometimes, he wondered where he was going to find a crew. Mum was

not one for sailing around the world; instead she might fly out to Rio to join him for some light cruising. I was thinking along similar lines. "Oh, you'll come," said Dad. "Once you see her finished you'll come."

He had been to the doctor the week before we came away. Indigestion was diagnosed, but the tablets he was given for it hardly helped. He mostly felt the pain first thing in the morning, but he always endured breakfast, drew on his old blue boiler suit, and made his way to the boat. On our last evening he felt much better; so much so that we drove out to a pub and worked our way through Dad's godchildren, wondering if there might be potential crew among them.

In the morning, I went into the small bathroom. I brushed my teeth in the yellow plastic mirror, lathered my face, and laid the razor blade against my cheek. The kettle whistled over the radio in the other room. I could smell toast. I was shaving beneath my chin when Dad called out.

"Your egg's ready, boyo," he said.

"Coming," I replied. I had just dipped the razor blade when I heard a loud impact from the other room, and a silence beyond it. I ran in to find Dad lying on the floor beside the table. He had knocked the teapot over as he fell. A large puddle of tea steamed on the tabletop, islanding the egg cups and the crockery and dripping between the table leaves. He had fallen on his side, both arms pinned beneath him. As I turned him over and raised him to a sitting position, to help him back to his feet, there was a peculiar noise from his throat, low-pitched and reflexive. Dad's eyes were partly open, but they had a milky, unfocused quality. There was a blow on his forehead where he had caught the table in his fall. Now I was supporting him so that he sat on the floor, in his tatty blue flannel dressing gown, his legs out straight, but his eyes had closed. I lowered him onto his back and ran from the flat. It was a still morning, with mist on the water. The man who was unlocking at the yacht broker's knew Dad, and also turned out to know something about artificial respiration. He returned with me to the flat, where Dad had not moved. The man removed the mirror from the bathroom wall and kneeled before Dad. He held the mirror to Dad's face to check for signs of breathing. Then, with stiff

palms, he began to pump Dad's chest. I stepped outside, and walked up
and down the wooden terrace. Through the slats, I could see the wet suits
swinging gently. There was an ambulance siren, then paramedics in yellow, and then a doctor who hurried into the flat. A few minutes later, he
came out.

"I'm sorry," he said. "Your father's passed away." I wanted to tell
him that the words would not do, and that it had been more sudden than
that. I carried myself back into the flat. The eggs were still warm in their
cups, but the surrounding tea puddle had turned cold and shrunk. Somebody had placed the mirror on the table and turned the radio off. They
had crossed Dad's arms over his chest and straightened his dressing
gown. I lay my hand upon his forehead for a while and, as I did so, I wondered if I'd ever touched his forehead during his life.

The two men at the foot of the steps fell silent as I left the flat, then
lifted the coffin and made their way up the steps. They took Dad to
Truro. I made some phone calls before somebody gave me a pack of cigarettes and put me on a train.

☨

I turned away, and followed the path back through the churchyard to
the car.

Chapter ❧ 26

Stevenson Peter, it seems, would have his name no other way. Indeed, in the mentions that survive, "John" makes its first and final appearance in Arbroath's register of births on October 7, 1813. Subsequently, there is not even a "J. Stevenson Peter" to acknowledge the name that his parents gave him, and by which his own father was known throughout his life.

Stevenson was certainly a popular second forename among the Peter family. It doubtless honored, in the nineteenth-century manner, a surname of family significance—the maiden name of a woman who had married into the family, perhaps, or that of a close friend or family benefactor. To Stevenson's nephew, James Stevenson Peter, we can add a cousin named Mary Stevenson Peter and another nephew, baptized John Stevenson Peter on October 6, 1840. In the census of 1841, this eight-month-old boy's name was given in the preferred manner of his uncle, as "Stephenson Peter"; the alternative spelling was perhaps due to the fact that the census clerk had in mind George Stephenson, builder of the "Rocket" locomotive in 1830. But by the census of 1851, his name was given as "John S. Peter." The name was fading along with the memory of his uncle, nine years dead.

Clearly, Stevenson's choice of name had caused contemporaries quite as much confusion as it would cause me 160 years later. References to the *Caledonia* in *Lloyd's List*—ship and master, as convention had it— conjure the bewilderment of nineteenth-century port clerks from Rio to Odessa. Time and again, they transposed his names, entering his ship as

"*Caledonia,* Stevenson" on his arrival at Marseilles in April 1841, at Rio in October of the same year, at Syra in March 1842, and at Smyrna the following month. He was given as Stevens at Constantinople, and as Stevenson at Odessa and on the ship's return to Constantinople. The master's name appeared as he would have wished it—"*Caledonia,* Peter"—only when he arrived at Falmouth in August 1842.

So why should he have fixed upon Stevenson so tenaciously? The question is unanswerable, of course, but that needn't deter speculation. Stevenson came from a seafaring family. His father was a sailor, and so were his brothers, Alexander and James. Like every Arbroath seafaring family of their generation, his parents would have long learned to fear the dreaded Bell Rock, eleven miles southeast of Arbroath, which made every approach to that port a perilous one and which had claimed scores of ships over the centuries.

The Bell Rock lighthouse finally had been completed just three years before Stevenson's birth by Robert Stevenson. Was that the answer? That any Arbroath boy with the sea in his veins would have called himself after the feted lighthouse engineer in those days if he'd had a reasonable excuse for doing so—like actually being named Stevenson? Was the adoption of his middle name a certainty waiting to happen?

If so, it was fitting: a name in which a sailor's gratitude for the lights that brought him home was enshrined. I could even forgive him the trouble he'd caused me trying to find him.

St. Just Pool, Carrick Roads, August 26, 1842
"Will you plug your confounded gullets?" The master's incensed whisper stilled the cram of men struggling for trim as they sought seats in the laden jollyboat. "And settle now—unless you want to go the way of last week's wretched brace of drownings."

The jollyboat drifted clear of the ship, where only William Tasker remained, a fading figure among the shrouds. Two pairs of hands began to row, but gently. The master sat in the stern, staring out at the evening from beneath the battered black tricorne that he had inherited from an uncle with obscure naval connections and reserved for solemn occasions. Each man had dressed with all the gravity at his disposal, although a stranger encountering the funeral party might have imagined otherwise, presuming a disembarkation of sunburnt scarecrows. The crew's canvas jackets and trousers, their straw hats and cotton shirts, were fast surrendering to the salt of sea and sweat, the damp and sun, the general stresses of ship work, and the hefting of cargo.

It was after eight bells, or eight o'clock, when the late-summer day had surrendered to darkness, with only the inky iridescence of the water to distinguish it from the plain black mass of the land. The air was heavy with the threat of storm. Noises arose now, as if bidden by the silence of the crew, but the master was thankful that they bore no trace of aroused suspicions. From their neighbors in the quarantine pool they could hear talk, the scraping of victualing bowls and the lazy rasp of anchor chains on the tide, and from the lazaret hulk itself the obscenities of the quarantine officers that the delirious ditties of the sick had provoked. A heron took flight, its rhythmic wingtips beating, then ruffling the water, before giving it a final skimming caress. A horse whinnied in the fields. Stevenson Peter brushed an insect from his face and comforted himself that it was no shame to have lost a single man after eighteen months away, not when that man had all but invited his own death. He shifted his bulk, seeking comfort. He had spread his legs wide, taking care not to scuff the makeshift coffin that lay in the bottom of the boat. Though the cortege might struggle for dignity, not least because there were those who must plump their behinds, albeit gingerly, upon the coffin, one assembled from old pine plankings and cutoffs that sagged alarmingly under their weight, the master would honor his cook as best he could in the manner of that man's obsequies.

Stevenson Peter had allowed the darkness to thicken until he could make out nothing beyond the lazaret's light—when its guard was no better placed to see the *Caledonia*. He then instructed the crew to muster in silence and to lower Tomaso Samuel's coffin, wrapped in an aged ensign, into the jollyboat. Before joining the men in the jollyboat, the

master left orders with Tasker to maintain lanterns and the impression
of onboard activity.

James Wallace sat in the bows, as far from the master as the boat
would allow. It had been seven weeks, he recalled, since the jollyboat was
last floated—to pluck the coffin's mortally wounded contents and the
drunken crew from the quayside at Galata. They had been at sea ever
since, making good time in Mediterranean weather whose summer glo-
ries—excellent breezes warm on the skin, dolphins on the bow wave—
only served to highlight a prevailing onboard atmosphere of ill temper and
resentment, to which William Tasker alone seemed immune. He pestered
his shipmates with peculiar queries about the price of a ship such as the
Caledonia, fully fitted, or, tiring of his time at sea, perhaps an Angus
manor farm with five hundred acres and a prize-winning beef herd.

The plight of the cook weighed heavier on the others; that and the
absence of coffee, which some had come to depend upon, not to mention
the loss of Samuel's victualing abilities, which the stand-in cooks signally
failed to emulate. Nobody would forget David Wallace's black olive and
ship's biscuit mash, nor forgive David McDonald his unholy salt beef
with flour. The apprentice, who knew nothing of flour's reliance upon
water, nor of the beneficial effects of the baking process, had coated the
meat in the powder, littered with occasional lumps, so that its texture was
that of Edward Le Dain's pockmarked face, which nobody could bring
themselves to touch.

It was upon Stevenson Peter, however, that the most explosive mood
had descended (so much so that Alexander Kent took to referring to him
as Saltpeter). The master berated the crew roundly, but his mate, whom
he considered responsible for the events of that night, he condemned to a
withering silence. The master had allowed himself to believe that the
curse of the coffee had been lifted; that it had actually led to the cook's
death only confirmed his worst suspicions about its malign influence.

Stevenson Peter could not know, of course, that Wallace had been
conceding a far deeper personal guilt in the privacy of his mind ever

since Galata. He understood what he had done; his repeated abuse of the cook for his coffee, to the craven appreciation of the crew, had served to further that man from the hope of their companionship. He had played Samuel with a callousness he was ashamed to discover he possessed, and had inexorably led that man to the worst of all ends, which was an arcane one; a fatal wound received championing the coffee preference of an admired officer was no kind of epitaph. The master, who was also his brother-in-law and had once been his friend, made no attempt to mask his contempt. All had gone amiss. Wallace wondered how he was to go about becoming the man he had once been, but saw no way of redeeming himself in the dancing blues of the passing Mediterranean.

And all the time the cook languished in the fo'c'sle. In the heat, the crew slept on deck. Besides, the smell of the man brought bile to the throat. Then there were the groans of such distress that they conjured visions of purgatory, and were endured only at a distance. It was the master who took it upon himself to attend to the cook. He received assistance from Le Dain, who knew what it was to lie in suffering darkness, and from McDonald, who had taken a tortoise into his protection. For the first few days, they allowed themselves to believe that the wound might somehow heal. But they were ignorant of medicine and had nothing with which to treat the injury. Nor could they know that the blade had ruptured the man's gut. The jagged wound turned purple, then black and lumpen. It began to suppurate, discharging a yellow pus that collected in his navel and crystallized there, and the man's stomach became swollen until it was hard as a drum. They brushed at the flies that gathered in the heat to feed at the wound. Every morning, for two weeks, they washed the wound with fresh water and bound Samuel's trunk with lengths of sailcloth. But the procedure caused Samuel greater pain until the day came that they abandoned the treatment as a futile gesture. They left the wound to fester.

After four weeks, as they beat toward the Straits of Gibraltar, Tomaso Samuel's condition had become unendurable. The slightest shift of position now cost him unspeakable pain. He was reduced to taking mere sips of water; rather than move him, it seemed kinder to leave the man to soil himself. They asked him if there was anything they could do for him, then winced at the Spanish delirium that spilled from him before returning to the deck, which was a kind of paradise where they could forget him in the brightness of the skies and the sparkle of the sea.

And now, rowing gently as if movement still hurt him, they were ferrying him across the water to a clandestine burial.

The cook had clung to life. It seemed for a while that he might live to see England. But the calmness, which they recognized as a sure prelude to death, had stolen upon him as they made splendid time past Ushant. The torment released him so that he no longer felt the pitch and yaw of the vessel like rake tines hauling at his poisoned innards. He settled back, breathing more easily, and let himself be lulled by the movement of the ship. He even asked to be moved so he might see the sky and the sails through the forehatch, and feel the sea breeze upon his face. And he asked to see the mate.

Wallace thus lowered himself into the fo'c'sle. The stench made him gag. His eyes soon adjusted to the gloom. The cook's shriveled figure was cocooned in the nest Le Dain and McDonald had fashioned from spare sailcloth, mattresses, clothes, rags, and the old flag in which they would subsequently wrap his coffin, to cushion him against the ship's movements. He squatted by the cook and affected jovial tones.

"So, when can we expect you back, Samuel? You should see what McDonald's been cooking. Now that really would kill you."

Samuel closed his eyes and smiled broadly, as if at a supreme joke. A film of sweat lay over his gray features. A glitter danced weakly in his eyes. He held a shivering finger upright.

"One thing you tell me, Mr. Wallace. You promise you telling me straight?" His weak voice rang, as if overheard from another room.

"One thing," Wallace nodded.

"That coffee, eh? What you thinking?"

"That *café au lait*. That heavenly morning. It was better than it ever was in Marseilles. You'll ship with me next time? First mate's coffee steward? If ever we're permitted the holy beverage again?"

"Not like tar, eh?"

"Nothing like tar, Samuel," said Wallace softly.

"Not muddy rubbish?"

Wallace shook his head.

"Not like saddle of hot gentleman riding too long," said Samuel. He breathed a sigh of satisfaction and closed his still-smiling eyes. After a moment Wallace rose to his feet and slipped from the fo'c'sle.

They discovered Tomaso Samuel's corpse at dawn, when the English coast was a gray ribbon on the northern horizon.

A kind southwesterly had ushered them to Falmouth by noon on August 24. They passed Pendennis Castle, flying the yellow flag from the main topgallant yard, and came into that great natural harbor, which was hemmed by wooded hillsides and dotted by merchantmen and men-of-war. On the *Caledonia*'s arrival at the quarantine pool, a boat put out from the lazaret, keeping the snow downwind on its approach. The boat drew to a halt and an officer rose to his feet; this action caused the boat to shiver like jelly, for it was a small boat and a capacious officer. The officer steadied himself and took hold of a weighted box. It hung from a rope that he swung with surprising deftness around his neck, like a lariat, before hurling it with a clatter onto the ship's deck. Stevenson Peter, who was familiar with the procedure, stepped forward and opened the box, which contained a scuffed and tarnished Bible. He held the book respectfully in both hands, rubbing the leather against his elbow as if to restore its shine.

"Place your hand upon the book," barked the fat officer, who was a young man but not without self-importance. "And answer the following questions upon oath."

Stevenson Peter answered the familiar questions: that he carried a clean bill of health, knew of no reason why his ship might carry contagion, had had no contact with others who might conceivably have succumbed to contagion, and could affirm that no signs of disease had been evidenced in the course of the voyage.

"And all your men are currently in good health?" the officer concluded in a brisk tone.

"All excellent," replied Stevenson Peter. "Barring the dead one."

The quarantine officer dropped the notebook in which he had been scribbling. A frantic flick of the wrist put his oarsmen into a reverse from which they did not rest until thirty yards of churning water separated them from the snow. The officer cleared his throat.

"A dead man, you say."

"I do."

"A dead man on board."

"Aye. Died of wounds cruelly inflicted while ashore in Constantinople."

"He exhibits no signs of contagion?"

"No such signs."

"No blistering carbuncles?"

"No."

"No black buboes?"

"He died of a knife wound, man, not of the plague. And we seek permission to bury him."

"But you're confined to your vessel until quarantine is completed."

"But we have a corpse on board, high as the summer. That it remains here offends our morals and begins to assail our senses. I would request that you or your superiors make an exception in this case."

"Rules are rules," the officer began, but was interrupted.

"It's a stinking bag of a corpse!" Stevenson Peter bellowed. "It's crying out for the earth."

The officer straightened his cap and made a note in his book. "I'll see what can be done," he said sourly and gestured at his oarsmen to be away.

It was two days later that the same quarantine officer returned with the *Caledonia*'s paperwork. The weather had remained unseasonably warm, and the stench of Tomaso Samuel's mortal remains had crept out of the fo'c'scle to envelop the entire ship. The approaching officer removed a handkerchief from his top pocket, which he plastered over his nose.

"Mr. Stevenson," he said, doffing his cap with his free hand.

"For the last time," the master retorted, "the name is Peter. What news of my request, officer?"

"No news, Mr. Peter."

"No news. What do you mean by no news?"

"The new postal service to London may be excellent, Mr. Peter, but it is too much to expect replies from the capital in two days."

"London? I'm waiting on word from London before I bury my cook?"

"Before you can break the quarantine, Mr. Peter," the officer corrected him, "which you can only do in exceptional circumstances."

"And how unexceptional, officer, is a corpse liquefying in my fo'c'sle? Have you really no nose beneath that kerchief?"

The officer shrugged. "I'll let you know the moment I hear, Mr. Peter. That's all I can do."

As the quarantine boat turned for the lazaret, Stevenson Peter called for Jones and asked the ship's carpenter how the coffin was progressing.

Later that morning, a boat bearing provisions came to call.

"Phew," said the boatsman. "Smells like the good crew of the *California* could do with some fresh fruit and vegetables."

"The *Caledonia*..."

"Carrots and cabbages. Tomatoes. Apples and potatoes I have. Just look at the size of them this excellent year."

"Not at those prices," said the master. "But I daresay you know the vicar here?"

"Mr. Carlyon. I do, sir. The rector baptized me, married me, and will surely bury me."

Stevenson Peter tossed the man some coin, then dropped a letter into the boat. "Deliver that to the vicar, you can rest assured it's fumigated, and bring me his reply forthwith."

*To the vicar of St Just in the county of Cornwall—for his private
attention. I, the master of the* Caledonia, *of the port of Arbroath
in Scotland and currently anchored at St Just, call upon your good
offices to inter our shipmate, departed some days since now. I should
advise you that though we presently perform quarantine, we carry a
clean bill and are all in good health, our departed brother excepted,
he being in desperate need of nothing but the hallowed earth. We
await your immediate reply.*
Yours
Stevenson Peter, master, the Caledonia

A reply reached the ship in the early afternoon:

Dear Mr Stevenson,
*Scotland! How delightful. One hears much to admire of the place.
The queen shortly leaves for a tour of your Highland home if I am
not much mistaken.*
Yours
Clement W. Carlyon, rector.
*PS: Another death, indeed. A month of untimely deaths in these
parts. Come to the south shore at eight o'clock tonight. Come
clandestine, for I would rather not have the quarantine officers at
my door. Your owners might wish to make a contribution to the
church roof. Shall we say ten shillings?*
PPS: Are you quite quite *well?*

"Steer for the shore," Stevenson Peter whispered. "And remember;
his name's Thomas. Any mention of Tomaso and there's sure to be awkward questions concerning his religion."

He could make out the widening mud flats, shiny wet in the moonlight. The tide was on the ebb, emptying the creek. They must land now
and make their approach on foot.

The jollyboat ran into the shallows and went aground with a gentle
scrape. The men hauled the boat high up the shingle. The mate and five

others bent to lift the coffin to their shoulders and set out along the shingle. Stevenson Peter straightened the ensign and fell in behind the coffin.

"There's a path through the woods," whispered McDonald, who had returned from a scouting foray. The cortege followed him up the beach to a steep slope that led to the path. As they manhandled the coffin up the rise, a sharp thud sounded from within.

"Ooh, his poor sodding head," muttered Jones, and Stevenson Peter hissed once more for silence. The path undermined their dignified progress, for it was overhung with low leafy branches and lively with exposed roots and snags, which caught at passing boots. Then a faint light appeared ahead of them, revealing the silhouettes of arched headstones and the squat tower of a church.

"This way," a whispered voice sounded in the darkness. "And please may I ask you to remain downwind of me."

The rector, dressed in a white cassock and carrying a lantern, led the procession to a far corner of the graveyard. A perspiring man clambered from a freshly dug grave.

"Shallow as my sock drawer," he muttered, "but I can see as I've run out of time." The vicar cleared his throat.

"Mr. Stevenson."

"Mr. Peter, Your Reverence."

"What of Mr. Stevenson?"

"I am he. Stevenson Peter."

"Stevenson Peter. How charming! Now, Mr. Peter, I'm advised to stand upwind of you."

Stevenson Peter nodded at the precaution. A silence followed.

"And where," asked the rector, "would upwind of you be exactly?"

"You'll be all right if you stand just there, Your Reverence."

"Thank you. You may put the coffin down. What was the name of the deceased?"

"Thomas Samuel," said Stevenson Peter firmly.

"'I am the resurrection and the life,' saith the Lord," Carlyon intoned, lifting his arms into the dark. "'He that believeth in me, yet though he die, he may live.'"

As Tomaso Samuel was lowered into the earth, James Wallace delivered up a silent apology into the night.

"You return to Scotland soon, Mr. Peter?" said Carlyon, rubbing the soil from his palms as he accompanied the master through the graveyard. Behind them, the gravedigger could be heard hammering at the topsoil with the flat of his spade.

"We await orders, Your Reverence. We know not where we are headed."

"Who does, Mr. Peter, who does?" They stopped at the gate.

"For the roof," said the master, holding out an envelope, which Carlyon took gingerly between between finger and thumb.

"God's speed," said Carlyon.

The crew made their way through the dark woods and pushed off the jollyboat. The night seemed closer yet. It was as if all its sounds had subsided under its great weight. Even the ships' hulls had ceased their groaning. So one could not fail but hear the sound of breaking glass, and the yell that accompanied it, as the oars drew the jollyboat close to the *Caledonia*'s side.

"Oh, buggery!" William Tasker exclaimed.

Chapter ✎ 27

Now that the *Caledonia* was just twelve days from Morwenstow, those words of the Bude man at the looting of the *Johanna* kept coming back to me. "It isn't as if we caused the ship to be wrecked," he had said, "which is what used to happen in times gone by."

The use of false lights to lure ships onto the rocks is a defining element of the West Country's moody past. The writer Claude Berry spoke for many, however, when he called "the viler suggestion that Cornish coast-dwellers lured vessels to their doom in order to plunder them . . . the very stuff of the sensational novel." Similarly, in a letter to the *Times* following the *Johanna* incident, the writer Winston Graham asserted that "the active inducement of wrecks by the deliberate waving of false lights . . . has no such evidence or even reliable hearsay to support it." Those who dismiss the practice as unsubstantiated lore also point to the fact that not a single case of wrecking by false lights was ever brought to the Cornish courts.

I had doubts of my own: namely, I could not see how the practice had possibly worked. Since time immemorial, shore lights had surely constituted an indisputable caution to steer clear. The first lighthouses constructed on the British coast were certainly effective in warning off approaching ships. Killigrew of Falmouth, a former privateer, remarked on the local resentment he had caused by building the first Lizard lighthouse in 1619, declaring that he had "taken away God's grace" from the local people who "now shall receive no more benefit from shipwreck.

They have been so long used to reap profit by the calamity of the ruin of shipping, that they claim it as hereditary."

Lundy Lighthouse was not lit until 1819, but there had been a tradition, albeit an irregular one, of cautionary lights for the benefit of shipping along this coast long before that time. A night light shone from the chapel at Stile, just south of Padstow. Another illuminated Chapel Rock, a dangerous protuberance at the entrance to Bude Harbor. St. Catherine's Tor, just south of Hartland Quay and shaped like a distinct cone on its land side but sheer cliff to seaward, was believed to be the site of another such chapel. And though the lighthouse was not built at Hartland Point until the 1870s, it was the custom of Hartland Quay's owner as early as the 1840s to keep a warning lamp lit in the window there. In the early days, these lights were intended as beacons to warn vessels off; they happened to be located at haven entrances because these were the only places along the shore where there were residents to maintain them. It was not until later that such lights regularly served to guide vessels into harbor, except *in extremis,* for few masters would have attempted entering North Cornwall's notoriously difficult ports at night under sail unless an unrelenting wind offered them no alternative.

It was also the tradition among more considerate locals to light warning fires on the cliffs. "We were aroused from our quiet by minute guns at sea," wrote Robert Hawker in February 1853. "We rushed up to the brow of Hennacliffe and there we kindled a cautionary Beacon of Furze. We have reason to think that a Russian ship had lost the Land in Harty Race and that by our Light she found it and made Bideford the next day." All of which made it hard to appreciate how lights might have been deployed as the main tool in the wreckers' locker—and used to lure ships shoreward.

The answer was to be found in the pages of fiction. In Daphne du Maurier's classic *Jamaica Inn,* set around 1815, a night storm sent the wreckers to Cornwall's north coast. They set a false light on the cliffs, which "danced and curtsyed, storm-tossed, as though kindled and carried by the wind itself." A crucially moving light, then. In his 1892 novel *In the Roar of the Sea,* Sabine Baring-Gould fictionalized the legend of the notorious Hartland wrecker Cruel Copinger. "A stationary light might serve as a warning," explains an old cove, "but a moving light misleads." The cove then describes "vessels coming up the Channel to Bristol" that "get lost as to their bearings, get near our cliffs without knowing it, and then—if a wind from the west springs up and blows rough—they are done for." Especially if there were landsmen intent on confusing them further: "The captain of a vessel, if he has lost his bearings—as is like enough in the fog—as soon as the mist rises, would see a light gliding along, and think it was that of a vessel at sea, and so make in the direction of the light, in the belief that there was open water, and so run directly on his destruction." According to Baring-Gould, Copinger's gang of wreckers simulated the movement of a moving vessel's lights by tying a lantern to the head of an ass ("Do you see how, as the creature moves his head, the light is swayed, and that, with the rise and fall in the land, makes it look as though the rise and fall were on the sea?").

Baring-Gould was notoriously cavalier with the truth—it was appropriate that he was Hawker's biographer in this respect. But he at least led me to understand how the passing mariner would interpret such a light not as a caution but as a come-on. The light indicated not land but sea, the mariner's element. It afforded a fatal illusion—of a fellow vessel marking out safe sea room—and to the mariner who had lost his bearings there was no sight more self-evidently reassuring. It was piracy by entrapment.

There was at least practical sense, then, in setting false lights—and plenty of voices from the centuries in question confirming that it had occurred. Some were no more reliable than the vicar of Morwenstow who claimed that such wreckers remained active in his time, describing them as "the cruel and covetous natives of the strand," who regarded it as "a matter of pastime to lure a vessel ashore by a treacherous light, or to withhold succour from the seaman struggling with the sea" (even as he utterly denied their presence in his own parish).

Others could not be dismissed quite so readily. In the introduction to a cautionary verse called "The Shipwreck," published in 1830, a writer for the Religious Tract Society alleged:

> ... vessels, particularly foreigners, have, in some countries been artfully decoyed on shore by the wreckers exhibiting false lights. Often, when the vessel strikes the ground, these wretches not only refrain from giving what assistance is in their power, but they go on board, and take such measures as inevitably to hasten the destruction of the ship. Nor have they always abstained from blood-guiltiness. Like the highway robber, they sometimes find it necessary for their own safety, to add murder to theft. Happy for Great Britain, the circulation of the Bible round its weather-beaten shores has swept much of this accursed practice from the land; but it is not yet wholly extinct!

Even the credible Report of the Constabulary Force Commissioners of 1839 asserted the continued existence of wrecking. "They would use every other endeavour to bring a vessel into danger rather than help her," one witness claimed, "in order that she should become a wreck, and exposed to their unchecked plunder."

None of which accounted, however, for the absolute lack of evidence. But the fact that no Cornish case of wrecking by false lights was brought to court may well have been explained by the fact that much must have gone unnoticed along this remote coast in the poorly illuminated past. Authority was by all accounts thinly spread and spectacularly ineffective. A letter to the Commissioner of Customs in 1804 referred to "the total incompetency of John Berry, riding officer, of Clovelly, who was appointed to guard the coast from thence to Bude. This officer is exceedingly infirm, being upwards of 70, and we understand has not been on horseback for 20 years past." With the likes of Berry patrolling the cliffs, wreckers had very little to fear.

There was, besides, a law against the practice. "If any person or persons," declared George II's wrecking bill of 1753, "shall put out any false lights or lights with intention to bring any ship or vessel into danger, then such person or persons so offending shall be deemed guilty of felony and . . . shall suffer death, without benefit of clergy." And when was a law ever passed against a nonexistent crime?

Had Hawker lied because he had seen things he should not have seen that September night? And when he sat down in his vicarage to pen "Remembrances of a Cornish Vicar" more than twenty years later, was he unable to face the truth? Was it his past he was rewriting?

Chapter ∞ 28

Tomaso Samuel would doubtless have preferred a daytime burial, the sun's rays falling warm upon his coffin, but I could find no way round his hugger-mugger interment.

Firstly, no certificate was ever issued on Samuel's death. Its absence was thoroughly unusual even in the early days of civil registration; death certificates would be issued for all seven of Samuel's shipmates when their bodies were recovered at Morwenstow and at Peppercombe. A death certificate was required from the local coroner before a burial could legally take place. Coroners were notorious, however, for their tardiness in the mid-nineteenth century. Applying for a certificate in Samuel's case would have entailed delays in the disposal of a body that had begun putrefying before death. The application would also have raised awkward questions regarding Stevenson Peter's obligations under the quarantine regulations.

The *Caledonia*'s last quarantine order lies deep in a ledger of the Falmouth Customs Service. The order, headed "The Council Chamber, Whitehall," states that the *Caledonia* "is arrived at Falmouth and there put under Quarantine, that the Master has brought a clean Bill of Health, and the Crew are all well; which . . . being taken into consideration, together with the Answers of the Master to the Quarantine Questions put to him;—It is thereupon Ordered in Council, that the said Ship with her Crew and the whole of her Cargo do perform a Quarantine of Ten Days from the Date of her arrival (and during that period the whole of her

AT THE COUNCIL CHAMBER, WHITEHALL,

THE *26th* DAY OF *August* 1842

PRESENT,

The Lords of Her Majesty's Most Honorable Privy Council.

WHEREAS there was this Day read at the Board a Letter from the Secretary of the Customs, setting forth that the *Ship "Caledonia"* *S. Peter* Master from *Odessa & Constantinople* with a Cargo of *Wheat*

is arrived at *Falmouth* and there put under Quarantine, that the Master has brought a clean Bill of Health, and the Crew are all well ; which Letter being taken into consideration, together with the Answers of the Master to the Quarantine Questions put to him ;—It is thereupon Ordered in Council, that the said Ship with her Crew and the whole of Her Cargo do perform a Quarantine of *Ten* Days from the Date of her arrival, *and during that period the whole of* (the Bedding and Clothing of all Persons on board be opened and aired daily on Deck,) and at the expiration of that Time be discharged from any further restraint on account of Quarantine, and permitted to proceed to the place of her delivery without opening and airing, in case all Persons on Board continue in good health, and that no new matter shall have come to the knowledge of the Commissioners of the Customs in objection thereto.

And the Right Honorable the Lords Commissioners of Her Majesty's Treasury, and the Lords Commissioners of the Admiralty, are to give the necessary Directions herein as to them may respectively appertain.

and directions to be given to the (Signed,) *C. C. Greville* *Superintendent of Quarantine to have the Bed and Bedding of the man who died on board destroyed, and the Berth well washed & the Body is removed.*

No. 451

CUSTOM-HOUSE, LONDON,
26 August 1842.

LET the *Collector & Comptroller at Falmouth* take care that the Directions contained in the Order of Council, (or which the aforegoing is a Copy) be duly complied with. *and the proper officer to see executed*

Care that that the Bed — **By Order of the Commissioners.**

and Bedding in question be totally destroyed
and the Berth well washed
& desire by their Lordships
decreed / (4)

pro Secretary.

Bedding and Clothing of all Persons on board be opened and aired daily on Deck)."

The official responsible for the order then appended a "memorandum" to the form, squeezing it, in a rather more crabbed hand, into the gap alongside his signature. "Special directions," he wrote, "to be given to the Superintendent of Quarantine to have the Bed and Bedding of the person who died on board destroyed, and the Berth well washed after the Body is removed." The directive is repeated in another hand at the foot of the page, where the quarantine officers are again charged to take "especial care that the Bed and Bedding in question be totally destroyed and the Berth well washed as decreed by their Lordships."

The quarantine order makes no reference to the disposal of the actual corpse, but comparable cases confirm that a strict procedure existed. At Bromboro, Liverpool's quarantine pool, it was ordered that same summer that the corpse of Simon Reid, a mariner on the *Agitator,* be placed on board a cutter that was to "tow the said corpse into deep water in order that it may there be sunk." So how else could it be that Samuel was buried ashore? And that the crew, specifically confined to their ship from the date of her arrival for ten days, attended the funeral?

Beyond the clandestine burial, the quarantine order conjures a final image: of the crew burning their shipmate's bedding and clothing, and washing and airing their own, as they waited out their confinement, and August turned to September, and, though they did not know it, eight of them entered the last week of their lives. Beyond their own sheltered view, meanwhile, of low wooded hills and the Carrick Roads bristling with shipping, the wider world was in foment.

England's political temperature had been rising steadily in the weeks prior to the *Caledonia*'s arrival at Falmouth. The depression deepened alarmingly that summer, with Chartists and Anti-Corn Law Leaguers at their most strident. There was a palpable feeling of revolution in the air, which the *Falmouth Packet* put down to "the increase of machinery and the general decline of morals." Others, less insulated against the wretched conditions prevailing in the industrial Midlands and North, blamed hunger and poverty, and a popular political awakening to the nation's plight. On July 23, *The Illustrated London News*, lately founded, observed how "the distress of the country is still the paramount theme.... We must awaken ourselves to the wretched condition of our poorer fellow-creatures, and probe the resources of the empire for the means of bringing them relief ... the grief and melancholy of the lower classes is truly heart-rending."

The governing classes, meanwhile, were partying. In May the young queen attended a masked ball at Buckingham Palace, wearing a pendant valued at sixty thousand pounds. A few days later, as she was driven down Constitution Hill a man drew a pistol on her; Victoria was to survive three assassination attempts that summer. "Poor little queen!" declared Thomas Carlyle. "I have some loyalty about me, and have no wish to see her shot."

Events came to a head in late July, when a wage cut caused colliers in Staffordshire to strike. They marched on the local factories, damaging boilers and extinguishing furnaces. The workers in the Manchester area, enduring daily wages of just seven and a half pence a day, were also at breaking point. On July 4, the spinners and weavers at a Stalybridge factory also came out on strike. They took to the streets and brought the town's mills to a standstill. The next day, when they marched on the center of Manchester, two policemen were killed.

On August 7, the rioting spread to nearby Stockport. Mills were attacked and bakeries, whose high prices made them a popular focus of resentment, were looted. On the tenth, eight thousand people marched on Manchester and had silenced most of the city's mills by eleven o'clock that morning. On the twelfth, three thousand people brought Heywood's thirty-three cotton mills to a halt. Soon, the country's manufacturing heartlands were paralyzed, with mills idle at Leeds, Saddleworth, Bury, Macclesfield, Bolton, and Stockport, and the Stafford, West Bromwich, and Potteries' colleries on strike.

By Sunday, August 14, with the local police forces and special constables powerless, the government called on the army. Seven hundred grenadier guards and 150 artillery men, equipped with cannon, were dispatched to Manchester by rail. Ten days later, as the *Caledonia* sailed into Falmouth, the insurrection was over.

It was ironic that Britain should have plumbed such depths just as relief was arriving, in the form of an unexpectedly excellent harvest. "Three months since," the *Globe* would declare in a mid-September editorial, "there was a strong possibility of a deficient harvest...A season more than commonly favourable for ripening and harvesting the crops has counteracted the unfavourable seed time." One newspaper even described it as "the most bountiful harvest that has, in the memory of man, ever blessed this country."

The Falmouth press abounded with stories of stupendous crops. A cabbage weighing 33.5 pounds was pulled from a garden in Helston; another, cut in Camelford in late August, "covered a spot of ground of five square feet." Potatoes weighing twenty pounds each were being dug up at St. Erth. An apple tree in St. Austell, which had already cropped twice, was blossoming for a third time by September. An apple measuring thirteen inches in circumference and weighing over fifteen ounces was found in an Exeter garden. And come November a Hartland man would pull a thirty-five-pound turnip, measuring forty-three inches in circumference, from his garden. Prospects appeared equally rosy elsewhere. At Wortley, near Leeds, a crop of oats "had stems which attained the extraordinary length of six feet, one measuring even seven feet six inches, the ear of which bore the almost incredible number of 240 corns!" At Applegarth, Dumfriesshire, thirty shocks of corn gave the extraordinary yield of "100 stones." A farm near Arbroath was reported as presenting "as rich a return as we believe was ever witnessed." "The crops, both for quantity and quality," declared the *Arbroath Guide*, "practical men readily agree, never held out better hopes of cheap food for man or beast."

The exceptional yields happened to coincide with unprecedented grain imports. That inauspicious spring "seed time" had spawned predictions of a poor harvest and consequent high prices, which, together with Sir Robert Peel's relaxed duties on imported corn, had sparked a heady rush for foreign wheat earlier in the season. By late summer, great quantities were unloading at Britain's ports. "Never has the port of London exhibited such a scene of activity as respects the transit of foreign grain as at the present time," reported the *Royal Cornwall Gazette* on September 2. Deliveries from the continent were running at fifty thousand quarters a week. Falmouth was also busy; the *Caledonia* was just one of twenty-one wheat cargoes from the Black Sea alone to arrive between August 24 and September 13, with many others arriving from Egypt, the Baltic ports, and elsewhere. Many speculators, who had purchased grain supplies back in the spring in the expectation of securing high prices and paying low duties in the British market, felt the first chill intimations of ruin as prices began to tumble.

Lord John Russell, debating the Corn Laws that February, had annotated the cost, before the imposition of duty, of shipping a quarter of Odessa grain to England. To the purchase price of the grain itself—twenty-six shillings—he added a ten-shilling freight charge and a further five shillings in additional charges, making a cost, per quarter, of forty-one shillings. And there was also the duty payable, which depended on the price received and was the major speculative element; to break even on Odessa wheat, the price received by the importer had to exceed the purchase and shipment cost of forty-one shillings by at least the amount payable in duty. In late August, when the average price being received was sixty-one shillings, on which eleven shillings duty was payable, the sums stacked up neatly enough: nine shillings clear profit was being made on every quarter imported. This converted, assuming an average ship's wheat cargo of twelve hundred quarters, to a tidy take of about £540.

The prospects were, however, improving daily. On September 1, the average wheat price officially dropped to sixty shillings, causing the duty to rise to twelve shillings; the erosion of the importers' precarious profit margin had begun. On September 8, the price dropped to fifty-eight shillings, hiking the duty to fourteen shillings. Importers were taking a hit. There was talk in the newspapers of foreign wheat being "forced off at ruinously low rates." "Immense losses, the result of a continuous fall in prices," were reported in the *Royal Cornwall Gazette*, which noted, "Serious failures have already been announced in the trade." On the fifteenth, the price fell again, to fifty-six shillings, pushing the duty to sixteen shillings.

By September 17, a corn trade reviewer would claim that the weather had "enabled the agricultural body to secure, in good condition, an immense quantity of wheat, barley, and oats." He was able, moreover, to account "the quality of the new grain as extremely good; indeed, it was seldom, or never, known to be finer." And in London, the Privy Council gave directions that special services of thanksgiving be held for the exceptional harvest.

But the grain importers were in no mood to celebrate by the end of September, when the price had slumped to fifty-three shillings, sending the duty to eighteen shillings. Now the sums involved in importing Odessa wheat to Britain made less palatable reading: forty-one shillings for purchase and shipment plus eighteen shillings duty added up to a cost of fifty-nine shillings per quarter, when wheat was fetching only fifty-three shillings. The importer, who would have made £540 just a month before, was now looking at a loss of £360.

The queen, meanwhile, suffered the indignity in late August of an intruder in her apartments at Windsor Castle. Thomas Quested, forty, of Maidstone, was dispatched to Tothill-Fields Prison, where he was visited by a medical officer who pronounced him perfectly sane except in his belief that he had title to a peerage.

"I am Lord Godolphin of D'Arcy,' Quested said, "and everybody knows it."

Amidst all this foment, Victoria resolved to depart for the relative peace of the Scottish Highlands. Meanwhile, its rapid depreciation was forcing the owners of the wheat cargo aboard the *Caledonia* to urgent decisions of their own. The paperwork does not survive to indicate whether the wheat belonged to Joseph Esplin in Arbroath or whether his vessel was merely the chartered carrier of another's interest. But that is of no immediate concern to us, who need only know that somebody was actively looking to minimize the loss threatened by the cargo's plunging value.

The solution was reported in the *Royal Cornwall Gazette,* which wrote that large quantities of grain "are passed upwards to be delivered by canal and railway to the interior of the country ... the holders trusting to find a better market for their corn." Wheat prices were holding up inland. Economics would decide the final destination for the *Caledonia*'s cargo, just as they had directed her to Odessa earlier that same summer. The market would dictate the *Caledonia*'s final orders: Stevenson Peter was to proceed, by way of the Severn and the recently completed Sharpness Canal, to the port of Gloucester, and land his cargo there.

Chapter ∞ 29

On the evening of August 29, 1842, as the crew of the *Caledonia* sat out their quarantine, the royal party boarded the *Royal George* at Woolwich Docks, disembarking at Edinburgh two days later. Victoria and Albert passed under triumphal arches erected in their honor and looked out on scenes "of peaceful industry, far removed indeed from those spectacles of outrage which have recently startled the peace of the English manufacturing districts." "Scotland," the prince wrote to his grandmother, "has made a most favourable impression upon us both. The country is full of beauty, of a severe and grand character." Five years later, the royal couple would confirm their lasting affection for Scotland by the purchase of Balmoral Castle to serve as the royal household's Highland retreat.

The royal party arrived one evening at Taymouth Castle, Perthshire, to a magnificent reception. Hundreds of spectators waved flags "from every spot and place on which a flag could possibly be placed." Bagpipers played, and at night the party was treated to "a splendid display of fireworks, and a blaze of bonfires from the heights." But the weather was set to change. Storms were already ravaging England, with lightning shows far outranking those artificial illuminations simultaneously witnessed over Taymouth. The broken weather reached Taymouth the following morning, with "dense clouds of mist completely concealing the summits of the surrounding hills and mountains.... Shortly after the sunrise, these misty clouds fell in alternate heavy showers and drizzling rain, filling the gravelly-bottomed ravines and beds of mountain rills with gushing streams of water."

It was the morning of September 8.

🕉

I had my own reasons for visiting Scotland. I took the train to Edinburgh and picked up a rental car, in which I bundled an overnight bag containing the few fragments I had managed to glean of my own unchronicled cast—newspaper cuttings, notes from Arbroath's church minutes, entries from the census of June 1841—hoping they might blossom in their rightful context and so put flesh on the spare bones of the *Caledonia*'s crew and their families.

Beyond Dundee the road followed the coast but at a distance, so stubbly wheat fields, freshly cut and pinned to the patchwork as if by the occasional trees or abandoned crofts at their corners, stretched to a distant sea glint. Approaching Arbroath, the road closed upon the shore and the fields gave way to an undulating golf links. Beyond a caravan park stood the mildewed barracks of a resort hotel, an amusement arcade, and a football stadium. Just before the harbor stood the Gothic signal tower, which housed the town museum but had once served as the shore station for the Bell Rock lighthouse, whose pencil form, far out at sea, winked through the soft summer afternoon.

I parked just before the harbor, near the lifeboat station. I looked over the sea wall onto a brief stretch of gently shelving beach. Stone steps led down to the ivory-colored sand. Nothing remained of the two bustling shipyards, proprietors Alexander Stephens and Arthur Smith, which had stood here during the 1840s. It was from Smith's yard that the *Caledonia* had been launched on Saturday, April 13, 1839. "The vessel," the *Arbroath Herald* reported, "breasted the billows in splendid style, amid the cheers of a large assembly of spectators. The *Caledonia* is as fine-looking a vessel as has been built here for many years. . . . We trust she may long 'plough the raging main' unscathed by disaster, and ever and anon return to her native port ladened with the riches of other climes."

So much for that.

I walked along the harbor front, a compact place with the forlorn air of a former bustle. A few remaining fishing boats were tied against the harbor walls, and lobster pots were stacked sporadically along the quay. Houses of red sandstone and slate roofs, with wide rows of chimney pots sprouting from their high gables, ran along the front. They must have been imposing once; now ferns and cactuses in plastic wicker containers, model sailing ships, and signs reading "Vacancies" showed through the net curtains. Plumes of smoke rose from shacks in small garden plots where racks of "smokies," the town's renowned smoked haddocks, were glimpsed. Streets stretched north, treeless canyons of red sandstone that culminated in bright glimpses of a chill sea.

I came to the foot of the High Street, hard by the shore, where noisy kids rode their bikes past the Golden Haddock fish shop and swerved to threaten the boldest of the gulls. In the window of the Mayfair hairstylists, a woman sat behind a magazine, behind sunglasses, and studiously ignored the crowd outside.

It was here, in a house long since demolished, that Bathia Wallace was recorded as living with her two-year-old son, Robert, and her mother, Hannah Buchanan, in the census of 1841. It is not much of a tableau, merely placing son, mother, and grandmother in a house on an Arbroath terrace on June 6, 1841. But to this brief family glimpse we can bring two additional facts: that Bathia was some three months pregnant with her second son; and that her husband, James, was aboard the *Caledonia*, en route from Marseilles to London. It may have been that Hannah had chosen to be close to her daughter during the pregnancy, to help with two-year-old Robert and to keep Bathia company in James's absence.

Hannah's husband was not listed as living at the house. John Peter, the father of Bathia, Stevenson, and four other children, variously gave himself as weaver and sailor. I guessed that he too must be away at sea, like his son and son-in-law, until I found him in the same census—but at an address on the other side of Arbroath, on Ponderlaw Street.

Nor was John Peter living alone. The census showed that another of his daughters, Ann, was living with him. And Ann had got herself into trouble. The Arbroath church minutes for June 29, 1841, recorded that "Ann Peter, unmarried, residing with her father, John Peter, a weaver, in Ponderlaw Street, confesses that she is with child and declares that the father of it is Charles Leitch, a baker."

Poor Ann; the nineteenth-century kirk's disapproval doubtless fell with formidable weight upon those who conceived out of wedlock. Poor Bathia, too, for the misfortune of one sister instantly reminded me of my doubts surrounding the other. Try as I might, I had been unable to place James and Bathia Wallace anywhere near each other in March 1841, when Bathia's second son, who I hoped had spawned a line of descent into the present, must have been conceived.

Not a portrait nor a single recollection survives of Bathia from which we might regretfully tease the suggestion of a wild destructive streak or reassure ourselves with some impression of her moral certitude. No choice, then, but to judge her by other nineteenth-century sailors' wives, who commonly bore illegitimate children during their husbands' lengthy absences. Such a misfortune had famously befallen Owen Chase, formerly mate of the Nantucket whaleship whose story inspired Melville's *Moby-Dick*.

Still, I did not wish such conclusions upon James and Bathia, and I cast around for the slightest indication of Bathia's innocence. Her best defense seemed to lie in the names by which she had christened the boy on January 5, 1842. Even the most brazen adulteress would have balked at naming an illegitimate son after her wronged husband. Moreover, by following the name James with that of Stevenson, she also recalled her brother and his close relationship with her husband, which, by her apparent infidelity, she was sure to have sundered.

Still, that argument constituted no kind of defense when set against the geographical distance that surely had separated them at the time of the boy's conception. That the mate had died without ever knowing his second son I could accept, but that the boy had not been his own struck me as a profounder tragedy, the brutality of domestic betrayal, than even what was to follow.

In a bid to save them, I went back to the original evidence one last time. The last crew list clearly stated that James Wallace had joined the *Caledonia* at London for the Marseilles voyage on March 4, 1841. From that day, it would be nine and a half months, or precisely 291 days, before the birth of the boy. A lengthy but entirely reasonable gestation period, this, but it did require Bathia to have been with her husband in London when he joined the *Caledonia*. Which seemed extremely improbable; no ordinary Arbroath woman, especially one with a two-year-old boy, would have made such a long journey in the late winter of 1841. It was more likely that Wallace had been home before joining the *Caledonia,* but the journey south to London, being a long one, pushed Bathia's gestation closer to ten months than nine and so only returned me to the unpalatable alternative.

I was about to resign myself to Bathia's disgrace when I noticed something. Halfway down the crew list, in the columns detailing where and when each man had joined the ship, a scribble broke the stack of dittos. Three crew members, David McDonald, Peter Sturrock, and Stephen Jones, had not joined up until March 18. And they had done so at Shields, Newcastle's port at the mouth of the Tyne. Marseilles may have been the final destination, but I had never considered the possibility that it was not the only one. The *Caledonia,* then, had initially headed north from London before making for her stated destination in the Mediterranean. She had called at Shields sometime in March (and was evidently there by the eighteenth), and left for Marseilles on April 3. Which meant that the *Caledonia* had been at Shields for at least a fortnight at precisely the time Bathia had most likely conceived. Which changed things, for Shields was only 160 miles south of Arbroath. Now James and Bathia were almost in reach of each other. There was a way of redeeming them. The question was this: would Stevenson Peter, a new master looking to impose himself, have granted his mate a few days' home leave during their time at Shields?

I was returning along Arbroath's front, past the harbormaster's office, when a modern memorial caught my eye. A brass plaque commemorated the crew of the motorized fishing vessel *Westhaven:* "Lost at Sea 10th March 1997. George Pattison (skipper), Mark Hannah, Alan Cunningham, Christopher Prouse." The hurt must still be keen. And for a moment, my pursuit of the *Caledonia* seemed like a distant indulgence.

Chapter ∽ *30*

And what of that cry, which could be heard across the quarantine pool as the returning funeral party bent their arms to the oars of the jollyboat?

According to "Remembrances": "The captain and all the crew, except the cabin-boy, went ashore to attend the funeral. During their absence the boy, handling in his curiosity the barometer, had broken the tube, and the whole of the quicksilver had run out." So it is that Hawker evoked William Tasker standing amidst the spilt mercury, which was scattered like silver buttons across the floor of the captain's cabin, and his cry of anguish seemed the natural consequence of his clumsiness.

The loss of the barometer, which measures atmospheric pressure, would crucially have deprived the master of his storm warning. We have, however, only Hawker's word that the incident happened. The barometer was certainly in widespread use by the 1840s. A naval officer who was called to the 1843 Select Committee on Shipwreck confirmed that "in all foreign traders, that is to say, ships that go distant voyages," there was "hardly one without a barometer." Add to this testimony the fact of the log-reckoners found in Stevenson Peter's dead grasp, which suggests some sort of reliance on nautical instruments, and it seems reasonable to assume the ship at least carried a barometer.

The fact of the breakage is more problematic, primarily because it was not mentioned by Le Dain. The Jerseyman was sure to have appreciated the significance of the barometer's loss in the light of subsequent events, and should therefore have recorded it in his wreck statement. Yet another Hawker invention, then, inserted to propel his narrative toward its tragic finale?

I could think of no reason Le Dain might have had for omitting the incident from his statement until I came across the letter of condolence Hawker wrote to David McDonald's kin in the aftermath of the wreck. Hawker wrote how Le Dain (together with McDonald) "used to attend upon the Captain in his cabin more than the rest." It seems that an understanding, even an affection of sorts, had existed between the master and Le Dain. Was it this that had caused Le Dain to omit the incident from his statement? Had he been protecting the dead master and his family from accusations of culpability—that the master had sailed without the replacement barometer that should have saved them all?

But just as we deal with one problem in Hawker's account of the barometer, another takes it place, this time concerning William Tasker. Hawker's mention of Tasker's "curiosity" toward the barometer strikes a false note, suggesting a boy fresh to the sea. But curious about a barometer after three and a half years at sea, as Tasker had been? Was it possible that something else entirely had drawn him to the barometer?

Could it be that word of the *Caledonia*'s final destination had already reached the crew by the night of the breakage? And had it occurred to William Tasker where the ship's route must take her—close to Lundy Island? Tasker had nothing but Lundy on his mind. He had to get there at all costs, and the only way he could see of even getting close was the possibility that bad weather would force the *Caledonia* to shelter in the island's lee. The east end of Lundy was certainly a recognized anchorage in weather from the north and west; according to one commentator, "on one occasion, 300 vessels were in sight, and 170 of good size anchored at once in the roadstead." Once there, there was always a hope he might be sent ashore and, slipping away, find his way to the mark on the map where the *Jenny*'s ivories and gold dust awaited him. Tasker knew that it was not in his gift to summon a storm, but he could do all in his power to ensure that should one arise, the master was surprised by it. Was it, rather than curiosity, that he knew the barometer's purpose only too well? Had he purposely broken it as the instrument that might keep him from Lundy? And cried out into the night, like a clumsy fool, to cover his tortured design?

It was certainly an obsessive's plan. Its success depended on numerous things, not least bad weather and the master's decision to make do without a replacement barometer. As it was, the weather on August 27, the day following the alleged breakage of the barometer, should have convinced Stevenson Peter of the excellent sense of replacing it. A fierce squall hit the area, which must have rocked the *Caledonia* in the quarantine pool. "At Falmouth, Penryn and in the neighbourhood," reported the *Royal Cornwall Gazette*, "the storm was fearfully near, the thunder in some cases following instantly on the flash." "In Falmouth Roads," the *Sherborne Mercury* reported, "such torrents of rain fell, with large pieces of ice, that small boats were obliged to be bailed to keep them from sinking." Lightning struck a mow of wheat at St. Anthony's, and one of oats at St. Just. Lightning killed two girls collecting blackberries near St. Austell and split the mast of a schooner at Par.

But Stevenson Peter had safely guided his ship across thousands of miles of ocean, and Gloucester being a mere three days away, he could surely make do without an expensive replacement barometer. He might, furthermore, have thought he had already suffered his share of bad luck, what with the loss of Tomaso Samuel. Besides, it had been an exceptional summer, and the weather once again seemed set fair when the *Caledonia* left Falmouth on the morning of September 7. It might even have been an auspicious omen that the port authorities got the master's name right—"*Caledonia*, Peter, Gloster"—on the departures list.

But it was September 10 before that same list was published in the newspapers. By then the *Caledonia* had run into a storm to dwarf that of August 27.

Chapter ❧ 31

I contacted David, who had cooked in the kitchens at Portledge before the sale of the house.

"Of course I remember the letter," he said. "And the nice wooden box it was displayed in, along with the bottle. It was on the stairs."

"But it's not there since they sold it."

"But the old owners will know exactly where it is."

"But they say they know nothing about it."

"But they can't do; they were so very proud of it. They were always going on about it."

"But they do." A pause.

"That is so very odd," said David.

The past was proving a tease. Facts rarely weathered confirmation; examine them, and they soon crumbled to presumption or speculation. Testimony seemed riddled by selective omissions. Even the words of the vicar did not keep their word, but freely indulged in fancies and untruths. And now a letter, preserved in a wooden display case in the sure confines of a country house only three years before, was somehow lost.

These were the times when only the promise of objects would do. Tangible and real, they felt like footholds on a teetering landslide. I imagined tracing them, and so felt my grip strengthen on the story. Some such objects—like the ship's portrait of the *Caledonia*—might never have existed. Others, like the Tasker letter bottle, had unaccountably disappeared. Which left me with the log-reckoners.

I might have been tempted to dismiss Stevenson Peter's log-reckoners as yet another of Hawker's imaginative flourishes. According to "Remembrances," the drowned master of the *Caledonia* was discovered—by Hawker—"lying placidly upon his back on the shore at Morwenstow." Each hand grasped "a small pouch or bag. One contained his pistols; the other held two little log-reckoners of brass." However, the 1903 edition of *Footprints* supplied a footnote that not only substantiated the log-reckoners, but confirmed their continuing existence some sixty years after the wreck. "These are still preserved," wrote editor Charles Byles. "They are little sand-glasses, shielded with brass, cylindrical in shape. The sand in one takes twenty-eight seconds to run, that in the other fourteen."

That the log-reckoners had evidently survived into the twentieth century, along with their stirring provenance, prompted the fleeting hope that I might even track them down, and by so doing hold the same objects that Stevenson Peter had grasped in his dying hand. Then I might even begin to feel I was getting close. I did not doubt that the log-reckoners had survived; such antiques were never thrown out, only exchanged or passed on. The danger was rather that they had been torn from their history, which was their only true asset, and had so become merely a pair of early-Victorian log-reckoners, without identifying marks, a fate from which it was most unlikely they could ever be retrieved.

The log-reckoners had the best part of a century to travel if I were ever to find them in the present. But I did not give up. One day, at the Bodleian Library in Oxford, I was reading the unpublished correspondence of Nicholas Ross of Kilkhampton and Cyril Wilkinson of Worcester College, Oxford.

Ross was actively seeking out new additions to his collection of Hawker memorabilia during the summer of 1956, when he had much to report to Wilkinson. It was what he wrote on August 13, however, that first sent my pulse racing: "I also hope soon to add to my collection those two log-reckoners which La Daine, Captain of the wrecked Caladonia, gave to Hawker for his services to the crew washed up on the

Morwenstow cliffs." No matter that the details were confused, and the spelling suspect; Ross clearly knew the whereabouts of the log-reckoners, and was bent on acquiring them. In a letter of October 4, 1956, he told Wilkinson that they were in the possession of Hawker's great-granddaughter: "While in London, we hope to contact Diana Byles again, and I expect to have from her the two log-reckoners mentioned in *Memories of a Cornish Vicar.*"

By November 5, when Ross wrote again to Wilkinson, the deed was done: "During our few days in London, we called—uninvited—on Diana Byles again.... I did manage to rescue those two little log-reckoners...." Diana Byles had a long history of mental illness. In 1957, Ross would write to Wilkinson how Diana had "got herself into trouble with her landlady and police before the Welfare people were called in. Miss Byles is now being well taken care of in a Mental Home. It is the best thing that could have happened." In the meantime, she was an unsuitable guardian of such treasures.

In the same letter, an adjacent asterisk directed Wilkinson to an additional description at the foot of the page: "Of brass, like two tiny hour-glasses or egg timers. They are much blackened, of course, but I hope soon to restore their nautical shine, as of old. These objects are perfect pets." Ross returned to the subject on April 15, 1958, when he described the log-reckoners as "most decorative ... They buzz with interesting associations." On April 26, Wilkinson replied, declining Ross's apparent offer of one of the log-reckoners. "I could not deprive you of it," he wrote, "and really should not know what to do with it. I am sure the pair should be kept together in your unrivalled collection, and should not be divorced."

The correspondence concluded with Wilkinson's death in 1960. But the letters had brought the log-reckoners another half-century closer to the present. And with their self-styled "rescue" by a guardian of the Hawker flame, there was now an excellent chance that they had survived, identifiable, into the present day.

The log-reckoners were not Ross's only acquisition in 1956. He had learned of the existence of a Miss Pitman, deaf, blind, and eccentric, who was said to possess considerable quantities of Hawker material; her sister had been married to one of the vicar's great-nephews. On July 4, Ross wrote to Wilkinson of a first visit to Miss Pitman, who lived in a hermit's isolation just south of Bude at Widemouth Bay, which even then was being hemmed in by caravans: "We found the little house completely hidden from view by tall battlements of pebbled concrete and the grounds so overgrown and wild that I almost expected to awaken the Sleeping Beauty.... We found her, a little, swarthy weazoned-up thing like an age-wrinkled wren, but charming and kind.... I took away as much as our bags could hold!" Ross's first haul, which included Hawker's Bible, photographs, letters, and first editions of several of his books, would prove a mere prelude to a later visit.

"Well, I've now again been through the briar and bramble and five-foot Valerian," Ross breathlessly told Wilkinson on July 11. "Eventually, I got in ... and her welcome was great! ... 'Take away anything,' she kept on muttering! I found Hawker's *Pickwick Papers* (1847 levant spine and corners) and a first edition of Baring-Gould's *Vicar of Morwenstow* ... then another first edition of *The Quest of the Sangraal*.... The afternoon was wearing on! ... And at this stage, something MOST strange—almost fey—came about. She ... seemed to become almost mischievous ... 'Pull aside that sofa for me,' she said with an impatient air. I looked towards the great grey sofa, and saw behind it a locked and closed and rather coffin-like, most forbidding cupboard. The sofa was shifted towards the window. She took from a bunch of keys at her waist—please do not think me romancing about these picturesque events—and opened the cupboard.... Really, if I had been at the mouth of an Inca mine, my excitement couldn't have been greater ... THE CUPBOARD WAS FULL OF MANUSCRIPTS! And I am far too much excited at this moment to go into any further detail or to even write clearly...."

Thirty years later, a pair of log-reckoners did not seem too much to expect.

Chapter ᪥ *32*

In the dawn, the rasp of anchor chain sounded across the water. It reached quarantine officers in their bunks on the lazaret, farmhands in the milking parlors, and servants raking hearth ashes in the rectory at St. Just as the rumble of distant thunder. The master of the *Caledonia,* squinting at the sky, made no such association. Though he knew he could not be sure, the weather seemed set fair.

The crew of the *Caledonia* were setting levers to the windlass and weighing anchor for the last time. In the quarantine pool, strands of mist snagged upon the trees where they crowded to the water's edge. A cormorant plunged into the still shallows, causing reluctant, oily ripples. Chimney smoke rose in vertical plumes that narrowed to the peak like cypress trees, reminding the crew, mustered on a foredeck glistening with the first dew of the autumn, of Mediterranean views they had lately seen. The men began to sing:

It's home and it's home, home fain would I be,
O, home, home, home to my own country.

The chain angled toward the vertical until the anchor lifted free of the seabed, and the ship's bows swung to face the distant harbor entrance where a ruffle line marked the open sea. But Stevenson Peter's practiced eye also made out the band of wind-chiseled wavelets running up the main channel of the Carrick Roads, signaling a southerly wind, with a touch of east in it. Slow progress as far as the Lizard, then, though, a wind that should serve them excellently if it were to hold.

The ebb tide carried the *Caledonia* across the quarantine pool. As she ran silently under the stern of the sleeping lazaret, where the quarantine boats were tethered, the *Caledonia*'s crew came to the gunwale. Remembering how the fat official had delayed burial of their shipmate, whom many of them had come to like, they emptied their night buckets into his boat.

The sails filled as the wind found them, and the *Caledonia* worked her way down the harbor. She left the Black Rock to starboard and came to the east. She passed St. Anthony's light and emerged from the headland's shadow into sudden sunshine. The crew turned their faces toward the sun's warmth, seeking it out for the first time since leaving England over a year ago. From deep in their sea chests they had turned out jackets, musty from disuse, to combat the unfamiliar chill of the morning, and turned up collars as they gathered about the windlass. David McDonald had wrapped the tortoise in Tomaso Samuel's spare trousers and stowed it in a hammock.

All morning the *Caledonia* worked her slow way to the south, where the rigs of fishing luggers, Yankee packets, fruiters, and men-of-war rose above the horizon. A haze was gathering in the western sky. Stevenson Peter observed his ship. The yards were braced close to the wind, the sails were trimmed, and the crew were hard at work. David Wallace was caulking the deck, where an oakum seam had worked loose. McDonald had squirmed his slim form into the main hold, where he was checking the cargo. The behind of William Tasker protruded through the galley's open door, where he scrubbed the floor with intent, as if to erase his recent disgrace by the vigor of his brushstrokes alone. Stevenson Peter noted the ordered industry with a profound satisfaction. He truly believed, in these last days of their long voyage, that the vessel was his once more. And for that, the first mate took much of the credit.

It seemed to James Wallace that he had been shaking off a dark dream for days now. The sensation, though he was not a swimmer and did not know the feel of the water, was of resurfacing into the light from great depths, bubbles trailing from him. Now he understood that the way back to himself had begun even at Galata. It was on the night of Tomaso Samuel's wounding, the darkest moment, that Wallace had resolved coffee would never again pass his lips. But it was not until Samuel's burial that the mate's guilt and self-loathing, acute as a blade, was blunted and the pain began to fade. For the last several nights he had been sleeping again, and with every morning his old spirit seemed further restored. Now, he remembered what it was to take a ship to sea, and to run her to her next port with all the excellence he could muster. He strode the deck with all his old ebullience and authority. Orders streamed from him, as if to make up for their long absence.

"The fo'c'sle hatch," he commanded. "Throw it open."

It was not that the place smelled of Thomas Samuel's rot—it had been emptied of the wretched man's soiled bedding, and thoroughly scrubbed some days since—but the salt smell of the sea had not yet repossessed it. Its very cleanliness was a discouragement to the crew, who only entered it to make brief forays to their sea chests and even preferred the shelter of the cramped galley when it rained. But though they might have shunned the fo'c'sle during their mild nights in port, they would need it in the sea nights ahead, as they made to the north through a waning summer where the chill gathered fast, prompting thoughts of home.

It was Wallace's memory that had suffered most markedly, blurring into a long dormancy. Whole regions of his mind had closed down, as if to allow that sleep-starved faculty to concentrate on the sating of his immediate needs. But it recently had begun to return, surprising him with its secrets, and as he looked out over the water, he suddenly found himself thinking of his woman for the first time in months.

Sixteen months earlier, with the crew gathered on the Shields quayside, the master had shaken his head.

"I can't spare a man of you," he said. "You've a ship to ready for Marseilles." Besides, he was new to the ship and the men must know him as he was.

"But Jones is only three months married," somebody murmured. The protest died away and the men returned to their tasks on leaden legs. It was not until the evening that the master called the mate to his cabin.

"So Jones is newly wed as that, Jim?" he asked.

"Aye. He is that."

"Then he should go. Three days. But only him, him and any other family men. Whoever that might mean." He shot a wink at his smiling brother-in-law.

"And you'll remember me to my sister," the master shouted as Stephen Jones and the first mate slung their bags and strolled down the quayside the next morning.

They took the steamer to Dundee, where they overnighted in a frozen inn. In the morning, though the tickets were dear, they traveled by the new railway for the first time in their lives. They sat gingerly on the seats, as if their sailors' trousers might mark them, and marveled at the frosted fields beyond the window, moving faster than they had ever known.

At Arbroath, the sky above the abbey ruins was full of mewing seagulls and a bitter wind funneled down the lanes. Wallace came to the little house at the foot of the High Street, and as he passed through the door, he heard her rising.

"Robert. Your father," she said, and they enfolded the boy between them in their embrace. In the night, as he lay beside her and the lighthouse flashed faintly at the window, James Wallace was blissfully aware of this soft time snatched from his seafaring life: his woman's love, but a ship waiting.

In the morning, when he said good-bye, his son had asked when he would be coming back. And now he was to see them again, and his new son for the first time, and his heart lifted with the rise of the bows.

"Closer to the south," he hollered at the helm, for it seemed the wind had shifted slightly.

In the early afternoon, as she rounded the Lizard, McDonald served up a spare lunch. As the great bight of Mount's Bay came into view, William Tasker bit into a large apple and nudged Edward Le Dain.

"Lundy," he whispered. "Can we see Lundy yet?"

They passed the Longships lighthouse at the Land's End in the afternoon and came to the northeast with a freshening wind, which now blew directly out of the west. The clouds, Stevenson Peter observed, had begun to thicken and turn a leaden color; they were in for rain. The sea had got up and where the waves crested, they now collapsed into ribbons of white. But the wind was astern, and the ship was making excellent progress under a full set of sails. Now they could make out the yellow slash that was the long beach at St. Ives and the boats awaiting the great pilchard shoals that were the season's boon, turning the bay to rust. As the sun set, it breached a gap in the clouds astern and flooded the face of the mate as he made his way aft. He took the wheel from McDonald, sending him forward so that only the master shared the quarterdeck. Wallace spoke after a pause.

"I'm sorry," he told the man at his back. "I'm truly sorry for the trouble I caused you."

For a long time he heard only the hiss of the waves, and the wind buffeting the canvas.

"My sister is your wife," said Stevenson Peter finally. "And your son, who is my nephew, carries our two names." He laid a hand upon his brother-in-law's shoulder. It had been nine months, he briefly realized, since he had laid his hand there, on their departure from Rio. Then the business of the ship was calling for his attention, and their reconciliation was done.

"We should get the royals down," he said, scanning a failing sky. "And a reef in the topgallants."

An hour later, somewhere off Boscastle, the storm hit them.

Chapter ∽ 33

From the drawer in the kitchen, Dennis Heard removed a small package wrapped in tissue paper and carefully unfolded it to reveal a shard of glass. "This came from a window in the house," Dennis explained. "It was broken before my birth but the family always kept it as a memento."

Dennis handed it to me; the unmistakable signature "D H Copinger" had been scratched across the glass.

I had walked north from Morwenstow that August morning, following a rutted inland track past isolated farmsteads where horseflies whirlpooled above the pats that crusted in the yards and glossy silage bales sweated within their plastic cocoons. A sheep dog barked at me from the doorway of a concrete farm shed before its unseen owner cursed it to silence.

The verges were thick with cow parsley, and the vermilion and vanilla rosettes of honeysuckle, fading now. Seed pods clustered around the stems of tottering foxgloves, burned out but for the last purple flowers at their tips. I trailed my hand in a field of ripening wheat that edged the path; the ear I picked had turned tawny along its spine, but the corns toward its edges were still flecked with green. Where the cliff contours allowed, the sea showed as a series of blue bowls, some deep, some shallow as plate. I dropped into the steep combes of Cornakey and Marsland, where a tangle of ash, oak, and sycamore cast a dank shadow over the fallen yellow stalks of old bluebells, and a silent stream that had not known rain for two weeks limped through dense foliage toward the sea.

Robert Hawker had often passed this way. I traced his route to Marsland Mouth, where he claimed to have seen a strange "swift, brown, rough shape" near the "all-but-ruined-hut" of the old mill there, which caused him to trace a shaky sign of the Cross in the air above the ears of his old gray mare. This morning, however, there was only a walker eating a chocolate bar on the shore. Outside the mill, which had long since been restored as a summer home, a pair of trousers hung to dry, its pockets turned out as if they had been rifled.

At Marsland, where Hawker would have turned inland toward Welcombe Church, I kept to the coast path. The path led to high ground where clot-black clouds strobed heather and bracken, then zigzagged seawards. At Welcombe Mouth a stream guttered toward a waterfall at the low cliff, and a ramped path led down to the shore. A big sea broke, then retreated with a sonorous mutter of back-raked pebbles. At the top of the beach, plastic bottles, driftwood, and an oil-smeared rubber glove missing its little finger had collected. Rounded gray stones, some large as cushions and mostly ribbed with a single vein of white quartz, had formed a barrage above the tideline, which landslided as I crossed. The half tide revealed waist-high rocks and sunken yellow sand that ran seaward in alternating aisles, patterning the bay with tiger stripes. With their uniformly canted sides that rose to crest before falling sheer away, the rocks were a petrified surf broadsiding the breaking waves they resembled.

It was said that the fabled West Country wrecker and smuggler Cruel Copinger had himself been wrecked at Welcombe Mouth. In Hawker's account, Copinger made the shore "with stalwart arm and powerful chest," and stunned those gathered at notice of the wreck by leaping into the saddle of a local maid and spurring the steed to her nearby home. Copinger was freely received into the home of the girl, whose name was Ann Hamlyn. But he did not return the family's kindness, bringing them brutally to heel, marrying Ann, and making a wreckers' den of their home. He turned this coast into his personal fiefdom, complete with secret lairs, caves in the cliffs where "sheep were tethered to the rock, and fed on stolen hay and corn till their flesh was required for a feast; kegs of brandy and hollands were piled around; chests of tea; and iron-bound sea-chests." Copinger's departure was quite as dramatic as his arrival. Even as the forces of law finally closed upon him, he was snatched from the shore by a barque, which faded from sight "like a spectre or a ghost."

A fiction plucked straight from the pages of a Gothic melodrama? But Copinger was not easily forgotten. Stories were still being told of him in the Hartland area into the early years of the twentieth century. The resonance has since faded, though the Copinger name is still employed as a psychological stick with which to caution badly behaved local children. He has become the region's bogeyman. The burning of a hay barn or a reckless driving accident may also invoke his name, as if such incidents were persistent legacies from his malign reign here in the final years of the eighteenth century.

A local Hartland historian, writing in 1903, cut a commendably factual swathe through the swirls of myth that cling to Copinger when he wrote that his ship was wrecked "probably at Welcombe Mouth, the end of the romantic glen which separates Welcombe from Hartland, on December 23rd 1792." A probable place and date, then, which seemed to imply that the Copinger legend's apparently fantastic content had a remarkable basis in fact. The historian even noted that Copinger's "chief cave was in the cliff at Sandhole," which still showed on the map two miles north of Welcombe.

Steps had been cut up the steep cliff path out of Welcombe Mouth. At the top, the path ran close to the cliff edge, where gray screes slung between outcrops of rock spilled into space. Fretful sheep, scraggy with blue dye, bumped the fence line as I approached. Hanging kestrels worked the bracken and gorse. Beyond Embury Beacon, Lundy rose steep from the sea. Inland, I could see the farmhouse, barns, and cottages of Southole gathered around the upper reaches of a wooded combe.

At Sandhole, the cliffs gave way to irregular terraces of rocky outcrops, which stepped down from the heights toward the shore. Initially, the path was hesitant, traversing the descent as a grassy sward, a gentle slalom edged by thickets of gorse, bracken, and thorn. But the moment it fixed upon a more direct descent and headed straight down the slope, the path choked. Undergrowth crowded in. The earth-cut steps' risers, staked planks, yawned forward, and the stairways that negotiated the steepest sections had broken free from their fixings to hang in space, bouncing and creaking beneath my weight.

The path ended at a landslide, which fell a hundred feet to the shore. I tested a boot on the slope of stone and damp soil beneath me. It gave way, but gradually, so that I entrusted myself to it, my weight carrying me downward at escalator rate. I reached the shore and looked out across rocky terraces. A jade-green fishing net lay in a crevice high above the water. It had wrapped itself around a tree trunk, barkless and gray, in a bolus of weights and plastic-football floats so knotted that the trawler-men, despairing of it, had cut it free. The net had snared a crab, whose feelers protruded from the carapace, stirring feebly in the wind.

It was some time before I noticed the wreck. Though it lay only yards away, the ship's barnacle-encrusted remnants had long begun to submit to the shoreline's contours. Not much remained: a rusted engine casing, a few scattered guardrails, and, farther out, slabs of pig-iron ballast that had dropped from the vessel's bilges as the rocks opened her up. It suddenly occurred to me that my fruitless search for Copinger's cave had brought me to the wreck of the *Goliath*.

The thirty-five-ton drifter, traveling from Lorient in Brittany, had come ashore in the early hours of March 16, 1969, a few months before the first moon landing. It was a misty night, with a twenty-knot north-easterly wind throwing up lumpy seas. The *Goliath* hit the Sandhole rocks with what the captain, Jean Montfort, would describe as *"un choc brutal."* He immediately left his bunk, ordered the engine to be cut, tried unsuccessfully to send an SOS signal, and ordered his crew to abandon ship. Montfort was about to follow his six crewmen into the inflatable when a heavy sea overturned it and swept it away. Montfort, huddled in a corner of his listing ship's flooded wheelhouse, could make out his crew clinging to the upturned dinghy.

Four of the men made it to the shore, crawling from the sea within yards of where I stood. They thus found themselves at the foot of the only recognized ascent between Welcombe and Speke's Mouth, and began to climb through briars and bracken in a chill darkness. When they eventually reached the road, the exhausted men divided into pairs and set off for help in different directions.

The two who headed north reached the farm at Elmscott after half a mile. John Goaman, one of the farmer's sons, had just left the milking parlor in the half-light of dawn when two strangers appeared from the direction of Welcombe. The men were soaked, their clothes in rags. Goaman initially figured them to have suffered a car crash. It was only when the men gestured that they had been in the water that Goaman rushed to rouse the family and called the coast guard. The sailors were given hot baths and were fed. An ambulance shortly arrived to ferry them to the hospital in Bideford.

If the whispered allegations and raised eyebrows that constitute local lore are to be believed, the pair who headed south encountered an altogether different reception when they first reached a habitation, the farmhouse at Southole. Southole had once been a well-tended place, with orchards and a stream that ran between cultivated fishponds. By 1969, however, it had deteriorated into a collection of ivy-swathed barns, shabby cottages, and rusted machinery. Southole, clinging to the narrow lane that runs south through ash trees and pine plantations to Welcombe Mouth, seems to have long since had something of a wreckers' notoriety, even amongst locals. A Hartland man wrote up his memoirs as an octogenarian in 1883, in which he specifically attributed to a Southole man the familiar wrecker's refrain: "Bad times indeed now, the sea is as poor as a millpond."

The popular, whispered version of the events surrounding the loss of the *Goliath* has it that the farmhouse door at Southole was slammed in the face of the two shivering survivors when they knocked upon it that March dawn. That slammed door has acquired considerable local resonance, serving to confirm how the entrenched suspicions of the past have endured unto the modern day. It recalls the Hamlyns, who once took in a stranger some three miles from here only to be made outsiders in their own home, and suggests that a lesson, once learned, was not forgotten in these parts. According to Hawker, a Morwenstow parishioner named Peter Burrow had expressed similar reservations about the survivor from the *Caledonia*. On the morning of the ship's loss, Burrow advised Hawker against taking Le Dain in by quoting the local saying:

> *Save a stranger from the sea*
> *And he'll turn your enemy.*

I scrambled back up the landslide and set off up the path. At the road that the French sailors had reached thirty years before, I turned north. I passed the farmhouse at Elmscott and followed the lane to Milford. There, I took a track that ran along the upper slopes of a steep combe until I came to a farmhouse of whitewashed stone that stood alone, and I passed through the garden gate. The house, called Galsham, had once been the home of the Hamlyn family.

Dennis Heard answered the door. He led me through dark passages into a high-ceilinged, timber-paneled sitting room. A wind bellowed in the chimneys and flogged the roses against the window. The television seemed like an intrusion from a future as yet undivined, for the past was palpable in this house where Ann Hamlyn had brought her shipwreck survivor two days before Christmas in 1792: the horse steaming in the yard, a brine-sodden stranger, towels and steaming broth, and unlikely company at Christmas.

The Heard family had farmed at Galsham for several generations. Dennis enthused over the Copinger connection, warming to the elemental figure whose memory wreathed the house in a dark romance. He had stalked Copinger in local libraries and record offices, and had found evidence of a real person. There was the register entry on the marriage, at Hartland parish church, of "Daniel Herb Coppinger and Ann Hamlyn of this parish married by licence this third day of August in the year One Thousand Seven Hundred and Ninety Three"—the summer after

Copinger had been shipwrecked at Welcombe Mouth. He had also found the will of "Ann Copinger, nee Hamlyn, late of Hartland but now of Barnstaple in the county of Devon, widow, made in January 1832." Ann Copinger had requested "to be interred in the Parish Church of Hartland, and to be laid by the side of my mother in the same grave with the remains of my late young friend Alice Western, and I desire to be born to my grave by twelve poor men who are to be paid two shillings and sixpence each and to have a pair of gloves." In the light of her request to be buried alongside mother and friend, the absence of reference to her late husband seemed pointed, as if she were well rid of that elemental malevolence. Then Dennis moved toward the kitchen drawer.

The dates, the places, the paperwork, and now the glass shard insistently made Copinger real, and in retrieving him from myth substantiated the allegations against him.

"I'd say it definitely happened," said Dennis Heard, pulling on a cigarette.

I was not sure whether he was referring to wrecking by false lights or to the Copinger legend. But the two seemed to have cohered. And if Copinger were true, what of his kind? Were they clinging to his practices fifty years later, when the *Caledonia* approached her end here? Was this what Hawker had been hiding? That the crew of the *Caledonia*, who had died on his glebe, had died at the hands of his men?

Chapter ∞ 34

The storm of September 7 and 8, 1842, raged across Britain for a day and night.

The first that the crew of the *Caledonia* knew of it was at nine o'clock on the evening of the seventh, when, according to Edward Le Dain, "a sudden squall of wind and rain came on." Nor was Le Dain alone in describing as sudden "the dreadful thunder storm of Wednesday night." The newspapers reported that the temperature that day in London had been only a "moderately high" 68 degrees Fahrenheit. A few drops of rain fell over the capital at five o'clock, but the skies "gave no indication of a storm at that time." At about half past eight, "the lightning became more brilliant and the flashes followed each other in rapid succession." One "flash of lightning struck a stack of chimneys in Ben Jonson's Fields," and took the back of a house clean away. The lightning also struck a postman, threw a woman into the Thames at Blackwall, and knocked a policeman to the ground on the Barking Road. The *Times* reported that the market gardens of Hackney, Bow, and Stratford "were completely inundated." Poplar and Limehouse suffered "serious destruction of property among the ships and wharfs of the river side."

Oxford suffered a lightning storm that seems to have far outranked that same night's illuminations over Taymouth Castle in Perthshire. "About half past eight," wrote a correspondent, "the effect of the electric fluid was truly magnificent. . . . From Magdalene Bridge, the whole of the churches and public buildings . . . were beautifully illuminated. As we

watched the sudden and quick returning movements of the sublime element, and its gradual growth in intensity as it darted to and fro, and higher
and higher among the masses of dark clouds amidst which it seemed to
spout, the thunder peels became louder and nearer, the clouds blacker and
denser, and the fast descending rain and the rising winds gave token that
no ordinary storm was preparing."

Along the east coast, where shipping found shelter from the worst of
the winds, damage was limited. Although several vessels "had their whole
suit of sails, rigging, anchors and cables carried away," no ships were reported lost. The *Mountaineer,* from Demerara, did go aground near Mar-
gate but was pulled off and, despite some damage, towed up the Thames
to safety. Along the exposed west coast, however, shipping felt the full
brunt of the storm. At Southport, Lancashire, the *Alfred and James Grif-
fifths* was driven ashore. In West Wales, the *Falkirk* was wrecked on
Skomer Island, the *Molly Lloyd* in Ramsay Sound, and "the mast and
part of the hull of a smack . . . supposed to have foundered and the crew
perished" was found near the North Bishop Rock. Of the brig *Cornubia,*
which had sailed from Swansea for Waterford in Ireland prior to the seventh, only the upturned jollyboat was found. A "poor fellow" was blown
from the crosstrees of the Milford Haven packet; another was lost off a
Dutch boat near Cardiff, and a mackerel fisherman was drowned off
Portmadoc in Cardigan Bay.

Many ships were lost in the Bristol Channel. The *Jersey Lass* went
onshore at the entrance to Bridgwater Bay. Two ships sailing from
Gloucester, the *Auckland* and the *Halcyon,* were wrecked on the Gore
Sands near Porlock, with all hands lost. The *Friendship* was wrecked in
Croyde Bay. The *Ann,* from Arklow to Newcastle, limped into Bideford
for desperately needed repairs. Her Majesty's cutter *Swan,* engaged in
smuggling prevention near Clovelly, was another victim of the storm's
sudden onset. "The vessel," reported the *Times,* "was riding at anchor,
apparently in perfect safety, when suddenly the weather grew tempestu-
ous and before the anchor could be weighed and the canvas set, she
was thrown among the breakers and became a total wreck. The crew,

with considerable difficulty, succeeded in saving their lives." The *Gazelle* went ashore in Shipload Bay, just east of Hartland Point. The *Alexandria*, headed for Neath, was driven ashore just south of Hartland Point, at Speke's Mill.

And the *North Devon Journal* reported that "a large vessel loaded with grain was wrecked at Sharps Nose, and with one exception, the whole of the crew were lost; the poor fellow who was washed ashore was in so exhausted a condition as to be unable at the time to give any information as to the name of the ill-fated vessel or number of the crew."

∽◌∽

I met Terry, master of the *Elsa*, on the quay beside the foot of Bude's canal, where the old lock gates sealed it from the sea. He kept his little red-and-yellow boat just below the gates, in the tidal creek where Bude's occasional fishing fleet congregated. The *Elsa* lay beached among orange mooring buoys and shallow puddles of stranded seawater. Weeds draped over bow ropes had dried into little wonky tents, green and threadbare.

The low tide also revealed a fine sandy beach. Wet dogs ran among striped windbreaks or squatted to coil down turds out in the open spaces where families played cricket. Toward the sea, where the beach narrowed, young men surfed the breakers that crowded the sandy entrance between the rocks. On the higher ground stood terraces of Victorian guesthouses and hotels, dilapidated now, which testified to Bude's popularity in the nineteenth century; it was less a lie than mere exaggeration when Hawker called the town "the Brighton of the West."

But the beach had been attracting crowds with quite different interests since much earlier times. The sand at Bude, with its high content of lime, salt, and crushed seashell, had long been considered an excellent top-dressing for the fields; wagons, packhorses, and herds of mules and asses thronged here at low tide throughout the spring tilling season. Bude sand's manuring qualities were so admired that a canal was built in 1828 to carry the precious fertilizer into the farming hinterland around Holsworthy.

The canal served a secondary purpose. It had always been to Bude's disadvantage that it was a drying-out port. In his 1602 *Survey of Cornwall*, Richard Carew recommended the place "only to such small shipping as bring their tide with them, leaving them dry when the ebb hath carried away the salt water." Low-tide beaching left hulls liable to damage; it also complicated the loading and unloading of cargoes including coal, manure, slates, and wood. Thus the canal also came to serve as Bude's improved port along its lower reaches where vessels could shelter within the sea gates, closed against the ebbing tide, and tie up against the wharves with permanent water beneath their keels.

The canal could do nothing, however, to ease the notorious sea approach to Bude. On either side of the narrow entrance lay treacherous rocks. To the north was the Coach Rock, and to the south the Barrel and Chapel Rocks; these last two had been incorporated into Bude's breakwater when it was rebuilt in 1839. Vessels of any draught could enter Bude only at high tide, and even so some high tides did not provide enough water for them to do so. When the so-called Tide Waiter finally flew his signal flag from Compass Point, ships were forced to follow the channel of the creek bed, which ran perilously close to the end of the breakwater. To help them into harbor, "hobblers" in rowboats met the ships at the entrance and took ropes from them, which they fastened to warping posts along the channel, and so gradually drew the ships to safety.

The *Elsa* drew only two feet, which meant Terry should be able to leave port two hours before high tide. We loaded fishing rods, diesel cans, and meat pies as the tide began to lap about the hull, and clambered on board.

"Now we wait for water," said Terry, who was originally from Launceston and worked in the building trade. He had moved here some years back, and took the *Elsa* out to fish for mackerel or for pollock, ling, and sea bass off the deep-water reefs when the weather allowed, which was not often.

"We're lucky today," said Terry, looking out at the low swell. "More than half the times I prepare the boat, and the sea gets up before I can get her out." The tide came under the hull, and after a few false bumps the *Elsa* began to float. Terry started up the aged diesel engine, and we cast off her mooring ropes.

She was about fourteen feet long and wooden, with a high gunwale and a bow window against the spray. Terry made his cautious way down the channel, following the breakwater toward the green-painted Bass beer barrel that perched high on a rusting post above its namesake rock. Here, in the sea squeeze, the swell built suddenly. Terry gunned the engine, and the *Elsa* lifted her prow toward the breaking waves.

"Sometimes," Terry shouted above the engine noise, "the sea's like a block of flats just here. Most times, I'm happier watching it from the quayside."

The *Elsa* rode two high waves before the swell moderated, and Terry turned to the north, following the coast toward Sharpnose. As he set his fishing rods and sat back in the warmth with a cigarette, I turned my gaze toward the shore. Beyond Bude, the cliffs had begun to rise again. They presented a gray wall to the sea, almost sheer, and were sometimes footed by sudden protruding slabs where waves broke. Among the layers of bedded sediment that constituted the cliff face, I could see sudden compressed folds and rocks strikingly patched with parallel scores. The lines of the cliff tops showed against the sky as gentle calligraphic undulations, broken only by sheep gathered on the sward of late summer. Below them, holidaymakers had colonized the brief beaches at Northcott Mouth, Sandy Mouth, and Duckpool. Then we were passing Stanbury Mouth, where a corpse which Hawker would bury had come ashore from the *Bencoolen* in 1862.

Now Sharpnose was in view. It showed quite as distinctively as it had from the north—until the great bulk of Henna Cliff loomed beyond to steal its silhouette. Soon I could see the rocks scattered about its foot, black protuberances where the white water spun and surged. Terry throttled back. He would go no closer. I stared at the rocks, waiting for something to happen. I had hoped that approaching this place from the sea, just as the *Caledonia*'s crew had once done, might help me to close on their experience—that this was the moment when I might come to know what the helpless men had felt as Sharpnose loomed above them. I now understood how foolish I had been to assume that merely taking to a boat might span our different circumstances. They had come here engineless, in a night storm, and found themselves on a lee shore they could not escape. I had bright skies and a moderate sea, and had a meat pie in my hand, and when Terry asked if I'd seen enough, I nodded and he gunned the engine, turning in a circle toward the south.

Still, the outing served to remind me that, even in these final few miles, it might have ended so differently. As I had learned from the newspapers, there had been two other ships in exactly the same predicament that ferocious night. Chance had it that the two vessels, headed in opposite directions, should converge somewhere near Bude. The brig *Elizabeth*, 186 tons, was making from London with passengers for Newport, where she was to load coal and iron for the West Indies. The sixty-five-ton schooner *St. Agnes*, of that North Cornish port, was homeward-bound from Port Talbot with coal. It seems, as the storm rose, that the two vessels settled upon the same plan of action. They would make for Bude.

In his 1835 *Pilot*, J. W. Norie made no mention whatsoever of Bude's port facilities, dismissing the place merely as "Bude Bay, in which there is little or no tide." Some masters cannot even have known of Bude's existence, and fewer yet would have considered the port an option in such conditions. The storm was funneling huge breakers into the narrow gap between the rocks, where they broke into furious seas of seething energy in the containment of Bude's harbor. Forget hobbler boats; there was no chance whatsoever of vessels reaching the quayside within the breakwater, let alone the greater shelter beyond the canal gates. Any such attempt was sure to have ended in disaster, most probably on the Barrel Rock at the breakwater's end.

As luck would have it, however, Captain Pearce of the *St. Agnes* had formerly been master of a trader out of Bude. He knew the port well. He also knew the neighboring coasts, which would have told him that Bude was his one chance that night, albeit a poor one; such wild conditions bent him to a course of absolute audacity. It was not his intention to try for the quayside, as he was perfectly aware that he could only fail in such an attempt. He would simply point his vessel up the beach north of the breakwater, hoping that she could avoid the worst of the rocks scattered there and drive high enough into the shallows that his crew, and even the ship herself, might be saved. He knew from experience the best line of approach to the harbor, and it was his great good fortune that the tide was full in the early hours of September 8, which should help carry his ship higher up the beach and so allow him a fighting chance of success.

The newspapers included the main narrative elements in their brief coverage of the drama. There was Captain Pearce's crucial familiarity with the port; the fact that no ship as large as the *Elizabeth* had ever entered that harbor; and the cheers of the assembled landsmen at the ships' safe arrival. But they omitted to explain how Captain Timothy Pike of the *Elizabeth* was persuaded to follow Pearce's brazen charge into Bude. It is inconceivable that Pearce could have successfully signaled his intentions to the *Elizabeth* in such conditions, or that he could have assured her master that he was at least qualified by his familiarity with that port to try for it.

And so I imagine Timothy Pike and the shambles of his ship—the shredded sails, the flailing sheets, the longboat snapping furiously against its lashings—as another curling wave broke over her windward bow and boiled along the deck, seeking out the hatches where whimpering passengers offered up prayers in the cabin darkness. Then, to the astonishment of the crew, the little schooner they had espied to the north sometime earlier, a shadow butting at the wind quite without impression, was a sudden specter leaping across their bows, running to leeward beneath those few sails that were not yet shreds of streaming canvas.

"In the name of God!" hollered Pike. "What is the holy fool doing?"

The driving wind was right behind her now, so she surfed the waves toward the shore, leaving a wide white train of trampled water. Pike looked beyond the schooner, but saw only breakers there and the shore's dark mass above them. And then it came to him, sure and strong, that they might save themselves:

Help me if he doesn't know something!

He ran to his helmsman. "Come off the wind!" he yelled and pointed in the direction of the schooner. "Follow her in!"

The helmsman started. The crew turned as one.

"Follow the schooner!" he insisted. The helmsman started again.

"Where, sir?"

To hell or salvation, thought Pike. "Wherever she's headed!" he shouted.

"She's headed for the rocks, sir!"

"Do it, man! Just do it! Stand by to square the yards!"

The helmsman put the wheel hard over, and the men rushed to free the sheets. As the ship came off the wind there was a terrible rending in the rigging. The trysail had gone with its mast, and lay in a chaos of streaming ribbons over the stern. For an instant the ship lay broadside to the sea before her bow turned away from the wind and, picking herself up, surged toward the shore. Pike could feel every pair of eyes turn toward him.

"The chart!" hollered Pike. "Bring me the chart!" *God help me if I'm wrong.* Then the forward lookout was running aft, urgent words spilling soundlessly from his mouth.

"A light, sir!" he shouted. "There's a light on the bow she making for."

"Good lad," thundered Pike. He staggered forward; the light that he could see, though he did not know it, was on Bude's Chapel Rock. Straining his eyes, he thought he could make out seething water just to port of it and a grayness above it that might just be a break in the cliffs. Then he was working his way aft again, and casting his arm toward the schooner for the helmsman's benefit when the chart he had requested, ripped down the middle by the storm, fled past him into the night like a great flapping bird.

Every moment, the shore appeared more distinct. The men could discern the breakwater now and the boiling white surge contained within

it. Then they could see the houses, and the swinging lantern lights clustering along the shore. They were barely a hundred yards behind the
schooner when she arrived at the harbor entrance. She had taken a line so
close to the rocks that it seemed certain that she must be lost there. But
at the very last moment, as the sea piled up around her and the rocks
loomed above her masts, the schooner came hard to port. For a moment
she was lost from sight in a deep trough. Then she was beyond the breakwater, the seas pouring from her decks. And as her wayward bow came
round again, the master finally understood where the schooner was leading them.

"He's running her straight up the beach!" he shouted. He ran to join
the helmsmen at the wheel.

"Passengers on deck!" the mate hollered. From the companionway, a
bedraggled, drawn, and unsteady crowd emerged. They looked about
them at the broken sky and the closing shore and felt the wind whistling
in their damp pockets and tugging at their hair, but nobody spoke. Hands
clamped around crucifixes and lockets as the master held firm to the
schooner's course.

"Hard a-port on my word," he cried. "On my word."

The rocks loomed above them, and it seemed the ship must burst to
pieces there until the master called out, and a huddle of men threw their
weight at the wheel. The ship came hard to port. She cleared the breakwater rocks, her bowsprit by mere inches, on the lift of a great cresting
wave that dumped the ship in a watery confusion. Now, as another wave
picked up her stern and the men at the helm heaved at the wheel to bring
her to face the shore, a chorus of prayers arose from the passengers.
Then the ship was racing into the breakers and at the last moment, as the
sea seemed to drain away from her sides, the master yelled out.

"Here we go! Brace yourselves!"

The *Elizabeth* slammed into the beach with a shudder, and the deck
dissolved in wails of distress. But it was the next wave that mattered, a
kindly one that lifted the ship's bow and drove her on, high up the beach,
until Pike knew that his charges were safe. Cheers burst from the shore,

where lantern glimmer revealed a mob of wide-eyed faces. As the passengers picked themselves from the deck, some burst into tears or took the hands of crewmen in clenches of gratitude. Then the passengers were assisted to clamber down the ropes that the crew had slung from the bow, into the outstretched hands of landsmen waist-deep in the surf. The master, with the ship's papers, was last to leave. In the morning he would learn what damage the *Elizabeth* had suffered. A watch would stand guard over her until then. The *St. Agnes*, beached neatly as his own vessel, lay just fifty yards to the south. A seaman stood beside her. Pike clapped him on the shoulder.

"Where's your master?" he asked; he owed that man some drinks. "And where the hell are we, by the way?"

∽

The *Elsa* entered Bude rather more sedately that afternoon. As we puttered up the channel and made for the buoy, I was left to wonder how close the *Caledonia* had come to spying those two ships making for a leeward light. And would Stevenson Peter have followed them in?

Chapter 35

The harvest was in by the time I went to see Joe Gifford's aunt, and the shorn fields were scattered with cylindrical bales of straw. Liz Gifford lived at Southole. Ash trees shouldered the narrow road that ran up the valley from Welcombe Mouth, their translucent foliage casting a weak dapple. A few modern cottages had recently sprouted in the hamlet, with tinted windows, fancifully leaded, and beside the old farmhouse gleamed the new owners' four-wheel drive.

But Liz Gifford drove an old hatchback, with bits of twine hanging from it and a bale of straw on the backseat. She kept livestock on a nearby plot of land. Her small white dog lay undisturbed on the pitted tarmac road outside her gate, sunning itself; though the road through Southole did lead to places, there were other roads that got there more quickly, and even these days few cars passed. Liz had lived in Southole for forty years, in a rough cottage, haphazardly extended, that had been built from the timbers of a wrecked ship.

Liz, now in her sixties, had arrived in these parts in the summer of 1955. She had bought a place in Welcombe, where she kept chickens and took in paying guests. She first met Jack Gifford when he turned up one day to try and sell her a horse. Liz had heard all about the Giffords.

"They seemed to have a bad name," she said. "That's probably what drew me to Jack. He was interesting. He didn't conform. He was an original."

Jack owned the farm at Southole with his brother, Stanley, but Jack wasn't one for farming. He preferred to spend his time hunting, breeding horses and hounds, and trapping rabbits. When the money was short he supplied local builders with sand, which he loaded into sacks and slung over the backs of donkeys down at Welcombe Mouth. Gipsy Jack they called him.

Jack had built the cottage before the war. Its frame was constructed entirely from timbers off the *Cambalu* of Liverpool, which had come ashore at Knap Head, between Southole and Welcombe Mouth, in January 1933. Jack had hacked the *Cambalu* apart and carted the timbers up the road from Welcombe Mouth. The cottage proved tough building, for the seasoned timbers were hard as stone; when a fire claimed part of the cottage some years later, the local fire brigade complained that they had blunted their axes on the smoldering frame.

Liz liked Welcombe, but she found it very quiet.

"It began when Jack offered me company," Liz remembered. "I was welcome to share his cottage if I'd help him out with his horses and hounds."

When Jack discovered Liz could cook and mend socks, he became more interested. They were married in 1959.

She showed me around her home. It was a scruffy place, chill in winter; flowers from the verges stood in tall vases of discolored water. But it housed an enquiring mind. There were books and journals, and a typewriter loaded with a half-written letter to the editor of the *Hartland Chronicle*. Liz pointed out doors and the mantelpiece made from ship's timber, and part of a ship's ladder with CAMBALU picked out in a faded red. One of the *Cambalu*'s rope lockers had been turned into a fitted cupboard. Liz motioned at the brass lock on its door, where the adjacent frame had evidently been repaired.

"Forced when the ship first came ashore," she chuckled, making me coffee on an old gas hob in the lean-to kitchen, "Someone after the ropes inside it, and someone not a million miles from here, I daresay."

I had come to see Liz for her memories of the *Goliath* wrecking in 1969; Stanley Gifford at the nearby farmhouse, now dead, had been her brother-in-law. Liz smiled, remembering the crowds and the newsmen that gathered at the cliff top after the wreck, their hats, foolishly lost to the wind, littering the shore. The first she knew of the wreck was when the two boys from the farmhouse turned up early at the cottage; there was a ship ashore, they said. Two soaked strangers had appeared at the farmhouse door in the dawn. I nodded; and they had had the door slammed in their faces.

But Liz explained: it had been a broken night at the farmhouse, what with the car rally that had come through Southole in the early hours. And the dawn knock startled the household, for people rarely had reason to call at such an hour. But it was what Stanley thought he heard as he stood in the doorway that gloomy dawn—two panicked strangers saying "sheep, sheep"—that had truly upset him; for a moment, he believed himself to be dealing with rally drivers who, not content with revving inroads into his hard-earned sleep, had woken him early with the news that they'd just run down some of his flock. So Stanley might have moved to slam the door on them.

It was barely an instant, however, before he was absorbing the shivering forms and bare feet, the soaked clothes and the life jacket that one man wore, and was opening the door again as he understood that what he'd actually heard was "ship, ship" in a foreign accent. The men were frightened, exhausted, and bloodied. Stanley ushered them inside and roused the house. The family found towels for the men and gave them dry clothes and boots. Stanley's wife heated a bowl of water and washed and bandaged their lacerated feet. They gave them tea. Liz called the coast guard from the cottage.

Stanley and the boys went to take a look for themselves. On the shore, not far from the wreck, they found an upturned dinghy, and a corpse beneath it. Another corpse lay to the north, naked and head down in a rock pool. There was nothing they could do but wait for the coast guard and, as the boys would admit to Liz, help themselves to a beached can containing what they mistakenly took for lubricating oil. They poured its contents away in disgust when they discovered its full vinegary smell; it was wine.

It goes without saying: it was not the story it had claimed to be. No descendants of Cruel Copinger's ilk would have poured away a flagon of French wine. Nor would they have taken in the two survivors and given them boots and clothes and cups of tea. Nor, finally, would they have knelt before them and washed their cut feet. That biblical detail finally persuaded me against the popular version of that morning's events, which claimed to confirm the wrecking notoriety of these coastal people, their atavistic suspicions of strangers from the sea enduring in the form of Stanley Gifford and a slammed door.

I had been struck, time and again, by the willingness of locals to believe that willful wrecking had taken place here. But the *Goliath* story had turned out differently after all, as cold and frightened men were taken in and cared for. Only ordinary kindnesses had been committed that morning. But ordinary kindnesses were of no special consequence. Did those who claimed wrecking had taken place do so out of preference for a colorful past over a clean one? Did the misinterpretation of that single moment in a March dawn allow the people of this coast to believe themselves directly linked to a wild and romantic past and to keep at bay the world in which they truly lived—a world of soap operas, shopping, and the keeping of VAT receipts?

They were not alone; I too had long since succumbed to the dark version. I had allowed myself to believe the worst of this coast. I had come to believe that all Hawker's lies and those missing bodies must hide a dark secret, and that some hideous end had actually befallen the crew of the *Caledonia*. I had almost wished them deaths at the hands of Morwenstow wreckers.

And now, in the moments before the ship loomed out of the storm and cudgels gleamed on the cliffs above Sharpnose, I was finally hearing the truth. I remembered how the crowd that had gathered at Bude on that very same night had cheered as the *St. Agnes* and the *Elizabeth* made it to safety. I remembered the gratitude of Edward Le Dain, who had named his first son after Hawker and even sent a gift of Jersey cows to Morwenstow. I remembered too the gratitude of others: the owners of the schooner *Primrose,* wrecked at Morwenstow on August 12, 1852, had presented a mahogany case to Hawker "as a grateful acknowledgement of his unwearied kindness and hospitality to the Captain and Mate, and for his preservation of the Hull and Stores of the said Vessel"; and a sailor saved from a wreck supposedly had sent Hawker a nugget of gold from California.

On September 7, 1838, four years almost to the day before the loss of the *Caledonia,* another storm had arisen. In deteriorating weather, the boilers of the paddle steamer *Forfarshire,* heading from Dundee to Hull with sixty passengers and crew on board, had failed off St. Abbs Head in Northumberland. In the early hours, the ship had drifted onto the rocks of the Farne Islands and broken her back there. In the dawn, the keeper of the Longstone lighthouse, William Darling, had sighted survivors among the wreckage across the water. Darling and his daughter, Grace, subsequently set off in their tiny boat across four hundred yards of mountainous seas to effect a successful rescue and so create a legend.

Twenty-two-year-old Grace rapidly became a remarkable icon of maritime heroism. Portraitists flocked to Northumberland to paint her. Poets including Wordsworth and Swinburne penned lines in her honor. Locks that purported to be of her hair were sold to souvenir hunters. And a fashionable black bonnet called the Darling hat was launched. Grace Darling died from consumption in October 1842, just a month after the crew of the *Caledonia* was lost. It was a curious coincidence that she and they should have died within weeks of each other, just as her act of heroism of September 7 and their deaths in the early hours of September 8 so nearly shared the same date. But I began to see that there was something else that connected her to Morwenstow.

I had not forgotten Hawker's obsession with the rescue and burial of Morwenstow's sea dead. I had not ceased wondering what could have induced those repeated tallyings, those numerous boasts of seamen saved, and his bitter scribbled observation: "a man writing about wrecks might have recorded that the Vicar of Morwenstow rescued with his own hands some at his cost all 33 corpses from the sea and laid them at rest. But fatal jealousy so obvious in all such things forbade—So I am d——d with the faint praise of ballad monger."

I could see it now. Hawker was already installed at Morwenstow when he would have heard word of Grace Darling; the papers of September 1838 were full of the girl who lived by the sea and rescued men from its jaws. Her example—and the extraordinary admiration she received—seems to have left an indelible impression upon Hawker. He wanted what she had, and his lies now began to make sense. He did not hide anything by them—no hideous crime, no foul cruelty had taken place that morning—but used them by falsely claiming extra burials and the discovery of the survivor to present himself, as far as possible, in the likeness of another. Frustrated by the "faint praise of ballad monger," he wanted to be recognized for his deeds down by the sea. He wanted to be lauded like the lighthouse girl.

And four years later, he would get his chance.

Chapter ∞ *36*

Robert Hawker has it that he was standing among the fragments of the wreck of the *Caledonia* on the shore at Morwenstow when he wrote a penciled note to the ship's owner on a leaf torn from his notebook, "with the brief and thrilling tidings" of her loss and all her Arbroath crewmen. According to the *Arbroath Guide*, this "melancholy intelligence" reached Arbroath just three days later, on September 11. The note does not survive; we might speculate that it was crumpled in Joseph Esplin's distraught fist that day, and tossed into a gutter outside his mill, manufactory, and weaving shop on East Mary Street, near where the town's job center now stands.

History does not relate how Esplin bore the loss of his crew and vessel. It may be relevant that he missed two consecutive meetings of Arbroath's town council—on September 21 and October 6, 1842—when he had barely missed one since his election to the council in 1837; and that, on September 30 of the same year, he took out a policy with the Scottish Equitable Life Assurance Company to the value of £1500, as if the loss of the *Caledonia* had reminded him of his own mortality.

Nor is there evidence that Esplin himself ever replied to Hawker. The vicar of Morwenstow never mentioned letters from the owner of the *Caledonia*, nor a gift of thanks of the sort he received from the men and owners of other ships lost at Morwenstow. The Arbroath newspapers did, however, recognize Hawker's efforts, describing him as "indefatigable in his attention on this sad occasion," and affording "every

detail possible to Mr Esplin." Le Dain, they stated, had been "most hu-
manely treated," although they did muddy this fulsome praise by reference to the "Rev. Mr Hawkin." But the *Arbroath Guide* made up for the
error, and more besides, on October 15, when they published the verses
of Arbroath medical man and poet David Arrott, entitled

LINES TO THE REV. R. S. HAWKER
VICAR OF MORWINSTOW,
Who so benevolently superintended the interment of
the bodies of the crew of the brig Caledonia, of
Arbroath, lost on the coast of Cornwall.

Arrott in the *Arbroath Guide* may not have been Wordsworth or
Swinburne in the *Times*, his poem containing as it did such gems as

> *No mother gaʒ'd on him who was her joy;*
> *But now, alas! her dead—her sailor boy.*

But no matter. Here was the recognition Hawker sought for his
shoreline deeds.

꩜

The few surviving walls of Arbroath's red sandstone abbey—a transept
in which a circular window was still contained and the immense west
front—tottered above the town. It was in the grounds of the abbey that
the people of Arbroath had been buried until the second half of the nineteenth century.

I passed through an arch in the west front. Hard by the high walls
that ran around the edges of the burial ground, the vaults of eminent
families moldered in the shade of horse chestnuts. Holly trees had long
since invaded the privacy of these damp alcoves, and the imposing iron
gates that once fronted them had lost their hinges to the rust and were
propped against the walls, where ivy now bound them.

The rest was a thicket of sunlit headstones whose ranks were broken
by the occasional obelisk or Gothic sarcophagus. There was an inland

smell about the afternoon air, of mown grass, though a briny wind from the sea occasionally lifted the fallen cuttings. The headstones, mostly in the same red sandstone, were badly weathered. The chiseling had evidently fissured many of the stones to the depth of the inscriptions, so that the weakened facade eventually had fallen away to leave the headstone rough and faceless above a pile of carved fragments on which words like "Died" and "Aged" could still be made out. Others had deteriorated more gradually, the facade sagging free of the stone behind it to leave a space so the epitaphs stood out like children's stencils.

Headstones commemorated George Simpson, whose eight children by his second wife were all dead by the age of five excepting Mary, who made it to seventeen; and Aikman Taylor and Catherine Dorward, who lost their children at eleven months, three and a half months, three years, four months, and three years respectively. On some headstones, the age of each child at the time of his or her death was entered in columns headed Years, Months, and Days, cursory as a scribbled note regarding the housekeeping.

Beyond infancy, however, lay Arbroath's second great hurdle to survival. Many of the stones commemorated shipowners and shipmasters, mariners and seamen, boatmen and sailmakers, ropemakers and light keepers, customs men and harbormasters. Anchors were carved on many of them; one even featured an intricately worked cutter on the starboard tack, her sails full and burgee fluttering. Many Arbroath men had not only devoted their lives to the sea but also lost their lives to it. I was struck by the contrast with Morwenstow, which rarely lost its own to the sea but contained in its graveyard the many strangers that washed up there. Where Morwenstow had bodies, Arbroath had memories; the headstones here commemorated the sea dead who lay elsewhere. I stopped counting when I passed a hundred, but a few of those lost around the time of the wreck of the *Caledonia* indicate the toll taken by the sea. David Patterson, a shipowner, was lost at sea on February 7, 1840; George Pearson, aged fifteen, was lost in the Thames on February 13 in the same year; John Patterson, aged twenty-seven, was drowned at Blythe on March 25, 1844; James Cargill, Captain of the *Reliance* of Arbroath, aged twenty-eight, was lost at sea on April 29, 1846; John Garland, aged forty-seven, was lost at sea on June 22, 1846; William Macomie, aged twenty-two, left Arbroath on board the sloop *Ann* on July 21, 1846, and was lost with the vessel; Walter Oliver, aged twenty-one, was lost at sea on July 29, 1846; William Mill, aged twenty-one, was lost at sea in 1847; James Porter, aged thirty-eight, was lost at sea on February 22, 1847, and his brother John, aged twenty-seven, on May 26, 1851.

It staggered me that anybody had survived the nineteenth century. Perhaps it was mere astonishment that compelled amateur genealogists to establish links from the past until they reached themselves. By their researches were they pinching themselves, marveling, even though it must be self-evident in the fact of their own lives, that their line had somehow sidestepped the carnage of previous centuries?

Then I began recognizing names. Here was Arthur Smith, who had died at fifty-nine on March 3, 1848. The builder of the *Caledonia*, he had also devoted himself to "educating neglected children," "circulating religious tracts," and "promoting Christian missions." And here was Joseph Sanderson Esplin, who had died on January 22, 1857, aged fifty-four.

Here was Stevenson Peter's uncle, David Peter, aged fifty-nine, drowned at sea on April 9, 1847. Here too was Stevenson's brother, James Peter, who had died in 1865, and his only son, John, aged twenty-three, lost in what was evidently the family manner with the brig *Catherine Ewan* in the Gulf of Finland in October 1860. Then I was standing before the stone of Stevenson Peter's grandfather, Alexander, who had died on February 26, 1823. It was in these few square yards of the graveyard that the Peter family had gathered the remains of their own. The adjacent headstone had, however, long since lost its entire facade. Beyond it stood a low stone to another "Alex Peter," whom I could not identify. And beyond that lay a space where headstones, two most probably, must once have stood. And that was it. I would never know from these stones, illegible or absent, whether the distant deaths of Stevenson Peter and his brother-in-law had ever been commemorated here.

But I at least knew who lay here; Arbroath's old parish register recorded burials even if the inscriptions that commemorated them were lost forever. I knew from the register that one of the stones had once marked the "lair," or burial plot, belonging to Stevenson's father, John Peter. It is not known when John Peter acquired the lair. He had no pressing reason to have hurried the purchase, if only because he was remarkably blessed that all his six children survived to adulthood, just as six of his own parents' seven children had done. But the family luck was about to run out.

The lair received its first corpse in 1844; it was John Peter's grandson. James Stevenson Wallace died of croup at age two on February 28, 1844, a year and a half after the father he had never met. He was buried on March 2, "one foot south from John Peter's stone."

Another grave, also recorded as lying one foot south of John Peter's stone, was dug two years later when Bathia's other child also died, from consumption, on May 6, 1846. Robert was seven years and seven months old. Another two years later, John Peter lost his wife, Hannah. She died on June 8, 1848, aged seventy-eight, and was buried here on June 13. Four years later still, John Peter himself died; he was buried before his stone, alongside his wife and grandchildren, on October 13, 1852.

So much for the miracle of descent. My last hope of a line to the present was snuffed out. I had had the idea that the memory of that distant shipwreck might have been preserved, to be passed down the generations as a stirring snapshot from the family past. Now the hope guttered and died. The only offspring from the crew of the *Caledonia* had been buried beside their grandparents in the abbey grounds at Arbroath long before they might have had offspring of their own. It was here that it finished.

But the boys' parents lay elsewhere. I thought of their mother, who had lost everything in the space of ten years. It's worth repeating, if only to comprehend the enormity of it, that she had lost her husband and brother in 1842, one child in 1844, the other in 1846, her mother in 1848, and her father in 1852.

Bathia is last glimpsed on February 25 in that dark winter of 1843, some five months after the loss of her husband, when "an aliment of two shillings and sixpence per week for widow Wallace and her children" was noted in the Arbroath church minutes; she evidently had the added burden of poverty to endure. Then she vanishes from the records. It may be she attended those family burials during the 1840s, but the only family members known to have been present were those whose names appear in the register as witness to the burials: Bathia's brother James in the cases of her younger son and parents, and her father-in-law, Robert Wallace, for her older son.

I looked everywhere for Bathia's death in the hope that its details— evidence of another husband, more children, a long life—would demonstrate that she had risen above the ordeal of her losses. But I never found her. Nothing would ever be known of her subsequent days. It was as if the effect of those successive tragedies, which had begun with the arrival of a grim-faced Mr. Esplin that day in September 1842, had been so great as to erase her completely. Her disappearance, like her husband's, was absolute.

∞

But something had turned up in the store at the Signal Tower Museum.

I walked down the High Street to the harbor. Outside the Commercial Bar, an empty cardboard box of Famous Grouse whisky had been dumped. Seagulls hovered above fishing boats with names like *Emu, Seacraig,* and *Keltic Lady,* or fell upon discarded french-fry wrappers on the benches by the memorial to the *Westhaven.* Blown plumes blew ragged above the smokehouses in the garden plots along the banks of the shallow Brothock stream, where it ran down a weedy sluice to join the sea.

The curator at the museum placed a package on the table before me and asked me to slip on a pair of white gloves before examining its contents. I unwrapped the protective foam to reveal an old painting. The canvas was coated in a cracked and weathered lacquer and nailed to a rough frame about nine inches wide by fifteen inches high.

It was not the ship's portrait that I had been looking for. The unsigned painting depicted an imposing classical monument. Its portico was decorated with an anchor and an inscription:

SACRED TO THE MEMORY

OF THE CREW OF THE CALEDONIA

OF ARBROATH;

ERECTED

MORWENSTOW CHURCHYARD

CORNWALL

WRECKED THERE

8TH SEPTEMBER 1842

Above the portico was seated a stately figure in helmet and kilt holding a shield, like a half-comprehended rendering of the ship's figurehead. Beneath the portico was a panel, framed in the black of mourning. Here, Hawker's own *Caledonia* poem was reproduced, and was signed "R.S.H." On the plinth of the monument was a triptych of images purporting to represent the loss of the *Caledonia*. In the first of these Victorian freeze frames, the ship was depicted as heeling heavily in ferocious seas. In the second, she had gone ashore below high cliffs, the surf breaking over her bow, which the seas had thrust high onto the rocks, and her masts were gone. The third merely presented an empty sea, but seething tellingly, which prompted the unintentional suggestion that some B-movie monster had devoured the *Caledonia*.

It had none of the accuracy and competence of a ship's portrait. It would certainly not tell me anything material about the ship. The painting was actually riddled with inaccuracies, not least in the triptych. It was perhaps allowable artistic license that the loss of the *Caledonia* should have been presented as taking place in daylight. But there was no justification that she should have been shown heeling to port when the wind and her route meant the opposite must have been true. Nor should she have sprouted a third mast. The painting was clearly not the work of a marine artist.

I looked at the memorial above the triptych, which was equally mis-conceived. It occurred to me that the artist had apparently imagined that a monument, something far more august and imposing than a battered figurehead planted in the soil, had been erected in the churchyard at Morwenstow. I began to realize that things might be learned from the painting's very mistakes.

As I stared at the painting, I was reminded of a description of the memorial in an article on Le Dain's "miraculous preservation," dated 1843, which I had stumbled upon in *Le Constitutionel* of Jersey. Though the article was in French, it struck me as the painting's precise verbal copy, complete with the same errors. *"La figure, le sabre et le bouclier qui etaient fixes sur la tete de ce navire,"* the article read, *"ont ete deposes sur le tombeau de ces hommes, ou se trouve en outre la pieuse et touchante Inscription suivante."* Or, "The figurehead, sword, and shield which were fixed to the prow of this ship, have been placed upon the tomb of these men, where the following reverent and touching inscription is also to be found": Hawker's poem then followed. Here, just as in the painting, the poem was mistakenly reproduced upon *le tombeau,* or the tomb (which significantly evokes something more grandiose than "grave"). And in the article, just as in the painting, the poem was signed "R.S.H."

The article thus informed the painting, which allowed the kin of the crew to imagine the grave they would never visit. The grave was as they would have wished it to be. They need never know the truth, which was a battered figurehead stuck above a mass grave, kindly meant and evocative but hardly monumental. Instead, they sought solace in a grand mausoleum, of marble or granite, with plinths, panels, and poetry. They would remember their husbands, sons, and brothers lying beneath a memorial worthy of remarkable men, one that would last through the ages.

Somebody, then, had mourned them.

One afternoon, I was checking some ships' entries in *Lloyd's List* when my own name leapt out at me from the pages. "Arrived at Standgate Creek, the Medway River, from Messina on 19th March 1841," the entry read, "the *Queen*, Seal." I was about to dismiss it as ocular reflex, the eye drawn to words with a personal resonance, when I remembered that my sister had mentioned a nineteenth-century master mariner in the family by the name of John Seal.

Still, all the odds were against it being the same man, rising from the past to snag quite by chance on the cursory glance of his great-great-great-grandson. They shortened when I checked *Lloyd's Register*, which gave the man's initial:

No	Ship	Rig	Master	Tons	Built	Year	Owner	Port	Voyage	Class
1	—	Bg	Christon	296	Qubec	1831	Alder & C	London	Lon. Mermc	6 Æ 1
				Srprs 38	Drp.4.1	S. S.	37—5Yrs	Cont.37—		2 41
2	—	Bk	Forrest	552	P.E.Isl	1837	D. Gibb	Liverp'l	Liv.	4 Æ 1
F.S.& YM.40 I.B.				651	BB.S.	P&H k Drp.39&4 0				40
3	—	Sw	J. Hart	275	Sndrld	1837	S Mease	NShilds	Shl. London	6 A 1
I.B.										39
4	—	Sr	G. James	59	Brxhm	1816	N. James	Brixhm	Drt.StMich	—
				50						39
5	—	Sr	R. Orford	81	Ipsw'h	1838	Suf& Nrfk	Ipswich	Ips. London	12 A 1
I.B.						Sh. Co.				38
6	—	Sr	R. Payne	93	Wdbge	1840	Row	Wdbge	Liv. Genoa	12 A 1
I.B.										2
7	—	Sr	T Sawden	105	Brdltn	1841	Sawden &	Brdlntn	Scr. London	10 A 1
				77						2
8	Queen	Sr	J. Seal	113	Bristol	1832	Mlhuish&	London	Lon.	10 A 1
	C.42				ND.TSds	& Srp rs41				5
9	—	Bk	A. Saul	421	Shi'lds	1808	Hawkins	Hull	Hul. Queb'c	— Æ 1
F.&s.41 I.B.					len.&lrp	35 Dr p.&lrp.41				41
20	—	Sw	E Thomas	189	Dndee	1839	E Thomas	Watrfrd	Lon.	5 A 1
YM.41				184	O.BhLh &E.	Drp41				41
1	—	Sw	Thurbell	203	Sndrld	1838	Penman	Sndrlnd	Sld.Shorhm	5 A 1
I.B.				235						38

It would prove to be him. My great-great-great-grandfather had been born in Poole, Dorset, in 1805, two months before the Battle of Trafalgar. He married Maria Martin in the early 1830s. By 1840, he was captaining the *Queen* on repeated voyages to St. Johns, Newfoundland, with calls at Gibraltar and Cadiz, and his mate was one Miles Martin. The *Caledonia* was not the only ship of the period to be commanded by brothers-in-law.

The discovery that the crew of the *Caledonia* shared the sea with Melville and Dickens had brought a shimmer to the tableau, but it was something else to learn that my own forebear had also been part of their strange and distant world. They had dates or place-names in common. The *Caledonia* and *Queen* visited Standgate Creek within three months of each other. John Seal's arrival, on March 19, 1841, was the day after the last of the crew of the *Caledonia* had joined up for the Marseilles trip at Shields; it may have been the very day of James Wallace's home leave. Once, both time and place brought them tantalizingly close. Certainly, they were both in London for much of July 1841. The *Queen* left London, for St. Johns, sometime after the twenty-fifth; it may even have been the thirty-first, which was the day the *Caledonia* left London for Torbay and Rio. All this time and space, and the ships commanded by Stevenson Peter and my great-great-great-grandfather might have sailed west together.

I followed the *Queen*'s progress. By the spring of the following year, 1842, when the *Caledonia* was unloading coffee at various ports in the Mediterranean, John Seal's ship was back in London. She again left for Newfoundland that May. But I needn't have worried; she was safely moored at distant St. John's on the night of September 7, 1842.

I would trace John Seal to his end. He had joined up as first mate on the *Adelaide*, master Longman, 640 tons, in 1859. He died at sea somewhere near Mauritius, of dropsy, on New Year's Eve 1861. But his first son had safely reached adulthood by then; that was my great-great-grandfather who would himself be married within five years, and would have six children of his own.

Bristol Channel approaches, September 7, 1842

At eight o'clock that evening, when the off-watch went below, the wind blew fresh but favorably over the port quarter and out of the darkened west, driving the *Caledonia* beneath big-bellied sails. The three men dropped through the hatch into the fo'c'sle. They had absented this dark place so long it seemed unfamiliar now, and they were silent for a moment as they remembered how Tomaso Samuel had died there. But the man suffered no longer and the dead had no place here, and Samuel's shipmates were gleeful to be heading home. They took to their hammocks in high spirits, as if determined to reclaim the place for the living by their irreverence.

"Charity!" exclaimed David McDonald, pinching his nose in disgust. "What else expired just now?"

"The offense is indeed rank," muttered Alexander Kent, lighting up a pipe. "It smells to heaven."

"The offense?"

"Why, the removal of your sea boots, Hamlet. Do as I advise and wash those feet of yours before you see your loved ones. Otherwise they'll wish you'd stayed at sea."

"As the proprietor of rotted gums, Kent, you're the one lucky man who's never smelt them," riposted McDonald, coming to the defense of the quiet Jerseyman.

"And so the mouse of Arbroath roars," chuckled Kent.

"Arbroath's worst-kept secret—Kent's imminent return," Le Dain weighed in. "'Here comes he,' the town'll say, noses all a-wrinkle, as they smell you all the way from Dundee."

"Or even Lundy," said McDonald.

"Or even the Bay of Fundy," said Le Dain.

"Very good," exclaimed Kent equably, puffing contemplatively on his pipe. "For a crater-faced Frenchie." And Le Dain threw the core of a large apple at him.

The off-watch had not been down an hour, disguising their fond thoughts of home as traded insults, when it began quite without warning.

Thunder cannoned over the ship. Sudden rain drummed against the deck, and the wind's low moan rose rapidly to a whistle. The fo'c'sle lurched heavily and the first sea of the evening broke over the bow.

"Well well," murmured Kent.

"A little wind, eh?" observed McDonald.

"Aye," said Kent. "And going to the north." The three men lay awake, their thoughts disturbed by creaking blocks and flapping canvas, hollered orders and the urgent stamp of boots, and as the squall grew in intensity they knew that it could not be long before they themselves were called.

"Aye. As we thought," said Kent wearily as the hatch was flung open and a flash of lightning illuminated Mr. Wallace, steam rising from his drenched oilskins.

"All hands," he bellowed. "Stand by to shorten sail!"

The mate's words boomed about the confines of the fo'c'sle, popping the men from their hammocks like podded peas. They were hauling on their oilskins when the ship slammed into a deep trough, which threw them to the floor. A bow wave bucketed through the open hatch and broke over them.

"At least that's your stinking feet washed," laughed Kent, picking himself up. The shipped water slopped about ankles, then took off across the bucking fo'c'sle to surge beneath sea chests, which briefly floated before being dumped with such force that they flew open to a strew of clothes and possessions. Then the water bucketed toward the bow, where it collected a mess of plates, pots, and sundry other objects, which it sluiced aft.

"The poor wee creature," murmured McDonald, grabbing the tortoise as it surfed past on its back. He turned it on its head as if to drain the animal of water, then threw it into his hammock before following the others through the hatch.

"Dieu," shouted Le Dain. "It means it tonight."

The three men clambered onto the foredeck and clung to the foremast ratlines, staring at the sea. There were snowcapped peaks of seething spindrift, but the men could see nothing of the waves beneath them until they appeared out of the blackness above the port bow, bearing down on the ship, a-dance with raindrops. They raised their heads to the heights of the foremast, where David Wallace and William Tasker were struggling to double-reef the topgallant.

"It won't do!" The mate pointed into the rigging. "Down the topgallants. And a reef in the topsails."

Le Dain followed McDonald into the forerigging, and he remembered being aloft with that frightened boy during the tropical squall that had sprung them from the dead of the doldrums all those months ago. But McDonald was a man now. He had nursed a dying shipmate and had learned to laugh with his mates and at the weather's worst alike; as they joined the men on the foretopgallant yard beneath a black sky cracked open by slivers of yellow lightning, McDonald looked up and scorned it for a wind of no consequence. The topgallant fought them like a mad dog, the sodden canvas lashing at their faces. Torrents of rain gathered in the flying furls and guttered from the sail ends. Eventually they secured it, and lashed it with extra preventers until its every flap was stilled. But they had hardly begun, and they dropped down to the topsail yard to reef that straining sail before heading up the mainmast to lend a hand.

The mate had turned out extra lashings to double the ties on the spars, the boats, and the water butts. Stephen Jones struggled forward to nail down the hold hatches. The second mate was at the wheel, straining to keep the ship to windward, but the rudder was fighting him so hard that James Wallace soon joined him there.

"What are you steering, Jim?" shouted Stevenson Peter as a sheet of spray tore across the quarterdeck.

The mate glanced at the compass.

"North north east," he replied. "Nearly."

Stevenson Peter clamped his sou'wester to his head and turned to look over his shoulder. It was as he'd feared; even as it dissolved among the seas, the ship's trailing wake clearly veered off to windward. The helmsmen were keeping her pointed close to the wind, but the gale was

causing the ship to drift sideways, to leeward, so that she was not achiev-
ing the bearing claimed by the compass. The master staggered below,
smelling the brine on him as he came out of the wind. The weather had
overturned his cabin. A sputtering lantern swung wildly against the bulkhead. Scattered garments lay everywhere. His chair was on its side and
his straw mattress was sprawled across the floor among chart rolls, his
Bible, scattered papers, and his tricorn hat, crumpled now. It was not how
he would have his cabin and he almost turned to call for Tasker to
straighten things, which was that clumsy boy's duty, before he remembered that Tasker had more pressing duties, battling livid canvas high in
the rigging. He grabbed at the charts and was freeing one from the roll
when a wave caught the ship broadside and threw him across the unmade
bunk. He clambered to his feet and spread Norie's *New and Correct Chart
of St. George's Channel* against the bulkhead, where the lantern cast its ca-
reening beam.

He sought the details of the Lundy lighthouse, which he noted—a
revolving light visible in clear weather at twenty-six miles—so he might
pass it on to the lookout when the time came. But there was something
else he had to know, and his eye was drawn to the bearing of the coastline, which was largely northeast. This he noted with some relief, since it
meant they were making roughly parallel to the coast (though slipping a
mite sideways) and had a good chance of staying offshore. Then his eye
ranged farther up the coast, and his heart lurched; at Bude it bore due
north and briefly northwest at a place called Sharp's Nose. He bent to
gather his fallen Bible and returned it to its drawer, resting his palm upon
it for a moment. Then he scooped up the log-reckoners, which lay beside
it, and slipped them into his pocket.

The wind had strengthened by the time Stevenson Peter returned to
the quarterdeck. The ship was heeling hard now, almost on her beam-ends.
White sea surged through her lee scuppers, and now and then the ends of
her main yard even dipped into the sea. Again, the men were called upon to
shorten sail. They double-reefed the topsails and reefed both courses—

mainsail and foresail. They dismantled the topgallant masts and yards, and somehow sent them down to the deck without mishap.

That night their calloused hands turned pink as those of babies, and their fingers welted where canvas and hemp lashed them, and their nails bled, but still they gave the ship all the work she asked of them. By midnight, they were chilled to the bone. Stevenson Peter sent McDonald below with instructions to break out the grog. A hearty slug to each man. The crew swallowed the fiery liquor, but even as they felt its warmth in their bellies some were struck that the master had never issued grog before, and they feared the meaning of it.

Then Stevenson Peter sent forward Tasker, whom he had not forgiven for the breakage of the barometer (and would not forgive until he understood its loss as fatal).

"Keep a lookout for the Lundy light!" he hollered.

Tasker nodded with an eagerness that confounded the master, since the foredeck was exposed to the very worst of the storm. But as the apprentice hauled himself along the steep-angled deck, clutching at shrouds and lashings, the spray coursing down his neck, he exulted at a single thought: the storm had arisen. Lundy lay close now, and the only place they might sit out the gale was in the island's lee. He thought of reasons, come the morning, why they might put ashore there. He patted his pocket through the oilskins and felt the green bottle and its dry stoppered contents there, and dreamed of all the riches of Africa. He reached the foremast shrouds, wove his arms among the ratlines to hold himself, and stared ahead. But Tasker could see no light there. In truth he could barely see beyond the bowsprit in the tumult of rain and sea spray, and the wind that threatened to rip his eyelids clean away. The smarting of his eyes soon became unbearable, and he turned away toward the lee side. And then he saw it, a light steady on the beam that he could not know as Bude, and would have reported it but for the bolt of lightning that illuminated the wider scene—a high black ridge, more substantial than even the darkest cloud, clearly visible off the starboard bow.

"Lee shore!" shouted Tasker as he scrabbled aft. But Stevenson Peter stayed him with his arm.

"We saw it, son," he said. "We saw it."

The storm grew to a pitch of violence that none of the men had known. Two weeks later, Edward Le Dain would describe it as rising to a hurricane at around one o'clock in the morning. The crew tried on several occasions to tack the ship, but it was quite beyond them to bring her to windward. The sea had turned entirely to white. The force of the wind had flattened it, scalping the tops of the waves and flinging them at the ship, where they shattered into spume. The air was frantic with flying water, and the whistle of the wind had given way to a merciless banshee shriek intent on breakage.

The mainsail was first to go, splitting from head to foot with a sharp crack. For an instant, the wind streamed through the gap it had made. Then the sail dissolved into ribbons that streamed from the boltrope along its base before the wind whipped them away in clutches, leaving only the reefs and the sheets that had held the sail, cracking like insane whips until they were hauled tight. Then the foresail, the ship's second sail, blew. Now only the spanker, the two topsails, and the jib were left. Once again, Stevenson Peter sent McDonald below for the grog bottle.

"Two rounds of grog, no less," shouted Kent to Le Dain. "Is it bad news he'll be preparing us for?" Then the sheets holding the foretopsail parted, and the freed sail seemed to take off, streaming to the lee from the mast with a flapping so wicked that it too was instantly reduced to shreds.

By half past two, they began to be able to see it without the benefit of lightning, a rearing blackness off the starboard bow blacker even than the night.

"What is that?" shouted McDonald, wide-eyed. "Where are we?"

But Le Dain only clapped the shoulder of his young friend and said nothing. The crew stared at the approaching land; the bulk of Sharpnose filled the sky above them. Again they crowded around the helm where James Wallace had stood all night until the feeling had left his exhausted arms and shoulders, and together they lent their weight one last time to bring the ship to windward. But she would not come round. She rushed onward, beneath a fragmented sky where a racing moon occasionally appeared, until the men could see the water boil where rocks broke surface. Some of the men had begun to sing the same song of home they had begun the day with, clustered around the windlass at St. Just.

They were singing when she grounded. There was a brief screech from her coppered hull before the rocks bit into her timbers with a rending and splintering sound that Edward Le Dain would never forget. The impact drove her bow skyward, snapped the bowsprit, which hung like a broken stem among its parted stays, and flung the men to the deck. As they scrambled to their feet, a sea broke over the stern, smashing through the windows of the officers' cabins and driving Wallace, the last man at the wheel, forward to the higher ground of the foredeck. The next wave flipped the ship onto her starboard flank, where a rock shattered the hull below the gunwale.

"All hands to the maintop," shouted the master. It was his last instruction. The men left the angled deck and returned to the rigging, where they gathered on the platform or clung to the ratlines nearby. Livid seas pounded the ship; the mast lurched with every impact. Nobody spoke. Each man's mind seethed with his own thoughts. Though the seas boiled about the deck and the mast groaned and the cliffs before them seemed mercilessly abrupt, few of them thought of death. They were so full of health and hope, and land was so near. Even David McDonald, who had been advised to reserve his dread for precisely such moments, found himself thinking only of the tortoise entombed in the black fo'c'sle. For his part, William Tasker had begun to presume a divine design; could this be Jenny's Cove itself?

There were among the older crewmen, however, better judges of their predicament. James Wallace thought of Bathia and the boys and took the hand of his nephew, David, and squeezed it hard. *The coffee, the knifing, the funeral, the barometer,* he told himself; *it was me who brought you here.* But nobody sought even in private to apportion blame—not to Samuel, with whose death it had all begun; nor to Tasker, who had broken the barometer; nor to the master, who had chosen to sail without a replacement—though Alexander Kent did allow himself a rueful smile as a final nickname occurred to him: *Of course! Peter the Rock!*

With every breaking wave, the ship's timbers were working loose. The galley swayed, then collapsed and went overboard in a mess of pots and boxes. The deck was quaking, planks punching free with the shrieks of sundering fastenings. Now the men could feel the mast moving like a loosening tooth, and with every shudder the rigging that supported it, ratlines, backstays, and braces, snapped and flailed away. When the longboat went over the side, Le Dain dutifully reported its loss. But the master only clasped the log-reckoners tighter in his fist and looked to his beloved ship's battered masts and yards, stripped of their sails, where he saw great crucifixes pointed to heaven. At the last moment, as a rushing sea pummeled the ship against the rocks and the mast began to teeter, it was the second mate who spoke, as if for the first time, in a louder voice than they had ever heard him use.

"You'll be all right, boys!" he shouted above the storm.

And Edward Le Dain was seized by the sudden unease that even now he did not know that man's name. But it was too late to ask. There was nothing to hold them of a sudden, and they were falling amidst spars and shrouds into an underwater silence.

But Edward would not stay there; he surfaced to gasps and shouts and sea roar. He looked about him and though he could see nothing of his shipmates in the tumult, he thought he heard from somewhere the voice of William Tasker shouting, "Lundy!" Then, through a spin of planks, barrels, and snaking shrouds, Edward Le Dain began to make his way toward the shore.

Chapter ഇ 38

I never did find the Tasker letter. It was lost, it seemed, between the Pine Coffins, who were certain it had been in its display case on the stairs when they moved out, and the new owners, who knew nothing of it. Nor did anybody who had worked at the house know what might have happened to it. I drew further blanks with local historians and the maritime museum at Appledore, but was eventually put in touch with the man who'd found the bottle back in 1967. And when I phoned Roger Cobley at his home in Northam, near Bideford, he laughed very loud indeed.

The newspapers, Cobley remembered, were regularly reporting spectacular recoveries from the seabed around the Gilstone Ledges in the Scilly Isles during the summer of 1967. Almost every day, it seemed, diving teams brought up bronze cannon and great anchors, brass pulley wheels and muskets, thousands of gold and silver coins including pieces of eight and English crowns, inkwells and silver spoons, candlesticks and pottery, dividers and uniform buttons. There was a gold ring with the inscription "God above increase our love." The haul was thought to be from the wreck of the *Association*, the fabled flagship of a British naval fleet returning from the blockade of Toulon. In one of Britain's greatest maritime disasters, the *Association* and several other ships hit the Scilly rocks in fog on an October night in 1707, and were lost with over two thousand men.

Roger Cobley eventually finished laughing.

"Nobody's asked me about the bottle for thirty years," he said. "So I suppose I can finally come clean." Cobley is an elderly man now, but in the summer of 1967 he had two imaginative children named Christopher and Penny.

"It was sometime in September," he remembered, "and the children were bored. They were also thrilled by all this talk of treasure in the news. Penny was jealous; if the Scillies had a treasure ship, she saw no reason why we could not have one of our own. Well, we began to hatch a plan. We did some homework and settled on our ship, along with other historical details which we thought would help our story along. We hunted around for an old bottle, green of course, and an even older cork. I had some old volumes in the attic, all dusty and falling apart, and I removed the yellowing blank page from the front of one. We made an ink of milk and lemon juice and inscribed the message and map across the page with it. The children thought it was great fun."

The first beach the Cobleys tried was at Westward Ho! One windy afternoon, they surreptitiously planted the bottle in the shallows where the beach was most crowded, and retired to await developments.

"But nobody even noticed it," explained Cobley. "Very disappointing, it was. After a while, we tired of waiting. We retrieved the bottle and decided to drive over to Portledge...."

"How did you know about Portledge?" I interrupted.

"Know?"

"That two bodies from the *Caledonia* had washed up there?"

"They did? Oh, we didn't know that. We merely figured that Portledge tended to attract a more refined beachgoer, types down from London, who might show more curiosity in our bottle. So we repeated the trick there, and waited."

But the Portledge crowd proved equally incurious, and the bottle rolled undiscovered in the surf for much of the afternoon. Eventually, the disgruntled Cobley family found the bottle themselves, and delivered it to the receptionist at the hotel. They didn't hear anything until the following spring, when the hotel manager at Portledge had become inter-

ested. He'd sent the bottle to the university at Exeter for their consideration, who duly sent it on to the maritime museum there. The researches
at Exeter proved inconclusive, but the museum staff held the bottle in
sufficient regard to have a wooden display case specially made for it. The
bottle was featured on local television. The *Bideford and North Devon
Weekly Gazette* took the letter to be genuine, and considered it "an incredible coincidence" that the bottle should have journeyed from Odessa
to within "a score of miles" of the ship's last resting place. The Cobley
hoax had succeeded.

"But why the *Caledonia* connection?" I asked. "How did you imagine
that a crewman from the *Caledonia* should have become interested in the
Jenny's treasure some forty-five years after she was lost on Lundy?"

"Oh, the two wrecks happened to be mentioned in the same reference book," Cobley explained. "That seemed reason enough."

"And how did you discover that William Tasker was on board the
Caledonia?"

"William?"

"Tasker."

"Oh, there really was a William on board, was there? What excellent
luck!"

So Tasker had known nothing of the *Jenny*. He had not courted
storm and shipwreck, nor endangered his shipmates' lives in a dream of
wealth. He was merely a clumsy boy (if it were indeed true that he had
broken the barometer). The dreamer was a girl named Penny who lived
by the sea. The old stories of shipwreck and buried treasure had captivated her, and led her to put the letter bottle on the beach 125 years after
William Tasker's death.

I subsequently happened to check the letter that Mark Myers had
copied into his notebook. I noticed for the first time that it was actually
dated "14 August 1843." Like the date on the poem and the sign in the
graveyard, the date was a year out. I might have known that it was a fake
from the very beginning—except that I simply had wanted to believe
in it.

Which left me with the log-reckoners, found on the shore in the clasp of Stevenson Peter's dead hand. I had successfully traced them to Nicholas Ross's possession in 1956. But just as they came within reach, securely preserved in a modern collection of Hawker memorabilia, their remarkable history established, circumstances actively set about erasing their every trace. Their disappearance began upon Nicholas Ross's death in 1967. Ross's widow, Adelaide, sold his Hawker collection to the Bodleian in Oxford the following year. But when I contacted them, the curators there were certain that no log-reckoners had been included in the acquisition.

Nicholas and Adelaide had had no children to inherit the log-reckoners. Nor was there any mention of them in Nicholas's last will, which was made prior to his acquisition of the log-reckoners. It was possible, of course, that Adelaide had kept them. She had continued to live at Kilkhampton and latterly at a nursing home in Poughill, near Bude, until her death in 1993. I checked her own will, which did make mention of a few objects and artifacts that she wished to bequeath to certain friends: paintings and portraits, scripts, letters and writings, the model of a Thames barge, table silver and cutlery, and a pair of black-and-white china Staffordshire dogs—but no log-reckoners.

I contacted the Bude solicitor who had visited Adelaide Ross several times during her decline and had supervised the clearance of the house at Kilkhampton after her death. He knew nothing of the log-reckoners. I discovered that Adelaide had donated some objects of value to a convent in Leeds that was raising funds for a home for the sick and elderly, and wondered whether the log-reckoners might have been included. But the Mother Superior told me that nobody at the convent knew of such things. Finally, I wrote to every one of Adelaide's beneficiaries in the hope that one of them might know something of the log-reckoners' whereabouts. Not one of them could help me.

There was nowhere left to go. The past rips at the clutch of the present, possessive of what it considers its own. There are museums, but there only the objects that attach to events and persons of import survive.

Most objects rot, are discarded, or get lost. Others lose their history, which is their very meaning. With each day, old homes are abandoned and forebears' memories fade. And with them goes all that has ever happened until we realize what we have lost, and the archives are full of us, armed with threadbare family trees, hunting down the past as if to make ourselves complete by it.

Still, I like to think that some day may bring a phone call or a letter, and sudden talk of old egg-timers. A pair of them, they'll say, and they'll describe the casings, made of brass and the size of shotgun cartridges, with "14 secs" or "28 secs" imprinted on the bases. They'll have to tell me something else, of course, some confirming fact about the origins of their log-reckoners that I can't even guess at until I hear it, when my certain heart will soar.

"I can tell you something about those egg-timers," I'll say.

Epilogue ঙ৯

I returned to Morwenstow in September and walked out to Sharpnose Point on a bright day, just as Edward Le Dain had done in the summer of 1845.

Le Dain had gone home to Jersey six weeks after the wreck of the *Caledonia*. He returned three years later to "see the very spot of his great deliverance." Hawker would remember the perfect weather of their reunion, with "the soft blue wave lapping the sand in gentle cadence, as though the sea had never wreaked an impulse of ferocity, or rent a helpless prey."

Edward Le Dain was not put off by his remarkable survival; on the contrary, he remained a sailor throughout his life. Edward, moreover, was shipwrecked a further two times, just as Hawker had claimed. He was serving on the Jersey ship *Day*, which had already suffered a battering by the time she reached Crookhaven, in Ireland, on January 1, 1847, "with loss of sails and bulwarks." After repairs, she left Limerick for New York on February 22, but was stranded on April 15 at Sandy Hook, on the approaches to New York, when *Lloyd's List* reported that she "is not expected off." *Lloyd's Register* for 1847 subsequently confirmed her as "wrecked."

Le Dain's third shipwreck was in 1854. "The *Navigator*, Le Dain, from London to Barbadoes," the *List* reported, "struck on a reef off the south point of that island, 3rd March, and became a total wreck; part of cargo saved in a damaged state." The master of the *Navigator*, an old hand in these matters, survived the experience. He died in 1885, leaving three children to do it all again.

I turned my back on the ocean and walked across the fields to the graveyard. I stopped at the figurehead. Grass obscured the low sign I had tripped against in the spring. I bent to uncover it and stopped short: *The figurehead of the Caledonia which marks the graves of the captain and crew . . . was wrecked in 1842,* it now read. Somebody had made the correction with a careful brush.

Appendix ⟡

I

Excerpts from "The Remembrances of a Cornish Vicar" by R. S. Hawker (1865). First published in *All the Year Round*, vol. 13, 1865, pp. 153–56.

It was not long after my arrival in my new abode that I was plunged all at once into the midst of a fearful scene of the terrors of the sea. About daybreak of an autumn day I was aroused by a knock at my bedroom-door; it was followed by the agitated voice of a boy, a member of my household, "Oh, sir, there are dead men on vicarage rocks!"

In a moment I was up, and in my dressing-gown and slippers rushed out. There stood my lad, weeping bitterly, and holding out to me in his trembling hands a tortoise alive. I found afterwards that he had grasped it on the beach, and brought it in his hand as a strange and marvellous arrival from the waves, but in utter ignorance of what it might be. I ran across my glebe, a quarter of a mile, to the cliffs, and down a frightful descent of three hundred feet to the beach. It was indeed a scene to be looked on only once in a human life. On a ridge of rock, just left bare by the falling tide, stood a man, my own servant; he had come out to see my flock of ewes, and had found the awful wreck. There he stood, with two dead sailors at his feet, whom he had just drawn out of the water stiff and stark. The bay was tossing and seething with a tangled mass of rigging, sails, and broken fragments of a ship; the billows rolled up yellow with corn, for the cargo of the vessel had been foreign wheat; and ever and anon there came up out of the water, as though stretched out with life, a human hand and arm. It was the corpse of another sailor drifting out to sea. "Is there no one alive?" was my first question to my man. "I think there is, sir," he said, "for just now I thought I heard a cry." I made haste in the direction he pointed out, and, on turning a rock, just where a brook of fresh water fell towards the sea, there lay the body of a man in a seaman's garb. He had reached the water faint with thirst, but was too much exhausted to swallow or drink. He opened his eyes at our voices, and as he saw me leaning over him in my cassock-shaped dressing-gown, he sobbed, with a piteous cry, "O mon père, mon père!" Gradually he revived, and when he had fully come to himself with the help of cordials and food, we gathered from him the mournful tale of his vessel and her wreck. He was a Jersey man by birth, and had been shipped at Malta, on the homeward voyage of the vessel from the port of Odessa with corn. I had sent in for brandy, and was pouring it down his throat, when my parishioner, Peter Burrow, arrived. He assisted, at my request, in the charitable office of restoring the exhausted stranger; but when he was refreshed and could stand upon his feet, I remarked that Peter did not seem so elated as in common decency I expected he would be. Taking me aside, he whispered in my ear, "Now, sir, I beg your pardon, but if you'll take my advice, now that man is come to himself, if I were you I would let him go his way wherever he will. If you take him into your house, he'll surely do you some harm." Seeing my surprise, he went on to explain, "You don't know, sir," he said, "the saying on our coast—

> *Save a stranger from the sea,*
> *And he'll turn your enemy.*

"There was one Coppinger cast ashore from a brig that struck up at Hartland, on the Point. Farmer Hamlyn dragged him out of the water and took him home, and was very kind to him. Lord, sir! he never would leave the house again! He lived upon the folks a whole year, and at last,

lo and behold! he married the farmer's daughter Elizabeth, and spent all
her fortin rollicking and racketing, till at last he would tie her to the bed-
post and flog her till her father would come down with more money.
The old man used to say he wished he'd let Coppinger lie where he was
in the waves, and never laid a finger on him to save his life. Ay, and
divers more I've heerd of that never brought no good to they that saved
them."

"And did you ever yourself, Peter," said I, "being, as you have told
me, a wrecker so many years—did you ever see a poor fellow clamber-
ing up the rock where you stood, and just able to reach your foot or hand,
did you ever shove him back into the sea to be drowned?"

"No, sir, I declare I never did. And I do believe, sir, if I ever had done
such a thing, and given so much as one push to a man in such a case, I
think verily that afterwards I should have been troubled and uncomfort-
able in my mind."

"Well, notwithstanding your doctrine, Peter," said I, "we will take
charge of this poor fellow; so do you lead him into the vicarage and order
a bed for him, and wait till I come in."

I returned to the scene of death and danger, where my man awaited
me. He had found, in addition to the two corpses, another dead body
jammed under a rock. By this time a crowd of people had arrived from
the land, and at my request they began to search anxiously for the dead.
It was, indeed, a terrible scene. The vessel, a brig of five hundred tons,
had struck, as we afterwards found, at three o'clock that morning, and by
the time the wreck was discovered she had been shattered into broken
pieces by the fury of the sea. The rocks and the water bristled with fragments of mast and spar and rent timbers; the cordage lay about in tangled
masses. The rollers tumbled in volumes of corn, the wheaten cargo; and
amidst it all the bodies of the helpless dead—that a few brief hours before had walked the deck the stalwart masters of their ship—turned their
poor disfigured faces toward the sky, pleading for sepulture. We made a
temporary bier of the broken planks, and laid thereon the corpses, decently arranged. As the vicar, I led the way, and my people followed with

ready zeal as bearers, and in sad procession we carried our dead up the steep cliff, by a difficult path, to await, in a room at my vicarage which I allotted them, the inquest. The ship and her cargo were, as to any tangible value, utterly lost.

The people of the shore, after having done their best to search for survivors and to discover the lost bodies, gathered up fragments of the wreck for fuel, and shouldered them away—not perhaps a lawful spoil, but a venal transgression when compared with the remembered cruelties of Cornish wreckers. Then ensued my interview with the rescued man. His name was Le Daine. I found him refreshed, and collected, and grateful. He told me his Tale of the Sea. The captain and all the crew but himself were from Arbroath, in Scotland. To that harbour also the vessel belonged. She had been away on a two years' voyage, employed in the Mediterranean trade. She had loaded last at Odessa. She touched at Malta, and there Le Daine, who had been sick in the hospital, but recovered, had joined her. There also the captain had engaged a Portuguese cook, and to this man, as one link in a chain of causes, the loss of the vessel might be ascribed. He had been wounded in a street-quarrel the night before the vessel sailed from Malta, and lay disabled and useless in his cabin throughout the homeward voyage. At Falmouth whither they were bound for orders, the cook died. The captain and all the crew, except the cabin-boy, went ashore to attend the funeral. During the absence the boy, handling in his curiosity the barometer, had broken the tube, and the whole of the quicksilver had run out. Had this instrument, the pulse of the storm, been preserved, the crew would have received warning of the sudden and unexpected hurricane, and might have stood out to sea. Whereas they were caught in the chops of the Channel, and thus, by this small incident, the vessel and the mariners found their fate on the rocks of a remote headland in my lonely parish. I caused Le Daine to relate in detail the closing events.

"We received orders," he said, "at Falmouth to make for Gloucester to discharge. The captain, and mate, and another of the crew, were to be married on their return to their native town. They wrote, therefore, to

Arbroath from Falmouth, to announce their safe arrival there from their two years' voyage, their intended course to Gloucester, and their hope in about a week to arrive at Arbroath for welcome there."

But in a day or two after this joyful letter, there arrived in Arbroath a leaf torn out of my pocket-book, and addressed "To the Owners of the Vessel," the Caledonia of Arbroath, with the brief and thrilling tidings, written by myself in pencil, that I wrote among the fragments of their wrecked vessel, and that the whole crew, except one man, were lost "upon my rocks." My note spread a general dismay in Arbroath, for the crew, from the clannish relationship among the Scots, were connected with a large number of the inhabitants. But to return to the touching details of Le Daine.

"We rounded the Land's End," he said, "that night all well, and came up Channel with a fair wind. The captain turned in. It was my watch. All at once, about nine at night, it began to blow in one moment as if the storm burst out by signal; the wind went mad; our canvas burst in bits. We reeved fresh sails; they went also. At last we were under bare poles. The captain had turned out when the storm began. He sent me forward to look out for Lundy Light. I saw your cliff." (This was a bluff and broken headland just by the southern boundary of my own glebe.) "I sung out, 'Land!' I had hardly done so when she struck with a blow, and stuck fast. Then the captain sung out, 'All hands to the maintop!', and we all went up. The captain folded his arms, and stood by, silent."

Here I asked him, anxious to know how they expressed themselves at such a time, "But what was said afterwards, Le Daine?"

"Not one word, sir; only once, when the long-boat went over, I said to the skipper, 'Sir, the boat is gone!' But he made no answer."

How accurate was Byron's painting—

"Then shrieked the timid, and stood still the brave"!

"At last there came on a dreadful wave, mast-top high, and away went the mast by the board, and we with it, into the sea. I gave myself up.

I was the only man on the ship who could not swim, so where I fell in the water there I lay. I felt the waves beat me and send me on. At last there was a rock under my hand. I clung on. Just then I saw Alick Kant, one of our crew, swimming past. I saw him lay his hand on a rock, and I sung out, 'Hold on, Alick!' but a wave rolled and swept him away, and I never saw his face more. I was beaten onwards and onwards among the rocks and the tide, and at last I felt the ground with my feet. I scrambled on. I saw the cliff, steep and dark, above my head. I climbed up until I reached a kind of platform with grass, and there I fell down flat upon my face, and either I fainted away or fell asleep. There I lay a long time, and when I awoke it was just the break of day. There was a little yellow flower just under my head, and when I saw that I knew I was on dry land." This was a plant of the bird's-foot clover, called in old times Our Lady's Finger. He went on: "I could see no house or sign of people, and the country looked to me like some wild and desert island. At last I felt very thirsty, and I tried to get down towards a valley where I thought I should find water; but before I could reach it I fell and grew faint again, and there, thank God, sir, you found me."

Such was Le Dain's sad and simple story, and no one could listen unmoved or without a strong feeling of interest and compassion for the poor solitary survivor of his shipmates and crew. The coroner arrived, held his 'quest, and the usual verdict of "Wrecked and cast ashore" empowered me to inter the dead sailors, found and future, from the same vessel, with the service in the Prayer-book for the burial of the Dead. This decency of sepulture is the result of a somewhat recent statute, passed in the reign of George III. Before that time it was the common usage of the coast to dig, just above the high-water mark, a pit on the shore, and therein to cast, without inquest or religious rite, the carcasses of shipwrecked men. My first funeral of these lost mariners was a touching and striking scene. The three bodies first found were buried at the same time. Behind the coffins, as they were solemnly borne along the aisle, walked the solitary mourner, Le Daine, weeping bitterly and aloud.

Other eyes were moist, for who could hear unsoftened the greeting of the Church to these strangers from the sea, and the "touch that makes the whole earth kin," in the hope we breathed that we, too, might one day "rest as these our brethren did"? It was well-nigh too much for those who served that day. Nor was the interest subdued when, on the Sunday after the wreck, at the appointed place in the service, just before the General Thanksgiving, Le Daine rose up from his place, approached the altar, and uttered, in an audible but broken voice, his thanksgiving for his singular and safe deliverance from the perils of the sea. . . .

Few, indeed, could have borne, without deep emotion, to see and hear Le Daine. He remained as my guest six weeks, and during the whole of this time we sought diligently, and at last we found the whole crew, nine in number. They were discovered, some under rocks, jammed in by the force of the water, so that it took sometimes several ebb-tides, and the strength of many hands, to extricate the corpses. The captain I came upon myself lying placidly upon his back, with his arms folded in the very gesture which Le Daine had described as he stood amid the crew on the maintop. The hand of the spoiler was about to assail him when I suddenly appeared, so that I rescued him untouched. Each hand grasped a small pouch or bag. One contained his pistols; the other held two little log-reckoners of brass; so that his last thoughts were full of duty to his owners and his ship, and his latest efforts for rescue and defence. He had been manifestly lifted by a billow and hurled against a rock, and so slain; for the victims of our cruel sea are seldom drowned, but beaten to death by violence and the wrath of the billows. We gathered together one poor fellow in five parts; his limbs had been wrenched off, and his body rent. During our search for his remains, a man came up to me with something in his hand, inquiring, "Can you tell me, sir, what this is? Is it a part of a man?" It was the mangled seaman's heart, and we restored it reverently to its place, where it had once beat high with life and courage, with thrilling hope and sickening fear. Two or three of the dead were not discovered for four or five weeks after the wreck, and these had become so loathsome from decay, that it was at peril of health and life to perform the last duties we owe to our brother-men. But hearts and hands were found for the work, and at last the good ship's company—captain, mate and crew—were laid at rest, side by side, beneath our church-yard trees. Groups of grateful letters from Arbroath are to this day among the cherished memorials of my escritoire. Some, written by the friends of the dead, are marvellous proofs of the good feeling and educated ability of the Scottish people. One from a father breaks off in irrepressible pathos, with a burst of "O my son! my son!" We placed at the foot of the captain's grave the figurehead of this vessel. It is a carved image, life-size, of his native Caledonia, in the garb of her country, with sword and shield.

At the end of about six weeks Le Daine left my house on his homeward way, a sadder and a richer man. Gifts had been proffered from many a hand, so that he was able to return to Jersey, with happy and grateful mien, well clothed, and with £30 in his purse. His recollections of our scenery were not such as were in former times associated with the Cornish shore; for three years afterward he returned to the place of his disaster accompanied by his uncle, sister, and affianced wife, and he had brought them that, in his own joyous words, "they might see the very spot of his great deliverance": and there, one summer day, they stood, a group of happy faces, gazing with wonder and gratitude on our rugged cliffs, that were then clad in that gorgeous vesture of purple and gold which the heather and gorse wind and weave along the heights; and the soft blue wave lapping the sand in gentle cadence, as though the sea had never wreaked an impulse of ferocity, or rent a hapless prey. Nor was the thankfulness of the sailor a barren feeling. Whensoever afterward the vicar sought to purchase for his dairy a Jersey cow, the family and friends of Le Daine rejoiced to ransack the island until they had found the sleekiest, loveliest, best of that beautiful breed; and it is to the gratitude of that poor seaman and stranger from a distant abode that the herd of the glebe has long been famous in the land, and hence, as Homer would have sung—hence came

"Bleethah, and Lilith, Neelah, Evan Neelah, and Katy."

Strange to say, Le Daine has been twice shipwrecked since his first peril—with similar loss of property, but escape of life; and he is now the master of a vessel in the trade of the Levant.

ᗡᗩ

II

Wreck statement of Edward Le Dain, made at Morwenstow on September 22, 1842.

"I joined the brig in the harbour of Rio de Janeiro, where I had been left by the ship *Mary Anne* of Jersey, sick with the small-pox three months before. I found that the Captain and all the crew were natives of Arbroath, except myself and the cook, who was from Buenos Ayres, and had joined the ship in London. We sailed from Rio, bound to Corfu, with a freight of coffee, which we dispatched at Corfu, and Syra, and Smyrna, and Constantinople. At the latter place we took in ballast, and sailed for Odessa, where we took in a cargo of wheat. We sailed from Odessa for Falmouth. At Constantinople, on our voyage home, the cook, Thomas Samuel, went on shore, and in a dispute in which he was engaged with the keeper of a public house he received a dangerous wound. We were upwards of five weeks on our voyage from Constantinople to Falmouth, with fine weather all the way. The cook was ill all that time. The crew were an orderly crew; they observed the Sabbath day; the Captain read the Bible in his cabin on Sundays. When we arrived at Falmouth the cook died. We attended his funeral in Falmouth church, and the next day we then performed quarantine. On the 1st of September we sailed from Falmouth for Gloucester, with a fair wind. We sailed about daybreak. We made the Land's End about 5 o'clock in the evening of Wednesday. We then stood up the Bristol Channel with a fair wind until about 9 o'clock, when a sudden squall of wind and rain came on, and all hands were called to shorten sail. The weather continued foul. All hands were kept on deck, and a good lookout forward for the Light Houses. About eleven we saw land on the starboard bow. We tacked ship, but from the violence of the storm we could make no way to windward. About one o'clock on the Thursday morning it blew a hurricane. Just at that time we carried away our square mainsail, our foresail, and our topsail sheets. About half-past two we saw that the danger was very great indeed. The crew were quite sober. The Captain only served out grog twice during the night. About half-past two we saw the point of land on which the vessel afterwards struck. We tried to weather it; we could not get the ship about. There was nothing said by the crew one to another except about the ship's work. Just before the ship struck I was going forwards, and I met David McDonald going aft. He took me by the hand and said, 'Where are we?' He was much moved. And then the ship struck. The Captain sent us to the main rigging. We went. We were there about a quarter of an hour. No one spoke, except once, when I saw the long boat was gone, I said to the Captain, 'Sir, our long boat is gone.' But he made no answer. Soon after the mast went overboard with the rigging and we in it. A heavy sea poured over us, and I was washed towards the land. Several seas struck me onwards. At last I felt a rock. I held on. I looked for my companions: they were not to be seen. The ship was going to pieces. I then climbed onto another rock, and then upwards, until I felt some grass, and then I rested and looked down to the sea for the crew. But there was no one to be seen. I then climbed higher, feeling my way. When morning came I found myself on top of a very high cliff, but I was very much exhausted, and did not then think I should live. But by God's great mercy I am alive. I am a native of Jersey. My Father is a Farmer named Philip le Dain."

(signed) EDWARD LE DAIN

dated Sept. 22nd, 1842

Witnesses {R. S. HAWKER.

{CHARLES MUGFORD.

෨෨

III

From *St Malo's Quest and Other Poems*, by John Adams, Vicar of Stock-cross (London: Henry S. King & Son, 1876).

LINES
ON THE CREW OF THE CALEDONIA
Who were shipwrecked on the Coast of Morwenstow in the
night-storm of September 8th 1842

They looked in dismay to the shore,
As they shot through the blackness of night;
And before them, on cliffs that re-echoed the roar,
The billows dashed foaming and white:
They quailed as they saw that Death's terrors were there
And clung to the mast with the grasp of despair.

They were hurled by the storm to their graves,
As though storming the door of that home;
They were dragged by waves harnessed like horses to waves,
Whose manes were white banners of foam;
Whilst voices of strife to a wild dirge were strung,
And loud the death-wail of the mariners rung.

But mourn not those moments of pain!
Those terrors which hung on a breath!
For the tempest-worn rocks and the billowy main
Grew smooth as a pillow in death;
And the surges that swept them to die on that shore,
Were chariots that bore them to rest evermore!*

---

*One only of the crew of nine men escaped death. He was thrown on a ledge of rock, and scrambled up a precipice so steep and rugged that no human being would have attempted to climb it in broad daylight. I found him, a few hours after the wreck, speechless and covered in bruises, in a gully a quarter of a mile from the sea, and had him conveyed on a stretcher to my father's house, where he was tenderly nursed for several weeks.

༄

IV

Poem by David Arrott, published in the *Arbroath Guide,* October 15, 1842

LINES TO THE REV. R. S. HAWKER
VICAR OF MORWINSTOW,

Who so benevolently superintended the interment of
the bodies of the crew of the brig *Caledonia,* of
Arbroath, lost on the coast of Cornwall.

Deem it not rude—a stranger dares to send
These lines to thee, who are the stranger's friend.
Feebly indeed, by words, can I impart
The humble tribute of a grateful heart;
A tribute due to him who strove to save
The sons of Scotland from the angry wave.
What though thine arm was impotent to wage
Th'unequal contest with the ocean's rage?
If Heav'n decreed that death should be their doom,
Thy pious care provided them a tomb.
To thee the ruthless sea gave up her dead,
That thou migh'st lay them in their lowly bed.

HAWKER! to thee a pitying heart is giv'n,
Worthy, indeed, a delegate of Heav'n.
No kindred came to pay the tribute due,
To the cold ashes of the shipwreck'd crew;
No mourning widow's burning tears were shed.
O'er him whom she deemed living—who was dead;
No mother gaʒ'd on him who was her joy;
But now, alas! her dead—her sailor boy.
No—and no train of kindred mourners come
To bear their kinsman to their last sad home.

'Twas thine to shed the sympathetic tear,
In pity bending o'er the strangers' bier—
Thine to fulfil the self-imposed trust,
To lay their bones in consecrated dust.
Thou need'st no thanks from me, a grateful bard;
Thy virtuous action finds its own reward.
What though on earth thou ne'er shalt cease to share
The mother's, widow's, and the orphan's prayer!
Such deeds as thine are register'd in Heav'n,
And there *alone can due reward be giv'n.*

Illustrations and Credits ☙

Frontispiece, New and correct chart of St. George's Channel, published by J. W. Norie, 1832, with additions in 1840.

Page 3, The figurehead of the *Caledonia*. Photo by Jeremy Seal.

Page 6, Sign below the figurehead of the *Caledonia*. Photo by Jeremy Seal.

Page 15, Morwenstow Church. Photo by Jeremy Seal.

Page 19, Stained-glass window, Morwenstow Church. Photo by Jeremy Seal.

Page 22, The *Caledonia* entry in *Lloyd's Register of Ships*, 1842. Courtesy of *Lloyd's Register*.

Page 26, Certificate of British Registry. Courtesy of the Public Record Office.

Page 37, Vicarage cliff. Photo by Jeremy Seal.

Page 52, "Stevenson Peter," Morwenstow Parish Burials Register, 1842. Copyright reserved to Cornwall Records Office.

Page 52, "Alexander Kent," Morwenstow Parish Burials Register, 1842. Copyright reserved to Cornwall Records Office.

Page 53, "David Macdonald," Morwenstow Parish Burials Register, 1842. Copyright reserved to Cornwall Records Office.

Page 53, "William Tasker," Morwenstow Parish Burials Register, 1842. Copyright reserved to Cornwall Records Office.

Page 53, "David Wallace," Morwenstow Parish Burials Register, 1842. Copyright reserved to Cornwall Records Office.

Page 59, Side view of cliffs. Photo by Jeremy Seal.

Page 62–63, *Lloyd's Register* Survey Report on the *Caledonia* of Arbroath, held at Arbroath in 1839. Original held at the National Maritime Museum, Greenwich. Courtesy of *Lloyd's Register.*

Page 66, *The Wave*, by John Ward of Hull, 1839.

Page 75, A List of the Crew. Courtesy of the Public Record Office.

Page 130, *The Wreck of the Caledonia*, © Mark Myers 1975. Courtesy of Mark Myers.

Page 131, *Clearing a Wreck at Cornwall*, by Rowlandson, 1805.

Page 151, The rocks at Sharpnose Point. Photo by Jeremy Seal.

Page 160, "A Stranger," Parkham Parish Burials Register, 1842. North Devon Records Office, Barnstaple.

Page 160, "A man. Name unknown," Alwington Parish Burials Register, 1842. North Devon Records Office, Barnstaple.

Page 175, "Thomas Samulle," St. Just in Roseland Parish Burials Register, 1842. Copyright reserved to Cornwall Records Office.

Page 199, "At the Council Chamber, Whitehall," Falmouth Customs Correspondence. Courtesy of the Public Record Office.

Page 255, The *Queen* entry in *Lloyd's Register of Ships*, 1841. Courtesy of *Lloyd's Register.*

Notes ⊗

Introductory Epigrams

ix "Every cove": J. L. W. Page, *The North Coast of Cornwall* (Penzance & Truro: John Pollard, 1897), 29.

"Significant, how an agricultural people": Charles Kingsley, "Morte," *Fraser's Magazine for Town and Country* (December 1849): 654.

Chapter 1

2 the stone Celtic cross: The cross was dedicated on 9 October 1924. *Hartland & West Country Chronicle*, 29 November 1924.

"He sent from on high": II Samuel 22, verse 17.

The figureheads of nineteenth-century merchant ships: C. Fox Smith, *Ship Alley: More Sailor Town Days* (London: Methuen, 1925), 118–19.

Chapter 2

7 a select committee: Select Committee on Shipwreck, April 1843, Minutes of Evidence, British Library, *Parliamentary Papers, 1843*, vol 9, 1 ff.

Goldsworthy Gurney: Sir Goldsworthy Gurney, inventor, died in 1875.

"a most dangerous coast"and subsequent quotes: Select Committee on Shipwreck, 1843.

8   "foul and rocky cliff": M. Oppenheim, "Maritime History," *Victoria County History of the County of Cornwall*, vol 1 (London: 1906), 475.

Longships Light: The name of the Land's End lighthouse.

"small lantern on the pier-head": Select Committee on Shipwreck, 1843.

"It ought to be generally known": J. W. Norie, *The New British Channel Pilot* (London: Naval Academy, 1835), 79.

"exhibited lights, tar barrels": Testimony of Mr. Johnson Hicks, Select Committee on Shipwreck, 1843.

"ships of 200 tons": J. W. Norie, *The New British Channel Pilot*, 81.

9   "If an unfortunate vessel": "A Cornish Church-Yard By the Severn Sea," *Chambers Edinburgh Journal* (July–December 1852): 317.

"how the coast and sea": Charlotte Chanter, *Ferny Combes* (London: Lovell Reeve, 1856), 26.

A previous shipwreck committee: Select Committee on Shipwreck, 1836, Minutes of Evidence, British Library, *Parliamentary Papers, 1836,* vol 17, 373 ff.

10   "Returning laden": Select Committee on Shipwreck, 1836.

"the increased value": Select Committee on Shipwreck, 1836.

Chapter 3

11   "The pier at Hartland": Lt. Henry Mangles Denham, *Remarks and Sailing Directions Relative to Lundy Island* (Liverpool: J. & J. Mawdsley, 1832), 16–17.

13   intriguing glimpse: Charles Kingsley, "North Devon," *Fraser's Magazine for Town and Country* (February 1850): 168.

14   "Whilst in other parts": Report of the Constabulary Force Commissioners, 1839 [subsequently CFC], British Library, *Parliamentary Papers, 1839,* 64.

15 fading black-and-white photograph: The photograph is on display at the Hartland Quay Museum. The *Jenny Jones* was lost on 19 February 1868.

the *Othello*: The *Othello*, Charlestown for Liverpool with cotton, was wrecked in February 1808.

"lately become the fashionable Watering Place": The map is on display at the Bude-Stratton Museum.

Chapter 4

18 "a mixed multitude": R. S. Hawker, "The Remembrances of a Cornish Vicar" [subsequently "Remembrances"], from *Footprints of Former Men in Far Cornwall*, edited by C. E. Byles (London: John Lane, 1903) [subsequently *Footprints*], 47.

19 A framed faded photograph: The photograph, by "Hawke, Plymouth," was taken on 7 August 1875.

20 first drafts of the vicar's poems: C. E. Byles, ed., "Morwenstow," from R. S. Hawker, *Footprints*, 25 footnote.

"the lonely Farthest North": Arthur Mee, *Cornwall* (London: Hodder & Stoughton, 1937), 144.

Chapter 5

23 carried *Lloyd's Register* for 1842: I was looking for the *Caledonia*'s loss there since the *Register*'s calendar year ran from July 1; ship losses occurring in the first half of 1843 were recorded in the 1842 edition.

24 later additions: Nineteenth-century subscribers were regularly invited to return their *Register* to the publishers so that Lloyd's clerks could update the pages by hand even as news was received.

25 "Certificate of British Registry": Port of Montrose, 1839, no. 16 (Ref BT 107/437) Public Record Office [PRO], Kew.

27 *"Lloyd's List* 10th Sept 1842": September 10 was the date the news of the wreck was published in *Lloyd's List*.

28 *"Caledonia,* Peter": The entry can also be seen in the *Lloyd's Losses and Casualty Book*, 10 September 1842, also held at the Guildhall, City of London. The wreck is given here as happening on the 7th, but the wreck actually took place in the early hours of the 8th.

Chapter 6

31 "The Figurehead of the Caledonia": R. S. Hawker, *Cornish Ballads* (London: John Lane, 1904), 101.

32 *All the Year Round*: "The Remembrances of a Cornish Vicar" originally appeared in this periodical in 1865, vol 13, pp 153–56. It appears on pp 46–78 in *Footprints*. The sections relating to the *Caledonia* are reproduced here in appendix 1.

Chapter 7

37 "Cargoes": From John Masefield, *Ballads & Poems*, 1910.

"glean enough to make": Hawker to Mrs. Watson, 4 September 1864. Piers Brendon, *Hawker of Morwenstow* (London: Jonathan Cape, 1875), 76.

"To me it is life": Piers Brendon, *Hawker of Morwenstow*, 76–77.

38 "to receive in the bread": C. E. Byles, *The Life and Letters of R. S. Hawker* (London: John Lane/Bodley Head, 1905), 171.

"the sufferings of man": Cecil Woodham-Smith, *Florence Nightingale* (London: Constable & Co., 1950), 35.

39 the average cost of a sixty-pound bushel of wheat: Mr. T. Smith, "Grain," *Encyclopaedia Britannica* 1911.

"bluff and broken headland": "Remembrances," 56.

40 "clusters of houses": Hawker letter of 1856, C. E. Byles, *The Life and Letters of R. S. Hawker*, 42.

Chapter 8

44   "quite unreliable": Thurston Peter, *History of Cornwall* (Truro: Netherton & Worth, 1906), 17.

"a man—and a not very scrupulous man": Charles Harper, *The Smugglers* (London: Chapman & Hall, 1909), 130.

"an element of fiction": C. E. Byles's preface to *Footprints*, vii.

"Hawker's antiquarian studies": C. E. Byles, *The Life and Letters of R. S. Hawker*, 42.

"another drawback": Margaret Jeune, *Pages from the Diary of an Oxford Lady*, ed. by Margaret Jeune Gifford (Oxford: Blackwell, 1932), 8.

45   *Morte D'Arthur*: From Tennyson's *Poems*, published May 1842.

"gathered together one poor fellow" and "During our search for his remains": "Remembrances," 61.

46   "In one or two minor details": C. E. Byles, *The Life and Letters of R. S. Hawker*, 159.

Chapter 9

48   "the body of a shipwrecked sailor": Morwenstow Parish Burial Register, 6 December 1823.

"a Mariner cast ashore": Morwenstow Parish Burial Register, 21 March 1855.

"A corpse cast ashore": Welcombe Burial Register, 5 November 1859, North Devon Records Office, Barnstaple.

49   Local man Sam Cleverdon: *Hartland & West Country Chronicle*, 29 November 1924.

"one of the seven acts of mercy": Hawker letter of 1868 quoted in Piers Brendon, *Hawker of Morwenstow*, 134.

50   "the message came at night": Hawker to Mr. Godwin, 12 November 1862, in C. E. Byles, *The Life and Letters of R. S. Hawker*, 398.

"It was on a solemn occasion": *London Standard*, 1 September 1875.

"pieces of ships": Hawker to Mr. Ellacombe, 27 November 1837, in C. E. Byles, *The Life and Letters of R. S. Hawker*, 80.

"The sea is casting up": Hawker to Rev. William Waddon Martyn, 19 January 1853, Ibid., 229.

"Two Bodies thus far on Shore": Hawker to Lady Acland, 8 March 1855, Ibid., 240.

50–51   "The search for the bodies": Hawker to Mrs. Watson, 11 December 1859, Ibid., 319.

51   "This is my dread": Hawker to Mrs. Watson, 13 October 1861, Ibid., 346.

"Next Morning the Watchers": Hawker to Mrs. Watson, 23 February 1868, Ibid., 566.

"treatment of the drowned": N. H. Lawrence Martyn to C. E. Byles, 16 February 1903, Bodleian Library 42885; MS. Eng. lett. e. 96.

"used to tell thrilling stories": Rev. W. Haslam, *From Death into Life* (London: Morgan & Scott, 1880), 37.

"the rescue from the rocks there"': undated letter, Bodleian Library 42882; MS. Eng. lett. d. 226.

"a man writing about wrecks": undated fragment, Bodleian Library 42883; MS. Eng. misc. b. 93.

52   "I saw Alick Kant": "Remembrances," 57.

53   "the first three bodies found": Ibid., 58.

54   "remained as my guest six weeks": Ibid., 60.

"And at last," Hawker reconfirmed: Ibid., p.61.

Chapter 10

57 "When a man or woman": Ashley Rowe, "Cornish Wrecking Fabrication of Fiction Writers," *Western Morning News*, 3 March 1952.

"Almost all the inhabitants" Report of CFC, 1839, 56.

"taught from infancy": John Robeson, *English Chronicle*, 1825, quoted in John Vivian, *Tales of the Cornish Wreckers* (Penryn: Tor Mark Press, 1989), 23.

57–58 A French brig, *Les Landois*, "pipes of wine," and subsequent quotes: Letter from Alexander Shairp, 4 October 1838, Report of CFC, 1839, 64.

58 "My situation in life": Borlase letter, 15 March 1753, *Journal of the Royal Institution of Cornwall* 23 (1881): 374–79.

"the bodies of the drowned," "cut off to secure," and "bitten off the ears": Report of CFC, 1839, 59.

"The daring outrages": Charles Collins Crump, *The Morte Stone* (London: Simpkin, Marshall & Co., 1850), preliminary notice.

Chapter 11

61 "survey held at Arbroath": Original held at the National Maritime Museum, Greenwich.

"excellent and commodious": *Arbroath Guide*, 17 September 1842.

Robert Stevenson's remarkable Bell Rock lighthouse: Robert Stevenson, grandfather of writer Robert Louis Stevenson, completed the Bell Rock project in 1810.

64 "the beautiful brig" and "a splendid brig": *Arbroath Guide*, 17 September 1842.

Chapter 12

69 the *Robert*, wrecked at Stanbury: The *Robert* of Christiana, bound from Bremen, was lost at Stanbury Mouth on 29 December 1894.

70 "A watcher of the sea": "Remembrances," 48.

"The people of the shore": Ibid., 53.

"eked out a precarious existence": Christopher Harris, "Morwenstow, " *John Bull*, 4 September 1875.

"wild folk": Charles Kingsley, "Morte," *Fraser's Magazine for Town and Country* (December 1849): 654.

71 "proceeded down the nave": S. Baring-Gould, *The Vicar of Morwenstow* (1899), 117.

"There are men in Morwenstow": Stanley R. Baron, *Westward Ho! From Cambria to Cornwall* (London: Jarrolds, 1934), 275.

"frequently the leader": Letter from O. B. Stokes, *Western Morning News*, 17 June 1965.

Chapter 13

73 a large cardboard document box: Montrose Agreements and Crew Lists, 1835–44 (PRO ref: BT 86/400).

74 "Within ten years of the peace": Basil Lubbock, "The Mercantile Marine, 1830–1865"in *Early Victorian England*, 1830–65, ed. by G. M. Young (Oxford: Oxford University Press, 1934), 379–80.

"The number of vessels": Goldsworthy Gurney, Select Committee on Shipwreck, 1843.

78 the *Forager*, Thompson: *Lloyd's List*, 25 September 1841.

she was again spotted: *Lloyd's List*, 14 October 1841.

"*Caledonia*, Stevenson, from London": *Lloyd's List*, 3 December 1841.

79 a registration ticket: Ticket no 78,184 (PRO ref: BT 113/40).

"the Bible in his cabin," "a good quiet lad," and McDonald's anguish: Le Dain wreck statement in C. E. Byles, *The Life and Letters of R. S.*

Hawker, 159–60. The wreck statement, made at Morwenstow on 22 September 1842, is reproduced here in appendix 2.

80 "you may get aground": Charles Wilson, *The Seaman's Guide* (London: 1851), 372.

Chapter 14

83 "substituting the more nutritious": Select Committee on Shipwreck, 1836.

86 "She sailed in September": The *Mary Ann,* master Payn, left Rio for Trieste on 28 November 1841 (*Lloyd's List,* 18 January 1842).

91 caulked with oakum: Hemp strands unraveled from ropes worn beyond further use were worked into the gaps between the deck planks.

Chapter 15

101 a week before Christmas 1841: The *Caledonia* left Rio on 17 December 1841 (*Lloyd's List,* 5 February 1842).

102 Herman Melville had embarked on a whaler: The *Acushnet,* which Melville joined in January 1841. He remained at sea until October 1844.

Charles Dickens: *American Notes* was published later in 1842.

Chapter 16

106 "A painted ship": S. T. Coleridge, *The Rime of the Ancient Mariner,* 1798, lines 117–18.

108 "A poison which God made black": Stevenson Peter's words here are shamelessly adapted from William Alcott, *Tea and Coffee* (New York: 1808), 63.

Chapter 17

112 over six hundred British vessels: Select Committee on Shipwreck, 1843, Appendix, 31–45.

William Huskisson's death: The British statesman was killed on 15 September 1830 at the opening of the Liverpool and Manchester railway.

"broadsides," the single-sheet flyers: the broadside quotes are taken from two collections; A Collection of Broadsides Printed at Bristol 1700–1840, items 591–612 (British Library, 1880.c.20) and from the collection of W. S. Thomas (1824) held at Bristol Library.

115 "in gaining his point": *Penzance Gazette & West Cornwall Advertiser*, 21 September 1842.

Chapter 18

116 "the most notorious of all": *Times*, 8 January 1983.

Sir Bevil Grenville: Sir Bevil Grenville was laid to rest in the crypt at Kilkhampton Church following his death at the Battle of Lansdown, Bath, in 1643.

117 the *Cambalu*: a Liverpool steamship, wrecked 30 January 1933.

the *Sjofna*: a 600-ton steamship, wrecked on 23 November 1944.

the *Saltburn*: HMS *Saltburn*, a minesweeper destined for a Welsh scrapyard, broke her tow and was wrecked just south of Longpeak on 7 December 1946.

118 The *Johanna*, traveling from: taken from *Daily Mail*, 3 January 1983; *Daily Telegraph*, 4 January 1983; *North Devon Journal*, 6 January and 13 January 1983.

119 "Sunday was like being": *Daily Telegraph*, 4 January 1983.

"most unfair that our community": Rev. Louis Coulson, *Times*, 12 January 1983.

"It isn't as if we caused": *Daily Mail*, 3 January 1983.

120 "There is still very much": Nicholas Ross to Cyril Wilkinson, 27 September 1957. Ross's unpublished letters to Wilkinson are held at the

Bodleian Library, Special Collections and Western Manuscripts (Ref MS. Eng. Lett. d. 523).

Chapter 19

122 "famine levels" and "when all will suddenly": Letter from "CONSERVATOR," *Times*, 14 September 1841.

A new bill: The new scale of duties was 20 shillings duty when the price of a quarter of corn was between 50 and 51 shillings; 19 shillings between 51 and 52 shillings; 18 between 52 and 55; 17 between 55 and 56; 16 between 56 and 57; 15 between 57 and 58; 14 between 58 and 59, and so on down to 7 shillings and 65 to 66. Then 6 shillings between 66 and 69; 5 between 69 and 70; 4 between 70 and 71, and so until the price exceeded 74 shillings, at which no duty was payable. *Annual Register*, 1842, p. 25.

123 arriving at Syra in the Cyclades: *Lloyd's List*, 6 April 1842.

Gulf of Smyrna, April 3 1842: The *Caledonia*'s arrival was reported in *Lloyd's List*, 27 April 1842.

a vessel out of Calymnos: *Illustrated London News*, 27 August 1842.

124 its hallucinogenic effects: James A. Henry, "The Narrative of a Gentleman," in *A Letter to the Members of the Temperance Society* (Dublin: Hodges & Smith, 1830), 16–19.

the allegations of women: Edward Bramah, *Tea and Coffee* (London: Hutchinson, 1972), 46.

Neglect it one moment: Robert White Stevens, *On the Stowage of Ships and Their Cargo*, 2nd ed. (London: Longmans, 1859), 47.

Chapter 20

133 "possibility of a hoax": *Bideford & North Devon Weekly Gazette*, 9 February 1968.

"We state with": *Times*, 9 February 1797.

134 "spoken" the brig *Mathew*: *Lloyd's List*, 26 August 1842.

Chapter 21

136 requested information on grain prices: *Annual Register*, 1842, p. 31.

She had arrived at Constantinople: *Lloyd's List*, 7 May 1842.

137 "carried to the coast of Roumeli": John Purdy, *The New Sailing Directory for the Gulf of Venice together with the Euxine or Black Sea* (London: 1834), 198.

The *Caledonia* eventually arrived at Odessa: *Lloyd's List*, 21 June 1842.

the bold granite steps: Work had begun on the Odessa Steps in 1837.

138 lest the cloth should imbibe: John Moore, *A Journey from London to Odessa, with Notices of New Russia* (Paris: 1833), 158.

139 Pushkin!: Alexander Pushkin spent much of 1823–24 in Odessa; he was killed following a duel near St. Petersburg on 29 January 1837.

140 "By thy long gray beard": S. T. Coleridge, *The Rime of the Ancient Mariner*, lines 3–4.

Chapter 22

147 "prepared for Burial": Hawker to David McDonald's parents, 22 September 1842, in C. E. Byles, *The Life and Letters of R. S. Hawker*, 162.

"sad processions" and "temporary bier of broken planks": "Remembrances," 53.

"now fallen into disrepair": E. A. Newell Arber, *The Coast Scenery of North Devon* (London: Dent, 1911), 139.

148 "Between Hennacliffe and the path": Ross to Wilkinson, 23 August 1957.

150 all kinds of cargoes: John Bray, *An Account of Shipwrecks on the North Coast of Cornwall, 1759–1830* (The Institute of Cornish Studies/The Trevithick Society, 1975).

153 "just where a fresh brook of water": "Remembrances," 50.

"the cliff, steep and dark" and "climbed up until": Ibid., 57.

"I made haste": Ibid., 50–51.

154 Newdigate Prize for Poetry: Adams's prize-winning poem was entitled "Prince Charles Edward after the Battle of Culloden."

Stories about Wrecks and Fairies: The Athenaeum, 25 March 1876.

155 "Lines on the Crew of the Caledonia": John Adams, *St Malo's Quest and Other Poems* (London: Henry S. King & Sons, 1876), 39–40. The poem is published here in full in appendix 3.

Chapter 23

157 "where the Coffins had lived": Charles Kingsley, *Westward Ho!* (London: 1855), 76.

159 Hawker had been performing burials here: Hawker buried Catherine Gregory at Welcombe on 13 March 1838. Welcombe Burial Register, North Devon County Records Office, Barnstaple.

"disfigured faces": "Remembrances," 53.

"manifestly lifted," and subsequently: Ibid., 61.

159–60 "A Stranger": Parkham Parish Burials Register, 1842, p. 50, no.394; North Devon Records Office, Barnstaple.

160 "A man. Name unknown": Alwington Parish Burials Register 1842, p.22, no.171; North Devon Records Office, Barnstaple.

Chapter 24

164 at Constantinople on July 6, 1842: *Lloyd's List,* 27 July 1842.

"would be to sign": John Purdy, *New Sailing Directory for the Gulf of Venice,* 174.

"Staid in all night" and "Englishman at dinner": diary entries, 12 and 15 December, in Herman Melville, *A Visit to Europe and the Levant* (Princeton: Princeton University Press, 1955).

"to Falmouth for orders": *Lloyd's List,* 3 August 1842.

Chapter 25

173 "as one link in a chain": "Remembrances," 54

"the *Montrose,* steamer": *Falmouth Packet & Cornish Herald,* 10 September 1842.

"Near the mouth": R. Thomas, *A History and Description of the Town and Harbour of Falmouth* (Falmouth: J. Trathan, 1827), 29.

Quarantine: For more on quarantine, see Select Committee on Quarantine, 1824. British Library, Parliamentary Papers 1824.

174 "Sickness to an alarming": *Times,* 16 August 1842.

175 Thomas Samulle, of the "Brig *Caledonia* in Quarantine Pool": Cornwall County Records Office, St. Just burials 1842, p.112, no. 894.

176 C. W. Carlyon: Clement Winstanley Carlyon, rector of St. Just from 1836 to 1888.

"I have blundered": H. V. Morton, *In Search of England* (London: Methuen, 1927), 81.

Chapter 26

181 Time and again, they transposed his names: The *Caledonia*'s arrival at Marseilles on 25 April 1841 is reported in *Lloyd's List* (LL) on 3 May 1841; at Syra on 20 March 1842 (LL, 6 April 1842); at Smyrna on 3 April (LL, 27 April); at Constantinople on 14 April (LL, 7 May); at Odessa on 12 May (LL, 21 June); back at Constantinople on 6 July (LL, 27 July); and at Falmouth on 24 August (LL, 26 August).

Chapter 27

193 "the viler suggestion": Claude Berry, *Cornwall* (London: Robert Hale, 1949), 29.

"the active inducement": *Times*, 15 January 1983.

"taken away God's grace": M. Oppenheim, "Maritime History" in *Victoria County History of the County of Cornwall*, vol. 1 (London, 1906), 498.

194 the custom of Hartland Quay's owner: Mark Myers and Michael Nix, *Hartland Quay* (Harland: Jamaica Press, 1982), 18.

"We were aroused": Hawker to Sir Thomas Acland, 7 February 1853. C. E. Byles, *The Life and Letters of R. S. Hawker*, 230.

"danced and curtsyed": Daphne du Maurier, *Jamaica Inn* (London: Victor Gollancz, 1936), 165.

195 "A stationary light": S. Baring-Gould, *In the Roar of the Sea* (London: Methuen, 1892), p.197.

"Do you see how": Ibid., 198–99.

"the cruel and covetous natives": *Footprints*, 48–49.

196 "vessels, particularly foreigners": Anonymous, *The Shipwreck* (London: The Religious Tract Society, 1830), introduction.

"They would use every other endeavour": Report of CFC, 1839, p.59.

"the total incompetency of John Berry": Letter to the Commissioners of Customs, 1804, Hartland Quay Museum.

George II's wrecking bill: "An act for enforcing the laws against persons who shall steal and detain shipwrecked goods; and for the relief of persons suffering losses thereby." British Library, *The Statutes at Large, 1753–56*, 54.

Chapter 28

198 civil registration: civil registration in England and Wales came into force on 1 July 1837.

The *Caledonia*'s last quarantine order: Falmouth Customs correspondence, Board to Collector (PRO ref: CUST 67/56, July–December 1842), 451.

200 "tow the said corpse": Letter of 23 June 1842, Quarantine correspondence, PRO.

"the increase of machinery": *Falmouth Packet & Cornish Herald*, 3 September 1842.

201 "the distress of the country": *Illustrated London News*, 23 July 1842, 166.

three assassination attempts: John Francis twice pointed a pistol at the Queen, on 29 May and on 30 May, when he was apprehended. A "deformed youth" called John William Bea also pulled a pistol on the royal coach as it left Buckingham Palace for the Chapel Royal on 3 July.

"Poor little queen!": Caroline Fox, *Memories of Old Friends*, ed. by Wendy Monk (London: Elek, 1972), 130.

Events came to a head: My main sources for coverage of the unrest of the summer of 1842 are the *Royal Cornwall Gazette*, 26 August 1842, and Arthur Bryant, *English Saga, 1840–1940* (London: Collins, 1940), 72–75.

202 "Three months since": *Penzance Gazette & West Cornwall Advertiser*, 21 September 1842, 2.

"the most bountiful harvest": *Sherborne Mercury*, 24 September 1842.

A cabbage weighing: *Falmouth Packet & Cornish Herald*, 3 September 1842.

another, cut in Camelford: *Royal Cornwall Gazette*, 2 September 1842.

Potatoes weighing twenty pounds each: *Falmouth Packet & Cornish Herald*, 10 September 1842.

An apple tree: *Royal Cornwall Gazette*, 9 September 1842.

An apple measuring: *Sherborne Mercury*, 24 September 1842.

thirty-five pound turnip: *North Devon Journal*, 10 November 1842.

"had stems which attained": *Sherborne Mercury*, 10 September 1842.

At Applegarth, Dumfriesshire, and "as rich a return": *Arbroath Guide*, 17 September 1842.

"The crops, both for quantity": *Arbroath Guide*, 24 September 1842.

203 "Never has the port": *Royal Cornwall Gazette*, 2 September 1842.

Lord John Russell: House of Commons speech, 14 February 1842, *Annual Register*, 1842, 29–32.

"forced off at ruinously low rates": *North Devon Journal*, 8 September 1842, 4.

203–4 "Immense losses": *Royal Cornwall Gazette*, 2 September 1842.

204 "enabled the agricultural body" and "the quality of the new grain": "The Corn Trade During The Past Week," *Penzance Gazette & West Cornwall Advertiser*, 21 September 1842.

Thomas Quested, 40: *Royal Cornwall Gazette*, 26 August 1842.

205 "are passed upwards": *Royal Cornwall Gazette*, 2 September 1842.

Chapter 29

206 "of peaceful industry": *Times*, 13 September 1842.

"Scotland," the Prince wrote: Letter to Duchess Caroline de Gotha, 18 September 1842 in John Raymond, *Queen Victoria's Early Letters* (London: Batsford & Co., 1963).

"from every spot and place" and "a splendid display of fireworks": *Sherborne Mercury*, 10 September 1842.

"dense clouds of mist": *Times,* 13 September 1842.

207 "The vessel": *Arbroath Herald,* 19 April 1839.

209 "Ann Peter, unmarried": Inverbrothock Parish Minute Book, Scottish National Archives, Edinburgh (ref CH2 903 1).

Owen Chase: Nathaniel Philbrick, *In the Heart of the Sea* (London: HarperCollins, 2001), 213.

Chapter 30

212 "The captain and all the crew": "Remembrances," 54.

"in all foreign traders": witness statement of Capt. John Washington, R.N., Select Committee on Shipwreck, 1843.

213 "used to attend upon the captain": C. E. Byles, *The Life and Letters of R. S. Hawker,* 162.

"on one occasion": John R Chanter, *Lundy Island: A Monograph* (London: Cassell, Peter & Galpin, 1877), 19.

214 "At Falmouth, Penryn and in the neighbourhood": *Royal Cornwall Gazette,* 2 September 1842.

"In Falmouth Roads": *Sherborne Mercury,* 10 September 1842.

"*Caledonia,* Peter, Gloster": "Shipping News," *Falmouth Packet & Cornish Herald,* 10 September 1842.

Chapter 31

216 "lying placidly upon his back," "a small pouch or bag" and "these are still preserved": "Remembrances," 60–61.

the unpublished correspondence: Wilkinson's letters to Ross are held at the Bodleian Library's Department of Special Collections and Western Manuscripts (Ref MS. Eng. lett. e. 97).

Chapter 32

219 *It's home and it's home*: The song is attributed to Allan Cunningham (1784–1842). It is famously sung by another contemporary, if fictional, Scotsman, Donald Farfrae, in Thomas Hardy's *The Mayor of Casterbridge*, set around 1845.

222 the new railway: The Dundee to Arbroath railway opened on 1 April 1840.

223 the great pilchard shoals: September was the height of the pilchard industry, with boats off St. Ives reported as being loaded with 3,000 to 6,000 pilchards that year (*Falmouth Packet & Cornish Herald*, 10 September 1842).

Chapter 33

224 a shard of glass: Hartland historian R. Pearse Chope writes in the appendix of *Footprints* (1903 edition) that "Copinger's name can still be seen, inscribed in bold characters, 'D. H. Copinger' on a window-pane at Galsham."

225 "swift, brown, rough shape" and "all-but-ruined hut": An encounter of 1856. C. E. Byles, *The Life and Letters of R. S. Hawker*, 100.

"with stalwart arm": R. S. Hawker, "Cruel Coppinger," *Footprints*, 127.

225–26 "sheep were tethered": Ibid., 132.

226 "like a spectre or a ghost": Ibid., 138.

"probably at Welcombe Mouth": R. Pearse Chope, *Footprints*, appendix F, 280.

"chief cave": Ibid., 281.

227 The thirty-five-ton drifter: for coverage of the loss of the *Goliath*, see *Times*, 17 March 1969; *North Devon Journal*, 20 March 1969.

"un choc brutal": Jean M. L. Montfort, H.M. Coroner's Notes of Evidence: Inquest on Christian Stephen and Francois Lautram, held at Bideford, 21 March 1969.

228 "Bad times indeed": William Heard, "Reminiscences of Hartland," 1883. Unpublished MS. Held at North Devon local records office, Barnstaple.

229 *Save a stranger from the sea*: "Remembrances," 51.

Chapter 34

231 "a sudden squall of wind": C. E. Byles, *The Life and Letters of R. S. Hawker*, 160.

"the dreadful thunder storm" and subsequent descriptions: *Times* (including *Oxford Times* extracts) 10 September 1842; *North Devon Journal*, 12 September 1842.

232 "had their whole suit of sails": *North Devon Journal*, 15 September 1842.

Along the exposed west coast: For coverage of the losses, see *North Devon Journal*, 15 September 1842; *Lloyd's List*, 12 September 1842.

232–33 "The vessel": *Times*, 12 September 1842.

233 "a large vessel": *North Devon Journal*, 15 September 1842.

"the Brighton of the West": Hawker to Sir Thomas Acland, 25 February 1834. C. E. Byles, *The Life and Letters of R. S. Hawker*, 36.

236 there had been two other ships: For coverage of the *Elizabeth* and *St. Agnes* incident, see *North Devon Journal*, 15 September 1842; *Lloyd's List*, 12 September 1842; *West Briton & Cornwall Advertiser*, 16 September 1842; *Royal Cornwall Gazette*, 16 September 1842. On 2 October, the *Royal Cornwall Gazette* reported that "the *Elizabeth*, the largest vessel that ever entered Bude, was towed out by the tug *Sampson* from Newport, and many hundreds of persons were collected to witness her departure."

"Bude Bay, in which there is": J. W. Norie, *The New British Channel Pilot*, 81.

237 the tide was full: *Lloyd's List* gave high water at London Bridge on 8 September 1842 as at 4 A.M.

Chapter 35

245 "as a grateful acknowledgement": C. E. Byles, *The Life and Letters of R. S. Hawker*, 223.

a nugget of gold from California: Ibid., 239.

Chapter 36

247 "with the brief and thrilling tidings": "Remembrances," 55.

"melancholy intelligence": *Arbroath Guide*, 17 September 1842.

he took out a policy: Joseph Esplin's will, made on 1 February 1848. National Archives of Scotland (ref SC47/40/24), 390–403.

247–48 "indefatigable in his attention" and subsequently: *Arbroath Guide*, 17 September 1842.

248 second half of the nineteenth century: Arbroath's Western cemetery opened in 1867.

251 Arbroath's old parish register: Deaths recorded in Arbroath's old parish register: James Wallace (272/18, no.52); Robert Wallace (272/20, no.104); Hannah Buchanan or Peter (272/21); John Peter (272/8, no.277, and 272/23, no.278).

even if the inscriptions that commemorated them: The only crew member known to be commemorated on a surviving headstone is David Wallace. A family memorial inscribed by his brother, "John Wallace, who was 26 years in the Australian colonies" stands in the churchyard at Inverkeilor. The relevant section of the inscription reads, "Also of

David, who was lost on the coast of Cornwall in Sept 1842, aged 24 years."

252 "an aliment of two shillings": National Archives of Scotland. Arbroath (Old Church) Session Minutes, 1834–54 (ref: CH2/1415/5).

254 "miraculous preservation": Mme Le Dain to R. S. Hawker, 21 July 1867, Welby collection.

Chapter 37

255 "Arrived at Standgate Creek": *Lloyd's List,* 20 March 1841.

260 Norie's *New and Correct Chart*: by J. W. Norie, hydrographer, published 1832, with additions to 1840.

264 Le Dain dutifully reported its loss: see Le Dain wreck statement, appendix 2.

Epilogue

270 "see the very spot of his great deliverance": "Remembrances," 62.

"the soft blue wave": Ibid., 63.

"with loss of sails and bulwarks": *Lloyd's List,* 6 January 1847.

"is not expected off": *Lloyd's List,* 8 May 1847.

"The Navigator": *Lloyd's List,* 1 April 1854.

Appendix

280 "On the 1st of September": this is the only clear error in Le Dain's wreck statement.

Bibliography

Adams, J. H. "New Light on R. S. Hawker," *Cornish Review*, Autumn 1967.

Adams, John. *St Malo's Quest and Other Poems*. London: Henry S. King & Son, 1876.

Alcott, William. *Tea and Coffee: Their Physical, Intellectual, and Moral Effects on the Human System*. New York: 1808.

Anon. *The Shipwreck, Showing What Sometimes Happens on Our Sea Coasts*. London: The Religious Tract Society, 1830.

Archibald, E. H. H. *Dictionary of Sea Painters of Europe and America*. Woodbridge: Antique Collectors Club, 1980.

Baring-Gould, Rev. S. *The Vicar of Morwenstow*. London: Methuen, 1876.

———. *In the Roar of the Sea*. London: Methuen, 1892.

———. *A Book of the West. Vol 2, Cornwall*. London: Methuen, 1899.

Baron, Stanley R. *Westward Ho! From Cambria to Cornwall*. London: Jarrolds, 1934.

Bere, Bennie. *The Story of Bude Haven*. Bude: Bude-Stratton Town Council, 1977.

Bowring, John. *Observations on the Oriental Plagues and on Quarantines*. Edinburgh: William Tait, 1838.

Berry, Claude. *Cornwall*. London: Robert Hale, 1949.

Blackmore, Edward. *The British Mercantile Marine*. London: Griffin & Co, 1897.

Bouquet, Michael. *No Gallant Ship*. London: Hollis & Carter, 1959.

Bramah, Edward, *Tea and Coffee*. London: Hutchinson, 1972.

Bray, John. *An Account of Shipwrecks on the North Coast of Cornwall, 1759–1830*. Edited by A. K. Hamilton Jenkin. The Institute of Cornish Studies/The Trevithick Society, 1975. Original at British Museum, ms. 37826.

Brendon, Piers. *Hawker of Morwenstow*. London: Jonathan Cape, 1875.

Bryant, Arthur. *English Saga, 1840–1940*. London: Collins, 1940.

Burney, Capt. C. *The Young Seaman's Manual and Rigger's Guide*. London: Kegan Paul, Trench, Trubner & Co, 1901.

Byles, C. E. *The Life and Letters of R. S. Hawker*. London: John Lane/Bodley Head, 1905.

Carter, Clive. *Cornish Shipwrecks (the North Coast)*. Newton Abbot: David & Charles, 1970.

Chanter, Charlotte. *Ferny Combes*. London: Lovell Reeve, 1856.

Chanter, John R. *Lundy Island: A Monograph*. London: Cassell, Peter & Galpin, 1877.

Chope, R. Pearse. *Book of Hartland*. Torquay: Devonshire Press, 1940.

Collins, Mortimer. *Sweet and Twenty*. London: Hurst & Blackett, 1875.

Collins, Wilkie. *Rambles Beyond Railways*. London: Richard Bentley, 1851.

Cornewall-Jones, R. J. *Ships, Sailors, and the Sea*. London: Cassell, 1887.

Crump, Charles Collins. *The Morte Stone: A Tale of the Coast Based on Fact, with a Remonstrance against the System of Wrecking*. London: Simpkin, Marshall & Co, 1850.

Dana, Richard Henry. *Two Years Before the Mast*. London: J. Cunningham, 1841.

———. *The Seaman's Manual*. London: Edward Moxon, 1853.

Denham, Henry Mangles. *Remarks and Sailing Directions Relative to Lundy Island*. Liverpool: J. & J. Mawdsley, 1832.

du Maurier, Daphne. *Jamaica Inn*. London: Victor Gollancz, 1936.

Duncan, Ronald. *Devon & Cornwall*. London: Batsford, 1966.

Finch, Roger. *Pierhead Painters*. London: Barrie & Jenkins, 1983.

Fox Smith, C. *Ship Alley: More Sailor Town Days*. London: Methuen, 1925.

Glover, Fred R. A. *Harbours of Refuge*. London: John Ollivier, 1846.

Godwin, J. G. *Prose Works of R. S. Hawker*. London: Blackwood & Sons, 1893.

Hamilton Jenkin, A. K. *Cornish Seafarers*. London: Dent, 1932.

————. *Cornwall and the Cornish*. 1933.

————. *Cornish Homes & Customs*.

Hansen, Hans Jurgen, ed. *Art and the Seafarer*. London: Faber, 1968.

Harper, Charles. *The Cornish Coast (North)*. London: Chapman & Hall, 1910.

————. *The Smugglers*. London: Chapman & Hall, 1909.

Haslam, Rev. W. *From Death into Life*. London: Morgan & Scott, 1880.

Hawker, R. S. *Echoes from Old Cornwall*. London: Masters, 1846.

————. *Footprints of Former Men in Far Cornwall*. 1870. London: John Lane, 1903.

————. *Cornish Ballads and Other Poems*. Edited by C. E. Byles London: John Lane, 1904.

Henderson, Charles. *Essays in Cornish History*. Oxford: Clarendon Press, 1935.

Henry, James A. *A Letter to the Members of the Temperance Society Showing that the Use of Tea and Coffee Cannot Be Safely Substituted for that of Spirituous Liquours*. Dublin: Hodges & Smith, 1830.

Herlihy, Patricia. *Odessa: A History, 1794–1914*. Cambridge, Mass.: Harvard University Press, 1986.

Hope, Ronald. *A New History of British Shipping*. London: John Murray, 1980.

Horder, Mervyn. "Amazing Grace" from *On Their Own*. London: Duckworth, 1988.

Jeune, Margaret. *Pages from the Diary of an Oxford Lady, 1843–1862*. Edited by Margaret Jeune Gifford. Oxford: Blackwell, 1932.

Langham. A & M. *Lundy*. Newton Abbot: David & Charles, 1970.

Lake's Complete Parochial History of Cornwall. London & Truro: 1870.

Larn, Richard. *Devon Shipwrecks*. Newton Abbot: David & Charles, 1975.

————. *Cornish Shipwrecks*. Newton Abbot: David & Charles, 1971.

Lindsay, W. S. *History of Merchant Shipping and Ancient Commerce*. London: Sampson Low, 1883.

Longmate, Norman. *King Cholera*. London: Hamish Hamilton, 1966.

Lubbock, Basil. "The Mercantile Marine," in *Early Victorian England, 1830–1865*. Edited by G. M. Young. Oxford: Oxford University Press, 1934.

Maclean, Charles. *Evils of Quarantine Laws.* London: T. G. Underwood, 1824.

Mee, Arthur. *Cornwall.* London: Hodder & Stoughton, 1937.

Melville, Herman. *A Visit to Europe and the Levant.* Edited by Howard C. Horsford. Princeton: Princeton University Press, 1955.

Meyer, K. F. *Disinfected Mail.* Kansas: Holton, 1962.

Mitchell, Alison, ed. *Angus Monumental Inscriptions.* Vol 2. Scottish Genealogy Society, 1981.

Monk, Wendy, ed. *Memories of Old Friends: Extracts from the Journals and Letters of Caroline Fox of Penjerrick, Cornwall, 1835–1871.* London: Elek, 1972.

Moore, John. *A Journey from London to Odessa, with Notices of New Russia.* Paris: 1833.

Moore, Rev. Thomas. *The History of Devonshire.* Jennings & Chaplin, 1832.

Morton, H. V. *In Search of England.* London: Methuen, 1927.

Mudd, David, *The Cruel Cornish Sea.* Cornwall: Bossiney Books, 1981.

Myers, Mark, and Michael Nix. *Hartland Quay: The Story of a Vanished Port.* Hartland: Jamaica Press, 1982.

Neale, John. "Only One Survivor From Brig Tragedy," *Arbroath Herald Review,* 1992.

Nix, Michael. *The Cruel Coast of North Devon.* Bideford: Badger Books, 1982.

Newell Arber. *The Coast Scenery of North Devon.* London: Dent, 1911.

Noall, Cyril, and Grahame Farr. *Wreck and Rescue Round the Cornish Coast.* Vol 1. Truro: D. Bradford Barton, 1964.

Norie, J. W. *The New British Channel Pilot.* London: Naval Academy, 1835.

Norway, Arthur H. *Highways and Byways in Devon and Cornwall.* London: Macmillan, 1922.

Oppenheim, M. Edited by William Page. "Maritime History," in *Victoria County History of the County of Cornwall.* Vol 1. London: 1906.

Page, J. L. W. *The North Coast of Cornwall.* Penzance & Truro: John Pollard, 1897.

Pardoe, Julia. *City of the Sultans.* London: H. G Clarke & Co, 1845.

Philbrick, Nathaniel. *In the Heart of the Sea.* London: HarperCollins, 2000.

Peter, Thurston. *History of Cornwall.* Truro: Netherton & Worth, 1906.

Philpotts, Eden. *Monkshood.* London: Methuen, 1939.

Protheroe, Charles. *Life in the Mercantile Marine.* London: John Lane/ Bodley Head, 1903.

Purdy, John. *The New Sailing Directory for the Gulf of Venice . . . together with . . . the Euxine or Black Sea.* London: 1834.

Raymond, John, ed. *Queen Victoria's Early Letters.* London: Batsford & Co, 1963.

Rendier, Jean. *Marine Navigation Instruments.* London: John Murray, 1980.

Ross, Adelaide. *Reverie.* New York: Robert Hale, 1981.

Rowe, Richard. *Jack Afloat and Ashore.* London: Smith, Elder & Co, 1875.

Runciman, Walter. *Before the Mast and After.* London: Ernest Benn, 1924.

Shearme, Rev. John. *Lively Recollections.* London: John Lane/Bodley Head, 1914.

Simmonds, P. L. *Coffee as It Is and as It Ought to Be.* London: 1850.

Stevens, Robert White. *On the Stowage of Ships and Their Cargo.* 2nd ed. London: Longmans, 1859.

Thomas, R. *History and Description of the Town and Harbour of Falmouth.* Falmouth: J. Trathan, 1827.

Vivian, John. *Tales of the Cornish Wreckers.* Penryn: Tor Mark Press, 1989.

Wilson, Charles. *The Seaman's Guide.* London: 1851.

Woodham-Smith, Cecil. *Florence Nightingale.* London: Constable & Co, 1950.

Acknowledgments ∽

The following were generous with their help: Rev. Richard Adams, Patrick W. Anderson, John Bartlett, Lt. Cdr. John Beck, Rev. W. Blakey, Lawrence R. Burness, David Clement of the South West Maritime History Society, Arthur Bryant, Roger and Christopher Cobley, Barry Cox, Robin Darwall-Smith, David Dithercott, J. E. Dykes of the Shipwrecked Fishermen and Mariners' Royal Benevolent Society, Jim Esplin, Joss Esplin, Brian Forsythe at the *Arbroath Herald*, Anne Garven, Robin and Enid Gauldie, Dennis Heard, Capt. G. A. Hogg, Margery Kelly, Harvey Kendall of the Bude-Stratton Museum, Margaret King, Terry Knight of the Old Cornwall Society, Richard Larn, Tim Longville, Lady Marshall, Hazel McKinnon, Paula Melville, Malcolm Miller, Alison Mitchell, Mrs. R. Nicholl, Capt. D. A. Parsons of the Merchant Navy Welfare Board, Chris Pollard, James Portman, Sir Hugh Stucley, Hilary Thompson, Richard Tregoning, Brenda Watson, William Waddon-Martyn, Frank Whitehead.

Thanks to the staff at the British Library, St. Pancras, and at the library's newspaper collection, Colindale; the Public Record Office, Kew; the National Maritime Museum Library, Greenwich; the Guildhall Library, City of London; the Family Records Centre, Farringdon; the Cornish Studies Library, Redruth; the Cornish County Record Office, Truro; the North Devon local studies library and records office, Barnstaple; Gail Davidson at the Signal Tower Museum, Arbroath; the Arbroath Library; Dundee City Archives; the library at the University of Dundee; the Tay Valley Family History Society, Dundee; the Scottish National Archives, Edinburgh; the

Bodleian Library, Oxford; Pembroke College Library, Oxford where the Goard Collection of Hawker material is held; and the Family History Centre, Whitchurch, Bristol.

Particular thanks go to André Bernard, Jen Charat, and Linda Lockowitz at Harcourt, Dr. Piers Brendon, Justin Creedy Smith, Malcolm Darch, Clare Dillon, Alan Giddings, Elizabeth Gifford, Terry Hodge, Nick Jouault, Philip Marsden, Richard Milner, John Moat, Douglas McKenzie, my late mother Jo Seal, and Sandy Wells.

Jane Bradish-Ellames and Jill Grinberg provided invaluable help with the original idea. Raymond and Valentine Sabin supplied repeated Southole humor and hospitality. Jill Welby allowed unlimited access to her Hawker material. Mark Myers was impossibly generous with his time, his unrivaled knowledge, and enthusiasm. On these people the book no less than depended.